Science, Jews, and Secular Culture

Science, Jews, and Secular Culture

STUDIES IN MID-TWENTIETH-
CENTURY AMERICAN
INTELLECTUAL HISTORY

David A. Hollinger

PRINCETON UNIVERSITY PRESS

PRINCETON, NEW JERSEY

Published by Princeton University Press, 41 William Street,
Princeton, New Jersey 08540
In the United Kingdom: Princeton University Press,
Chichester, West Sussex

Library of Congress Cataloging-in-Publication Data

Hollinger, David A.
Science, Jews, and secular culture : studies in mid-twentieth-
century American intellectual history / David A. Hollinger.
p.   cm.
Includes bibliographical references and index.
ISBN 0-691-01143-5 (cloth : alk. paper)
1. Jews—United States—Intellectual life.   2. Science—
United States—History—20th century.   3. Secularism—
United States—History—20th century.   4. United States—
Intellectual life—20th century.   5. United States—
Ethnic relations.   I. Title.
E184.J5H646   1996
305.5'52—dc20   95-39843   CIP

This book has been composed in Baskerville

Princeton University Press books are printed
on acid-free paper and meet the guidelines
for permanence and durability of the Committee
on Production Guidelines for Book Longevity
of the Council on Library Resources

Printed in the United States of America by
Princeton Academic Press

10 9 8 7 6 5 4 3 2 1

To my son, Jacob, and my daughter, Julia

Contents

Preface

THIRTY YEARS AGO one of the most respected public moralists in the United States identified academic intellectuals as vital agents of the future of the nation, and of the entire modern world. Now that human beings are "emancipated and thus deprived of the guidance and support of traditional and customary authority," the aging Walter Lippmann told readers of the *New Republic* in 1966, "there has fallen to the universities a unique, indispensable and capital function in the intellectual and spiritual life of modern society." Cultural leadership belongs to the academy "rather than, let us say, to the churches or the government," because behavior depends on what people believe to be "true." And when we want the truth we now know better than to look to priests or politicians. Instead, we rely on "the universal company of scholars supported and protected and encouraged by their universities." Lippmann, who was not himself a professor, professed to be uncertain whether the era's men and women of learning were up to the challenge. But he did not doubt that the challenge was theirs, and that the rest of society stood to benefit from their effort to meet it.

Such sober respect for universities and their faculties has largely passed out of fashion. Lippmann's successors among journalists are rarely idealistic about academic intellectuals. Today's professors are not the first to be accused of bias, foolishness, triviality, political dogmatism, and unjustified hostility to religious belief, but in the 1990s these complaints have become staples of opinion-page and talk-show discussions. No doubt the failings of the professors have something to do with this change. But today's jaundiced assessments of academia are also facets of the culture wars of our own time, which are, in turn, as rooted in contemporary politics as Lippmann's more generous view of the professoriat was rooted in the struggles of his own generation. *A faith in the unique importance of secular inquiry to the making of a good society* had been inherited from the people who built the American universities between the Civil War and World War I, and was then renewed and expanded during the prodigious growth of American higher education that followed World War II. This faith, which Lippmann reasserted at a moment in the mid-1960s when even cautious men and women were not afraid to display hope, was felt deeply by most of the intellectuals whose strivings are the subject of this book.

Science, Jews, and Secular Culture: Studies in Mid-Twentieth-Century American Intellectual History invokes "Science" because so many of its cast of characters believed that natural science set the standard for secular inquiry, and also because some of them understood science to be a vehicle for a certain cluster of liberal, democratic values they thought appropriate for American society as a whole. The title invokes "Jews" because a unique feature of the era was the demographic transformation of academic communities by immigrant Jews and their children, and because, further, many of these Jewish intellectuals were conspicuous in their devotion to science and to the building of a culture liberated from the Christian biases that barred Jews and other non-Christians from full participation in American life. "Secular Culture," finally, marks the line between the religious cultures inherited by the bulk of the midcentury intellectuals studied here—non-Jewish as well as Jewish—and the kind of culture a number of them were concerned to expand as a common, public possession of Americans independent from private spiritual orientations. Although the title conveys the volume's principal themes, some of this book is addressed to additional facets of the discourse of intellectuals in the midcentury decades, and to institutional and political matrices of that discourse.

The studies collected here are more of a single piece than the methodological and monographic essays I brought together more than a decade ago under the title *In the American Province: Studies in the History and Historiography of Ideas* (Bloomington, Ind., 1985). But this new collection is, like the earlier one, made up of articles and lectures produced for separate occasions. I do not want to exaggerate the thematic unity of *Science, Jews, and Secular Culture.* These inquiries are forays into domains within the recent American past that deserve the more systematic exploration I trust they will receive as historians devote more attention to this terrain. I took each inquiry in its own direction, while drawing sometimes on several of the same sources and building upon one or more of the studies I had completed earlier. This results in some overlap, which I hope will not be too distracting to a reader who proceeds directly from one essay to another.

I have corrected a few errors made known to me in the interim and I have edited down to a size appropriate for this volume one article of excessive length, but otherwise these essays remain exactly as first published. I have written a brief introduction and have prefaced each essay with a headnote indicating its chief concerns and sometimes clarifying its relation to the other studies collected here.

These pieces are of two distinct genres. One is the narrowly focused, monographic inquiry into a highly specific case: a single career (Oliver Wendell Holmes, Jr.), a single text (an influential article by Robert K. Merton), a single event (a conference held at New York University in 1932), and a single campus (the University of Michigan). The second genre is the wide-ranging essay sketching certain developments visible in a number of domains across several decades, and trying to assign histor- ical significance to these developments in the larger context of United States history. Writing in this second genre, I analyze the use of science as a weapon in a sequence of cultural conflicts, trace the transition from individualist to communitarian terms for the public representation of the scientific enterprise, and explore the role of Jewish intellectuals in the process by which the cultural program of Christianity loses some of its public standing.

Parts of this book were written at the Center for Advanced Study in the Behavioral Sciences in Stanford, California, and at the Rockefeller Study Center in Bellagio, Italy. I am grateful for the opportunity to work under the ideal conditions provided by both of these institutions. I want also to express my appreciation for the stimulation and critical support I have received from colleagues on two splendid faculties, first at the University of Michigan and later at the University of California at Berkeley.

I want to acknowledge my debts to several individuals. It has been a pleasure to work with Diana Wear and her staff at Berkeley's Office for the History of Science and Technology, and with Emily Wilkinson and her staff at the Princeton University Press. Of the many colleagues and friends who reacted to drafts of one or more of these essays, I especially want to thank Thomas Bender for his unfailingly helpful critical advice over the course of many years. For suggestions about how best to orga- nize these essays for presentation in a book, I am grateful to Ronald Numbers and Daniel T. Rodgers. My wife, Joan Heifetz Hollinger, has contributed to the studies collected here in more ways than I know how to adequately acknowledge.

Berkeley, California
June 1995

Science, Jews, and Secular Culture

CHAPTER ONE

Introduction

WHEN J. ROBERT OPPENHEIMER received the Atomic Energy Commission's Fermi Award from President Lyndon Johnson at the White House in 1963, he quoted Thomas Jefferson on "the brotherly spirit of science which unites into a family all its votaries." That spirit of brotherhood, conceded the physicist in charge of the scientific team that had built the atomic bomb, may be hard to see amid the great struggle to get beyond "war as the great arbiter of history." Oppenheimer was alluding to disputes over weapons development that had raged since World War II. In the course of these quarrels, Oppenheimer's prewar associations with Communists had been maliciously invoked by opponents within the government to discredit him and even to deny him a security clearance in 1954. On the occasion of his political rehabilitation, Oppenheimer thanked the president for his "charity" and "courage" in presenting the award, and invited the assembled dignitaries to remember that science was a cultural as well as a technical presence in modern life. Science embodied an ideal of fraternity congruent with the larger hope that human beings could find means less ghastly than warfare to resolve their conflicts.[1]

Oppenheimer was at once a physicist, a political actor, and an agent of what he took to be the culture of science. If he was exceptional among American academic intellectuals of his generation in the extent, visibility, and volatility of his public political entanglements, his career can still serve as a reminder that the experience of academic intellectuals generally is embedded in the larger society. Yet Oppenheimer also reminds us that academic intellectuals, like other groups within the United States, engage the society on distinctive terms. Oppenheimer was a representative of an academic intelligentsia more secular, more liberal, and more Jewish than any comparable professional and cultural cohort in the United States.

The historical study of this cohort from the 1930s through the 1960s, to which this book is primarily devoted, is best advanced if we keep in mind two points that can serve as a common frame for the essays collected here. One point concerns chronology; the other, ethnoreligious demography. Many of the significant episodes in the history of academic intellectuals during Oppenheimer's generation stand somewhat apart from "the fifties" and "the sixties" as popularly invoked. Among these episodes is the transformation of the ethnoreligious demography of American academic life by Jews, of whom Oppenheimer was one. First, to chronology, then to demography.

An understanding of the history of American academic intellectuals during the midcentury decades requires that this history be liberated from historiographic monsters that threaten to devour most of what happened culturally in the United States from World War II through the 1990s. The most formidable of these monsters is The Sixties, long since a singular noun denoting a series of highly visible, contentious movements and events that dominated the public life of the United States during the second half of the 1960s and the very early 1970s. Prominently at issue were the Vietnam War, the persistence of poverty and of antiblack racism, the perceived constraints of American family life, and the propriety of the political behavior exhibited by people in conflict over these issues. How should we interpret this legendary segment of modern American history? How does it figure in the more narrow history of American academic intellectuals? These are worthy questions now extensively pursued by scholars,[2] and by critics and politicians eager to assign The Sixties credit—or, more often, blame—for deconstruction, feminism, multiculturalism, postmodernism, and other enthusiasms of the final third of the century.[3]

One need not doubt the importance of The Sixties to look, in the meantime, at the part of the 1960s that came before The Sixties. The distinctness of this historical moment becomes more apparent with the passage of time. It is a moment etched the most vividly in popular memory by the assassination of President John F. Kennedy near the end of 1963. As it happened, the shooting took place on the very afternoon of a day the White House had begun by announcing Kennedy's decision to present the Fermi Award to Oppenheimer. Ten days later Johnson was no doubt exaggerating when he told Oppenheimer that signing the award had been "one of President Kennedy's most important acts."[4] But Kennedy's decision to rehabilitate Oppenheimer was at least one of a series of steps Kennedy had taken to acknowledge the value to the nation of intellectuals of many sorts, even those who had run afoul of McCarthyism. This rapprochement between the country's political leadership and its intellectuals is one reason why the early 1960s, when viewed with the history of the American academic community in mind, is a distinctive point in time. By way of sorting out The Sixties from the 1960s,[5] it is possible to list a number of long-term transformations in the circumstances and engagements of American academic intellectuals, and to note their stage of development in the early 1960s.

By the early 1960s, many Jews had quietly entered the social scientific and humanistic disciplines from which they had been almost entirely excluded only two decades before. But affirmative action programs for women and for African Americans (then usually called "Negroes") were yet to be developed, and the reopening of immigration that eventually fostered new attention to the status of Asian Americans and Latinos had yet to take place. Mutual suspicion between Catholics and secular intellectuals was rapidly diminishing in the wake of Vatican II and of Kennedy's election as president in 1960, but the large-scale entry of Catholics into American intellectual life had scarcely begun. Faith in the epistemic unity of all humankind remained widespread and was still contrasted to Nazi and Stalinist theories of the racially and socioeconomically situated character of knowledge, rather than to poststructuralist critiques of "totalizing strategies." The modernist literary canon was at the peak of its spiritual and curricular authority and had only begun to receive, at the hands of Lionel Trilling and other critics who had celebrated modernism for a generation, the skeptical scrutiny that within a few years would be turned by Paul de Man and others in postmodernist directions alien to Trilling. American democracy, imperfect as it was known to be, remained highly valued for having survived the McCarthy era and for its superiority to Soviet totalitarianism, and was yet to be tested by bitter conflicts over the issues that produced The Sixties. Indeed, the early triumphs of President Johnson's Great Society in 1964 and 1965 reinforced a certain idealism about American institutions, and even about electoral politics, which was to be widely and vociferously scorned by 1966 and especially in the years immediately following.

The ideals of tolerance, "brotherhood," and cosmopolitanism were more strongly entrenched in the early 1960s than they had been a generation before; they remained untouched by the multiculturalist complaint that these ideals, as interpreted throughout the midcentury decades, were too narrow, that they had served covertly to maintain in America the cultural hegemony of Europeans in general and of Anglo-Protestants in particular. Margaret Mead, Hannah Arendt, and several other women were among the most respected of American intellectuals, but the feminist theory that was to flourish in the 1970s and after was less prefigured in departments of anthropology and political science than in the journalist Betty Friedan's *The Feminine Mystique* (1963), which feminists of later decades would patronize as "a fifties book." Many academic communities prided themselves on providing a humane working atmosphere for a colleague believed to be homosexual, but the Stonewall Riot was yet to take place and what public discussion there was of gay and lesbian sexuality remained evasive when it did not speak in the categories of sin, crime, and disease. Thomas S. Kuhn's *The Structure of Scientific Revolutions* (1962) caused many people to alter their conception of science, but the implications of this epochal work for the political and cultural relations of science were still widely believed to be compatible with a host of traditional assumptions soon to be challenged by radically relativistic "Kuhnians" later disowned by Kuhn himself. Social scientists were finally enjoying a substantial measure of the prestige—and opportunities to advise governments and corporations—that seemed to come so easily to physical scientists, but these enthusiastic, confident new "policy experts" had yet to confront on a regular basis the insistent and angry charge that their claims to ideological neutrality were false and served to conceal their contributions to American imperialism. Ken Kesey's *One Flew over the Cuckoo's Nest* (1962) was a campus bestseller, but the public LSD parties over which Kesey presided were not to begin until the fall of 1965.

Such was the status, at the instant immediately prior to The Sixties, of a number of important transformations, trajectories, and tensions. Sorting out The Sixties from the 1960s demands awareness that among the foundations for The Sixties was an honest frustration with the inability of the received wisdom to deal more effectively with deep injustices within American society and with outrageous iniquities in the conduct of the United States in the world. But another, less widely enacted phase of this sorting out is the comparable recognition that the men and women who made the early 1960s were still responding to challenges rather different from those that animated The Sixties. This could hold true even when the same people were involved: many of those who made the early 1960s were, after all, the same people who later made The Sixties.

Of this remarkable mini-era so often overshadowed by The Sixties we sometimes say, "That's just the fifties, extended a few years." In this view, there is a "long 1950s," stretching from 1947 or 1948 to about 1963 or 1964, defined in part by the pre-Vietnam Cold War but characterized more decisively by something this era was not, namely, The Sixties. There is something to this idea that we can deal with the early 1960s by calling it part of the 1950s. But not much. While some of the historical importance of the early 1960s does indeed consist in the culmination of developments that gained their defining character only within the previous "long" decade, The Fifties is as overweight with meaning as The Sixties, in relation to which it has been articulated dialectically in the American popular historical imagination.

Hence the singular noun, The Fifties, has become a historiographic monster almost as distracting as The Sixties. The shadows cast by Dwight Eisenhower, tail-finned Plymouths, "consensus history," and the *Ozzie and Harriet* show are as oversized as those cast by the Chicago Democratic Convention of 1968, the murder of Martin Luther King, Jr., "repressive tolerance," and the Woodstock rock concert. The names of these two decades, even more than The Twenties and The Thirties, have become codes for highly specific clusters of American historic phenomena, which are, in turn, commonly assigned enormous powers of determination. These mystified calendrical entities are too often incanted as substitutes for analysis. What explains this or that? Well, it was part of, or a consequence of, The Sixties. Or, The Fifties.

The chronological referents in this book are intended to be literal, not symbolic. Separating the early 1960s from The Sixties and even from The Fifties helps to situate the major themes of this volume in a chronology that was more truly theirs, frees them from extraneous associations, and makes room for more specific terms of description and analysis. The early 1960s is not the topic of this book, yet it was then that several debates and transformations addressed in this book either came to a climax or were significantly redirected. Between 1962 and 1965, for example, American scholars suddenly published a host of books and articles about science that radically reoriented learned discussion of the entire scientific enterprise. The early 1960s was also a point when the increased number of Jews on many faculties became statistically significant. But both of these developments got their momentum earlier in a history that included the 1950s while having little to do with The Fifties. And both produced legacies beyond the 1960s not limited to the contributions they made, in the meantime, to The Sixties. Several of the studies gathered here do touch upon The Fifties and The Sixties, but these two abstractions illuminate only faintly the themes in the intellectual history of the midcentury decades to which this book is addressed.

The ethnoreligious transformation of the academy by Jews—the demographic point to be discussed in this introduction—demands special attention here because it has received remarkably little systematic discussion by historians. Other basic features of the period addressed in this book, including the increased authority of science and the decline of a Protestant establishment, are staples of the historiography of modern American intellectual history. But the arrival of Jewish intellectuals within academic institutions long hostile to them has remained at the margins, even in a multiculturalist era during which sensitivity to ethnic distinctions and to the relative fate of various ethnic groups within American society has been a matter of intense public concern. In view of the fact that in many of the studies collected here I take up this ethnoreligious transformation in specific contexts, here I want to provide a sketch of this event in the round.

The specific case of Yale University instructively illustrates the experience of American higher education generally. Yale has been the subject of one of the most rigorous, scholarly treatments yet completed of academic anti-Semitism and of the pressures finally brought against it, Dan A. Oren's *Joining the Club: A History of Jews and Yale*. There were a scattering of Jews in the university's professional schools prior to World War II, but Oren found that within the faculty of Yale College itself—the culturally strategic core of the university—no Jew held the rank of professor until 1946. In that year the philosopher Paul Weiss was appointed, after deliberations in which Weiss's Jewishness was very much on the minds of Yale officials and of the philosophers to whom Yale turned for advice. In 1950 Weiss remained Yale College's sole Jewish professor, although by then eight other Jews held that rank in Yale University as a whole. But by 1960 the transition was visibly underway: 28 of the university's 260 professors were Jewish, including 6 out of the 95 professors in the college. A decade later the ethnoreligious demography of Yale was strikingly different. In 1970, 22 percent of the professors in the university were Jewish, as were 18 percent of the professors in the college.[6]

Not all major universities were as slow as Yale College to hire Jews to begin with, nor as decisively changed ethnoreligiously once the reluctance to hire Jews was overcome. But much of American higher education at the end of the 1960s looked like Yale. In a study carried out in 1969, the Carnegie Commission on Higher Education concluded that while Jews accounted for only about 3 percent of the American population, the barriers to their participation in academia had collapsed so thoroughly that nearly 9 percent of the combined faculties of 303 colleges and universities surveyed were Jewish. The same study reported that when only the most highly ranked of American universities were considered, the proportion of Jewish faculty was much greater. More than 17 percent of the combined faculties of the seventeen most highly ranked universities represented themselves as Jewish. The percentage of Jewish faculty differed greatly from discipline to discipline. Jews were common in psychology and in many biomedical fields, for example, while in agriculture and physical education the Carnegie Commission found almost no Jewish faculty. In selected disciplines within the faculties of the seventeen leading universities the Carnegie study reported the following percentages of Jews: law, 36 percent; sociology, 34 percent; economics, 28 percent; and physics, 26 percent. Even in the humanities, where Jews had been the most persistently excluded, Jews were found to constitute 22 percent of historians and 20 percent of philosophers in this same group of elite universities.[7]

One important truth contained in these figures is that the integration of Jews into American intellectual life was a phenomenon much broader than the one phase of it to receive the most notice, the rise to prominence of the writers and critics known as "the New York intellectuals." This group is now the subject of countless monographs and memoirs. The greatest impact of the New York intellectuals was in the realm of public discourse about literature and politics. But the Jewish intellectuals who altered the ethnoreligious demography of American intellectual life during this era were not only novelists, poets, editors, and critics. Within the humanities, these men and women were also philosophers, historians, art historians, and literary scholars. Their number included not only humanists, moreover, but also scientists, social scientists, and professors of law, medicine, and engineering. And many of them were not New Yorkers.

Why did American higher education open its doors to Jews when it did? The integration of Jews into liberal arts faculties after World War II followed in large part from the discrediting of anti-Semitism by Hitler's "Final Solution," the dimensions of which became widely known during the years immediately following the war. Opinion polls showed that anti-Semitism declined sharply in 1947, having maintained prewar levels throughout the war itself. But this change in public attitudes, especially as it affected higher education, was directly stimulated by a campaign mounted by liberal journalists and politicians against "un-American" discriminatory practices in the context of a victorious war against Hitler. After decades of only episodic public discussion of anti-Jewish quotas in the admissions policies of undergraduate colleges and professional schools, magazine and newspaper articles of 1945–1947 exposed in detail the practice of excluding Jews. It was revealed, for example, that Jewish enrollment at Columbia University's medical school had declined from about 50 percent in 1920 to less than 7 percent in 1940. Anti-discrimination policies soon adopted by the governments of New York City and New York State—political constituencies with a large bloc of Jewish voters—prefigured federal efforts led by President Harry S. Truman, who accompanied his recognition of the state of Israel in 1948 with his own statements condemning anti-Jewish prejudice within American society.[8]

Precisely at the time anti-Semitism was being discredited, academic jobs in unprecedented numbers suddenly became available in the wake of the "GI Bill." The Serviceman's Readjustment Act of 1944 is one of the most far-reaching yet least appreciated events in the history of the relationship between intellectuals and American society.[9] Two million veterans quickly doubled undergraduate enrollments nationally and increased student-fee revenues on some campuses as much as fivefold. The federal government's decision to finance the college education of veterans led to a much more broadly based expansion of higher education than the military and technological requirements of the Cold War demanded. Government priorities that took form in response to the sharpening of the Cold War did affect the size and specific shape of many intellectual projects, including scientific fields funded by the National Science Foundation and the foreign area studies programs de-

veloped in response to the decolonization of Asia and Africa. But to simply invoke the Cold War in explanation of the increased economic base
for American intellectual careers in the postwar era is to miss the sprawling character of this expansion, its motivation within the political and
moral economy of the war against the Axis powers, and the range of
opportunities it created for a great variety of kinds of intellectuals.
Among these intellectuals, of course, were Jews who had long awaited
such opportunities. Hence it was the convergence of two major developments—the discrediting of anti-Semitism by Hitler and the expansion of
higher education under the aegis of the GI Bill—that most directly facilitated the entrance of Jews into American academia in such large numbers after World War II.

Yet there is an additional circumstance, less direct in its impact, that
should be taken into account. The intellectual atmosphere of the Cold
War in the United States promoted the idea that ideology, rather than
race or class, was what divided the great, historic blocs in the world from
one another. Solidarities based on race had been rendered suspect by
the spectacle of the Third Reich. Solidarities based on class consciousness, never strong in the United States, had been discredited by what
had happened to socialism under Stalin's leadership of the Soviet
Union. The enemy in the Cold War was understood to be an ideological
entity, Communism. To be sure, Communism was embodied in a particular regime, but the Soviet Union was understood to be neither a genuine working-class state nor a state organized on an ethnoracial foundation. And the "free world" opposed to Communism was understood to
be, again, essentially ideological in character. World leadership outside
the Soviet orbit had been transferred from the most racist of the regimes
of Europe and Asia—Nazi Germany and Imperial Japan—to the United
States, a power that defined itself with Enlightenment universalist abstractions. Hence the Cold War was in part a worldwide "battle for men's
minds," as the slogan went, waged in the decolonizing "Third World," in
the territory reached by Radio Free Europe, and, of course, in American
classrooms, theaters, and publishing houses. The specific conditions of
the Cold War militated against a resurgence of anti-Semitism.

Nothing better illustrates the implications of this ideological atmosphere for American Jews, including Jewish academic intellectuals, than
the fact that Senator Joseph McCarthy was not anti-Semitic. The most
powerful of the anti-Communist extremists of the Cold War certainly
earned his lasting reputation as the era's archvillain. But one thing he
did not do was to actively perpetuate the old association of Jews with
Bolshevism. Indeed, McCarthy's most visible coworker was the Jewish
lawyer Roy Cohn. The Communism McCarthy understood as his enemy
was created by pernicious acts of mind, not by blood or by historic cul-

tures. Anybody could be a Red. Well-bred Anglo-Protestants like Alger Hiss turned out, in McCarthy's view, to be just as likely as Americans of other backgrounds to have made the wrong political choices. The espionage case of Julius and Ethel Rosenberg did keep before the public an important Jewish image of American Communism, but McCarthy himself rarely mentioned the Rosenberg case.

Whatever the dynamics by which academic intellectuals' ethno-religious demography was transformed, awareness of this transformation's scope prompts additional questions. What difference did it make? Did the culture of the American professoriat and the role played by that professoriat in American society change because so many more of its members were Jewish by the end of the 1960s than a generation before? Historians have scarcely begun to consider these questions. In several of the essays collected here, I point to instances in which there is good reason to believe that Jews did make a difference. Jewish intellectuals were a secularizing influence in certain contexts, and many of them were significant agents in advancing an ideal of cosmopolitanism.

To make even such modest claims is to risk falling into the "booster-bigot trap" that tempts the scholar to choose between the uncritical celebration of "Jewish contributions" and the malevolent complaint about "Jewish influence."[10] This is an old dilemma. Concern about it fueled Lionel Trilling's much-quoted declaration in 1944 that he would take offense if people found either "faults or virtues" in his work as a writer and critic that they called "Jewish."[11] Even physics had been divided into "Aryan" and "Jewish" categories by Nazis; and a common strategy for combating anti-Semitism was a celebration of Jewish accomplishments that Trilling and many of his contemporaries found chauvinistic and parochial. The best way to avoid both boosterism and bigotry was, and is, to avoid talking about Jews.

This way of dealing with the booster-bigot trap concerning Jews is increasingly anomalous in an era when analysis of the role of many groups in the development of American culture is commonplace, and when the study of ideas in their sociocultural matrices is carried out with unprecedented resolve and rigor in most fields of historical scholarship. The booster-bigot trap is not, after all, peculiar to claims about Jews, nor is it found only in the study of academic intellectuals. It is potentially a problem for scholars studying virtually any cultural enterprise in which any group marked by a history of prejudice has attained a presence. Within the multiculturalist mood of recent years, students of American life have often assigned historic agency to such groups. African Americans, Latinos, and various European and Asian ethnic groups have put their own stamp on many aspects of the national culture of the United States; if that culture was largely created by Anglo-Protestants, it has been altered, contemporary scholarship frequently shows, by other groups, including many who have been the victims of Anglo-Protestant prejudice.

The same willingness to analyze cultural enterprises in terms of the group identities of its participants applies more than ever to the specific enterprise of academia. The increased presence of African Americans, Asian Americans, and Latinos in the humanities and social sciences, especially, has placed the booster-bigot trap in the path of anyone who might want to attribute a given aspect of academic culture to these groups. The same applies to changes in gender demography and to the role of women. Indeed, the belief that members of specific groups—women and ethnoracial minorities—would bring distinctive perspectives to the study of a given discipline has sometimes been advanced as a reason for diversifying faculties. Insofar as these new perspectives correct blind spots in a discipline, those blind spots themselves can be subject to a certain amount of ethnic and gender explanation: communities of historians and literary scholars missed certain truths, it is said, because so many of their members were, after all, white European-American males.

Scholars working within a late-twentieth-century atmosphere of heightened consciousness of group identities have sometimes blunted the jaws of the booster-bigot trap by ascribing "influence" of even the most remotely problematic sort only to the most fully empowered groups, and by appreciatively recognizing the "contributions" of groups who have been most disadvantaged. Yet empowered groups, too, can be credited with contributions in the multiculturalist milieu. No group, not even Anglo-Protestants who bear the chief responsibility for the perpetuation of racism in the United States, is normally denied positive contributions. Persons not bound by the civil conventions of the academy sometimes repeat the old complaints that the excessive influence of this or that group is destroying Norman Rockwell's America, or that whites are carrying out cultural genocide against a minority group. But mainstream scholars in the age of multiculturalism are more generous. Echoing the "immigrants' gifts" argument that some liberals brought to the defense of immigration in previous epochs—each immigrant group brings its distinctive "gifts" to the United States—multiculturalist scholars have proven much more willing to accept the risks of appearing akin to the booster than the risks of appearing akin to the bigot. This is no doubt as it should be, when we really must choose one or the other. But often, we do not.

The booster-bigot trap diminishes if we renounce several assumptions that helped to create it. The group in question is almost never a cultural monolith, nor defined by timeless dispositions. Nothing did more to set the trap than the mistaken idea that a given group possessed an enduring cultural essence grounded in blood and history, implanted in each of its individual members and capable of having an unmediated impact on any object it encountered. Although some multiculturalist scholarship has perpetuated this idea, the bulk of that scholarship in the 1990s has quarreled with this "essentialism" and has emphasized instead the internal diversity of ethnoracial groups and the contingent, historically specific character of the culture these communities present to the larger society at any given moment.[12] It is in this "anti-essentialist" atmosphere that the study of the role of Jews in American life—and within American academia—might be expanded without falling directly into the booster-bigot trap. Four specific points are of special salience for the study of Jews whose increased prominence invites historical study.

First, these Jews were of diverse origin within the Jewish Diaspora. Although a majority derived from the immigration of 1880–1924 that drew largely from the villages and small cities of Russia and Eastern Europe, others descended from the more urban, socially assimilated, and well-to-do German-Jewish families that had immigrated earlier. Still others immigrated directly from Hitler's Europe.

Second, the men and women in question oriented themselves in a variety of different ways to Jewish ethnicity and to Judaism. Some adopted anglicized names and displayed no connection to Jewish identity during most or all of their careers, whether or not they had been shaped significantly by any distinctly Jewish cultural experience or by any injuries resulting from anti-Semitic prejudice. Others, like Oppenheimer, were known to be of Jewish origin but had been educated in the Ethical Culture Society. Countless others affirmed Jewish identity to one degree or another in private contexts but not in public ones, and still others made a point of publicly asserting Jewish identity and, like many contributors to *Menorah Journal* and *Commentary*, wrote about Jewishness in relation to life in the United States.

Third, generational differences could be profound. No matter how he or she felt about Jewish identity, a new Ph.D. beginning a career as a twenty-five-year-old assistant professor in virtually any academic field in 1967—the year the writer Norman Podhoretz published his triumphant Jewish-generational memoir, *Making It*—could not help but bring to that career a "Jewish" experience of American society and of academic culture very different from that brought to such a career by a counterpart of twenty years before. But what it meant to be an aspiring Jewish intellectual of twenty-five in 1947 was also distinct from what it had meant in 1937, or 1927, or 1917. At each chronological point, Jews entering American academia carried different generational experiences conducive to different expectations and different sensibilities. This continues to be the case today: one reason Jews have rarely been treated as a distinctive group in discussions of academia during the multiculturalist 1980s and 1990s is that Jews have long since come to be perceived as part of an empowered white, or European-American, demographic bloc. Any inquiry into the possible intellectual consequences for the disciplinary community of sociology, for example, of that community's suddenly becoming more Jewish in the 1950s would need to take account of the generational experience of the parties.

Fourth, Jewish intellectuals absorbed greatly differing amounts of the prevailing culture of educated Americans that owed much to Protestant Christianity. Recognition of this assimilation fostered lively debates over who was and was not "really" Jewish, and over the relative costs and benefits of "liberation." Assimilation and resistance to assimilation took many forms, and these forms varied, in turn, from decade to decade. If Jews affected the culture of the United States in some respects, America also changed Jews. The study of the coming of Jewish intellectuals into American intellectual and academic life is the tracing of a dialectical process; it is not the mapping of a one-way street.

Nor is it the charting of more than a fraction of the intellectual history of the United States during the midcentury decades. That history ranges well beyond the topics emphasized in this introduction, and well beyond the additional ones explored in the studies collected within *Science, Jews, and Secular Culture*. But to bring into focus the historical episodes to which this book does attend there can be no better individual lens than the remarkable figure with whom this introduction began, J. Robert Oppenheimer.

When Oppenheimer reminded President Johnson and his other auditors in 1963 that science was an enterprise of cultural significance, and one that carried a "spirit of brotherhood," he was sounding yet again a point he had repeatedly voiced since he had become a public figure at the end of World War II. Even when audiences expected the "Father of the Atomic Bomb" to talk about physical theory or about concrete dilemmas in weapons policy during the Cold War, Oppenheimer often delivered himself of sober philosophical-literary meditations on the mission of science in the modern world. Among the most insistent of these meditations were Oppenheimer's Reith Lectures, delivered in London in 1953 and published the next year as *Science and the Common Understanding*.[13] Early in these lectures Oppenheimer quoted a sweepingly universalist manifesto from Bishop Sprat's 1667 history of the Royal Society of London:

> It is to be noted that they [the members of this organization of savants] have freely admitted Men of different Religions, Countries, and Professions of Life. This they were oblig'd to do, or else they would come far short of the

Largeness of their own Declarations. For they openly profess, not to lay the Foundation of an *English, Scotch, Irish, Popish,* or *Protestant* Philosophy; but a Philosophy of *Mankind.*

"Reading this today," Oppenheimer confessed, "we can hardly escape a haunting sense of its timeliness and a certain nostalgia" on account of the gap between the state of the world and the "agreeable and noble" ideals of the Royal Society. Oppenheimer was also quick to display an awareness that Bishop Sprat and his contemporaries did not fully see their own cultural particularity, including the distinctly Christian lineage of the universalism they espoused: the scientific communities of the seventeenth and eighteenth centuries "took for granted" a "way of life and a history," and owed much, specifically, "to the long centuries of Christian life and Christian tradition." Sprat, Boyle, and their comrades had no idea, moreover, how their "program" of universalist science, once launched, would eventually revolutionize their society and change "the very men and the very minds to which their program would in time become entrusted."[14]

That program was of course Oppenheimer's own. Throughout his Reith Lectures he endorsed the ideal of a universal brotherhood of honest inquirers aloof from religious and ethnic sectarianism. He also connected this ideal to the development of democracy and associated it with the political culture of the United States. He took every opportunity to identify his ideal community of science with his ideal community of humankind. Oppenheimer was not an especially gifted theorist of science's relation to culture, but he bore consistent witness to what he described, in the very last paragraph of his Reith Lectures, as "our faith—our binding, quiet faith—that knowledge is good and good in itself." That goodness assured the ultimate "harmony" between the interests of science and the interests of humankind, advanced by any and all who "bring a little light to the vast unending darkness of man's life and world."[15]

NOTES

1. "Oppenheimer's Remarks," *New York Times,* December 3, 1963, 23.

2. The state of the art of "Sixties studies" is well represented by a valuable collection of original articles, David Farber, ed., *The Sixties . . . From Memory to History* (Chapel Hill, N.C., 1994).

3. For an influential example of blame-the-Sixties discourse, see the chapter entitled "The Sixties," in Allan Bloom, *The Closing of the American Mind* (New York, 1987), 313–335.

4. Nuel Pharr Davis, *Lawrence and Oppenheimer* (New York, 1968), 355.

5. One of the first students of the period to insist on the importance of a break within the 1960s was Godfrey Hodgson, whose *America in Our Time* (New York,

1976) was also unusual, among books addressed largely to the 1960s, in the interest its author took in academic intellectuals and their role in American politics and society.

6. Dan A. Oren, *Joining the Club: A History of Jews and Yale* (New Haven, Conn., 1985), 261–268, 326. Oren's work is focused on the institutional exclusion, and later inclusion, of Jews at all levels of Yale life, including undergraduate admissions. Although Oren deals briefly with the impact of Jewish faculty on the culture of Yale, his book is less a study of the ethnoreligious transformation of the academy than of the dynamics of discrimination and antidiscrimination.

7. These figures were based on the self-identifications of respondents to questionnaires distributed by the Carnegie Commission. This study served as the chief basis for Seymour Martin Lipset and Everett Carll Ladd, Jr., "Jewish Academics in the United States: Their Achievements, Culture and Politics," in *American Jewish Yearbook 1971* (New York, 1972), 89–128. The study itself was made public and analyzed in a volume published by the Carnegie Commission, Stephen Steinberg, *The Academic Melting Pot: Catholics and Jews in American Higher Education* (New York, 1974); see esp. 101–103, 122–123.

8. For the specific points in this paragraph I am indebted to the informative article by Leonard Dinnerstein, "Anti-Semitism Exposed and Attacked, 1945–1950," *American Jewish History* 71 (1981): 134–149, esp. 139, 143, 146. Dinnerstein (136) also cites examples, as late as 1945, of fears that "one racial strain" will take over certain schools.

9. A helpful study is Keith W. Olson, *The G.I. Bill, the Veterans, and the Colleges* (Lexington, Ky., 1974).

10. I have called attention to the bigot-booster trap in my *In the American Province: Studies in the History and Historiography of Ideas* (Bloomington, Ind., 1985), 56.

11. Lionel Trilling, "Under Forty," *Contemporary Jewish Record* 6 (1944): 15.

12. For an engagement with this and related issues within multiculturalism, see my *Postethnic America: Beyond Multiculturalism* (New York, 1995).

13. J. Robert Oppenheimer, *Science and the Common Understanding* (New York, 1954). These lectures were later reprinted, along with several of Oppenheimer's other essays of the same era, as J. Robert Oppenheimer, *Atom and Void: Essays on Science and Community* (Princeton, N.J., 1989).

14. Oppenheimer, *Atom and Void*, 13–14.

15. Ibid., 75; see also 29, 65, 67, and 70–71.

CHAPTER TWO

Jewish Intellectuals and the De-Christianization of American Public Culture in the Twentieth Century

This essay began in response to a question I agreed to address at a conference of specialists in the history of Protestant Christianity in the United States: What accounts for the relative decline in cultural influence of the generic Protestantism so clearly dominant at the start of the twentieth century, and its replacement by a general acceptance of religious pluralism? The organizers were kind enough to let me scale down my paper to the more modest task of calling attention to one factor in this transformation, but one rarely confronted in the existing scholarly literature. What had been missing from the discussion was a forthright exploration of the role played in this transformation by immigrant Jews and their progeny.

The resulting essay tries not only to expand the Protestant-culture-to-pluralism inquiry in this way but also conveys my belief that this classical issue in modern American Protestant historiography is less important than another, prior question. Why is there so much Christianity in the United States? When the culture of other highly industrialized societies in the North Atlantic West is considered, the remarkable fact about Christianity in America is not that its hold on American culture has weakened but that this hold remains so strong. The task of explaining this persistence should be more prominent on the agenda of historians of religion, and of modern America in general. Countless books and articles have been written about the relative failure of socialism in the United States, but the relative failure of secularization also demands attention. To this large and demanding question I offer here no more than a prologue listing some obvious starting points. But it is within this frame—a presumption that de-Christianization is the norm in the modern West, not the exception—that I nest both the question of Protestantism's relative decline in America and my own inquiry into the role played in that decline by Jewish intellectuals.

To call attention to the relevance of Jewish intellectuals need not entail exaggerating their role. Religious pluralism would have flourished in the United States even in the absence of a Jewish population. Many of the Anglo-Protestant intellectuals who became engaged with the ideas and careers of specific Jewish intellectuals, moreover, were already well on their way down a secular path before they encountered Jews. These encounters took place in a number of settings, but this essay focuses on the academic intelligentsia. This intelligentsia was the site of especially concentrated interaction between Americans of Jewish and Anglo-

Protestant origin, and was the scene, too, of an unusually extensive de-Christian-
ization sometimes resented by Christians, especially those of a more conservative
orientation.

The concluding pages speak to contemporary efforts to advance the cultural
program of Christianity in academic and political spaces where this program has
lost the influence it once had. My aim in these closing reflections is to suggest that
an understanding of the story told in this essay should inspire caution in those
who lament secularization today and look for ways to reverse some of its effects.

This essay was first published in New Directions in American Religious
History: The Protestant Experience, *ed. D. G. Hart and H. S. Stout (New*
York, 1996).

"ANY LARGE number of free-thinking Jews" is "undesirable" if one wants
to maintain or develop a society in which a Christian tradition can flourish, said T. S. Eliot in 1934. He was right. At least he was right if the
standard for a flourishing Christian tradition is the one Eliot took for
granted. This conception of an ideal, racially and religiously homogeneous society Eliot illustrated with his ancestral New England and with
the Virginia whose self-image he flattered by respectfully invoking, in the
presence of his Charlottesville audience, the agrarian manifesto *I'll Take*
My Stand. It was an inauspicious time for a sophisticated and internation-
ally minded intellectual to send off to the press a suggestion that there
might be any context at all in which Jews should be declared undesirable; a full year had passed since Hitler had begun his notorious purge
of Jews from German universities.[1] Amid the dismay now routinely regis-
tered about Eliot's anti-Semitism, we risk losing touch with two insights
embedded in this, his most lamented public utterance. Eliot was right to
suggest that community building and maintenance involves at least some
drawing of social boundaries. And he was correct to single out Jews, especially freethinking Jews, as a unique threat in the 1930s to the realization
in the United States of a Christian community of the sort in which
Eliot—and not Eliot alone—would have preferred to live.

Religious and nonreligious Jews were far from the only agents and
referent points in the story of American Protestantism's encounter with
diversity and the consequent attraction of Protestantism's leaders to
"pluralism." But this story will not be accurately told until the role of Jews
is explored more extensively than it has been in previous tellings.[2] Although Catholics had long been a more numerous non-Protestant presence in the United States, and a more formidable threat to Protestant
religious leaders, these Catholics were, after all, Christians. The challenge they presented to Protestant hegemony was less absolute than the
one presented by an entirely non-Christian demographic bloc, even if
this non-Christian bloc was made up of "People of the Book." Despite the

existence of the American Jewish Committee and the several councils of rabbis, Jews were not so easily categorized as a single religious entity. Jews threw themselves more directly into American cultural life and embraced the public schools with enthusiasm, while Catholics developed their own comprehensive educational system supervised by a single network of organizations ultimately responsible to the Vatican. Moreover, substantial segments of the Jewish population were in possession of greater capital holdings, higher class position, and stronger technical skills than were the bulk of their Catholic counterparts. Although Catholics developed effective political bases in some urban localities, the political visibility of Jews within the circles of the nation's old Protestant elite was signaled by the appointment of Louis Brandeis to the United States Supreme Court in 1916. This Jewish presence was also concentrated to a large extent in the most conspicuous of places: New York City, the closest thing to an American cultural capital. By 1920, nearly one-third of New York's population was Jewish.

In addition, there arose from within the Jewish population an articulate and energetic minority of intellectuals—the "free-thinking Jews" of Eliot's most pointed concern—who took little interest in Judaism but did not become Christians, and who, even more portentously, brought a skeptical disposition into the American discussions of national and world issues that had been the all but exclusive domain of Protestants and ex-Protestants. To these freethinking Jews there was virtually no Catholic equivalent.[3] Even if Protestants managed to mentally shoehorn religious Jews into the categories of religious particularism—another peculiar "denomination" like the Mormons or the Seventh-Day Adventists—the cosmopolitan, Enlightenment-inspired Jews refused to stay put. It was not adherence to some un-American "tribal" faith that created a problem here; rather, what made these intellectuals special was their manifest failure to be Jewish parochials. This applied to many of the Zionist as well as the non-Zionist intellectuals in the group. Their transcending of conventional religious categories rendered them a problem for Protestants quite distinct from the challenge presented by Orthodox, Conservative, and Reform Jews.[4] Like their European prototypes Marx, Freud, and Durkheim, these emancipated Jews engaged the same "universal" discourses that American professors and authors had reproduced in terms more distinctly Protestant than would be widely acknowledged until later. This Protestant matrix was cast into bold relief first by Jews, then by Catholics who had long resented it but did not confront it very directly until the era of John Courtney Murray and Vatican II,[5] and eventually by a third, very different set of critics: the multiculturalists of our own time, for some of whom the exposure of the parochially Anglo-Protestant character of earlier American intellectual life has become an almost sacred calling. Before the role of Jews in this process can be properly assessed, however, it is important to clarify the question to which American Jews are part of a satisfactory answer.

No one doubts that the public culture of the United States was more decisively Protestant at the beginning of the twentieth century than it is today. The point is not simply that the overwhelming majority of religiously affiliated Americans had always been identified with one or another of a host of Protestant denominations. Nor is it that American ecclesiastical institutions were dominated in the early and middle decades of this century by a loose "Protestant Establishment" consisting of the recognized leaders of the most socially prominent of these denominations (especially Congregationalists, Baptists, Methodists, Presbyterians, Disciples, Episcopalians, and Lutherans). The question is not thus situated in "religious history," narrowly conceived.[6] The starting point for the inquiry lies instead in the larger history of the United States itself, and in the influence there of a generic Protestantism for which the ecclesiastical "Protestant Establishment" was assumed to be a reliable voice. This generic, transdenominational Protestantism had come by the end of the nineteenth century to be taken for granted by nearly all of the Americans in a position to influence the character of the nation's major institutions, including those controlling public education, politics, the law, literature, the arts, scholarship, and even science.[7] This confident spiritual proprietorship lay behind the continued currency well into the century of the idea that the United States was a "Christian nation." In recent decades Protestants, increasingly aware that the old, generic Protestantism is taken for granted by fewer and fewer of the people running the relevant institutions, have tended to acknowledge that the religious character of the nation is contested. They have been inclined to describe themselves as but one of a variety of parties to a "pluralism" that accepts the legitimacy within the American nation not only of Catholics and Jews, but, more recently, of a vast expanse of cultural units defined by ethnoracial as well as religious principles.[8] What accounts for this transition from "Protestant culture" to the acceptance, however gradual and in some cases grudging, of a pluralism in which Christianity is acknowledged to be but one of several legitimate religious persuasions in America? This is the question.

The place to begin is with a recognition that this question should be nested within another one that lies beyond the scope of this essay. Why is there so much Christianity in the United States in the twentieth century? What most needs to be explained is surely not the decline of Protestant cultural hegemony in one of the most socially diverse and highly literate of the industrialized nations of the North Atlantic West, but rather its persistence in such a setting. It would be implausible to expect the generic Protestantism of 1900 to be able to maintain its authority for long against the aggressive expansion of scientific culture, against the pluralizing force of massive migrations of Catholics and Jews down to 1924, and against the particularizing pressures of social diversity within the ranks of American Protestants.[9] The relative slowness and limited extent of de-Christianization in modern American history even down to the present is an event of the same order as the failure of the American Left to develop social democratic movements comparable to those of Great Britain, France, and Germany. The historiography of twentieth-century America has wrought many variations on the classic question "Why is there no socialism in the United States?" but this relative "failure of the Left" has a less widely addressed counterpart in the relative "failure of secularization." Why, indeed, is there so much Christianity in America today?

We do have a literature on this question,[10] although it is not always cast in these terms. The parallel to the Sombartian interrogative beloved of political historians has never, to my knowledge, been made explicit.[11] Treatments of the persistence of Christianity under implausible circumstances fall into some of the same patterns as do interpretations of the failure of the Left. It is often said, for example, that what appears superficially to be Christianity really is not—Harold Bloom's recent book on American "post-Christianity" is a convenient example[12]—just as a range of ostensibly nonsocialist protest movements are revealed by close study to have had sufficient anticapitalist content to render them American equivalents of social democracy. What shall count as "real" socialism and "real" Christianity is, of course, at issue in all of these studies. Yet the question of Christianity's persistence in twentieth-century America has not been as much in the foreground of inquiry as a world-historical perspective demands. The historiography of American religion since 1900 is more caught up in a master narrative of declension within an isolated national tradition than in a narrative of persistence informed by a comparative perspective on the destiny of Christianity in other highly literate, industrialized societies.

This is not the place to attempt an answer to the question "Why is there so much Christianity in the United States?"[13] *But awareness of some of the historic conditions that make this question compelling can help guide an examination of the transition from Protestant culture to pluralism.* The most salient of these historic conditions are part cognitive and part demographic.

Cognitively, refinement of the critical tradition of the Enlightenment created structures of credibility within which many of Christianity's truth-claims looked highly suspect. This sharpening of Enlightenment-inspired critique was visible in the historical study of the Bible, in the

Darwinian revolution in natural history, in the development of materialist analyses of the human self and of society, and in a multitude of efforts to substitute "science" for other authorities in a variety of specific contexts. Throughout the nineteenth century most of the Americans who welcomed and helped to advance the Enlightenment in these respects were, of course, Christians, many of whose descendants were in turn able to retain or to reconstitute their faith in relation to the increased cultural authority of science. But some were not. By the turn of the century many of the leading intellectuals whose professional work was most associated with the defense of a religious sensibility—Josiah Royce and William James are convenient examples[14]—knew better than to count biblical evidence as among the reasons for accepting a given idea as true. Careers like those of Margaret Mead, David Riesman, and Daniel Bell indicate the extent to which social scientists replaced the clergy as the most authoritative public moralists for educated Americans. The simple notion that the Enlightenment diminished the place of Christianity in the West may be banal, but it is also true.[15] It applies in an arena stretching far beyond twentieth-century America, but it applies there too, and formidably so.

Demographically, the immigration to the United States between about 1880 and 1924 and again after 1965 brought directly into the polity large numbers of people who were not only non-Protestants, but who also lacked the Protestant past that churchgoers shared with those who, like John Dewey, rejected or drifted away from the faith. Although a majority of the non-Protestants in both of these historic migrations were Catholic—from Europe in the first instance, from Latin America and the Philippines in the second—there were, of course, many Jews in the earlier one and many Muslims, Hindus, and Buddhists in the more recent one. Multiplicity as a social condition does not always produce pluralism as an ideological persuasion, but it often generates some effort in that direction. It did in both of these cases, although the pluralism inspired by the 1880–1924 migration—the pluralism of Brandeis, Randolph Bourne, and Horace Kallen—was aborted.[16] Indeed, the old Protestant establishment's influence persisted until the 1960s[17] in large measure because of the Immigration Act of 1924: had massive immigration of Catholics and Jews continued at pre-1924 levels, the course of American history would have been different in many ways, including, one may reasonably speculate, a more rapid diminution of Protestant cultural hegemony. Immigration restriction gave that hegemony a new lease on life.

Demographic diversification threatened Protestant predominance in some contexts without much reference to cognitive demystification, and vice versa. The challenge presented by Catholic immigrants from Italy, Poland, and elsewhere in Europe entailed very little Enlightenment resonance; on the contrary, Protestants generally felt that Catholics were not enlightened enough. But as prejudice diminished and as Protestant leaders worried more about secularism, one cohort after another of Protestant leaders came around to recognizing in their Catholic coreligionists a force that could be mobilized against religious indifference and even against the de-Christianizing influence of secular intellectuals and, some felt, of Hollywood. The same alliance was extended, with some theological adjustments, to religious Jews through the popularization of the idea of a "Judeo-Christian Tradition."[18] In the meantime, the secular modes of thought descending from the Enlightenment found constituencies among the sons and daughters of the old Protestant Establishment, even when such people were sheltered from social diversity. Cognitive demystification was a comprehensively Western and ultimately a global movement; secular inquiry could feel liberating in Peoria as well as in Paris, in Baltimore as well as in Berlin.

Yet the cognitive and demographic pressures on Protestant hegemony were not altogether unconnected. One leitmotif of Enlightenment commentaries on Christianity, after all, had been the diversity of the world's religions, and the extent to which some of the most esoteric of these actually contained myths similar to those basic to Judaism and Christianity. This diversity of credible religious witnesses was a staple of nineteenth-century free thought driven home to American Protestants by Col. Robert Ingersoll's scandalous public lectures during the Gilded Age, and reinforced in a more benign voice by William James's prodigious *Varieties of Religious Experience.* The difficulty of establishing Christianity's superiority to other religions—once they were really scrutinized with a modicum of honest sympathy—bedeviled many in the wake of the 1893 World's Parliament of Religions. And foreign missionary experience, too, sometimes had the effect of undermining a confidence more easily maintained within the confines of a small town in rural America.[19] Moreover, it was the secular intellect's claim to be able to handle any experience that came along that most distinguished it from its apparently more parochial rivals. All methods of "fixing belief" other than science will eventually fail, Charles Peirce explained in the pages of *Popular Science Monthly,* because of the social world's diversity: the tenaciously faithful may try to hide from the diversity of human testimony about the world, but they will be unable to ignore it forever.[20] "The scientific method is cosmopolitan," insisted a representative ideologue of science at the turn of the century, because it is truly "worldwide" and tries to take everyone's reports into account.[21] Immigration brought to the United States a tiny fraction of the world that the ideologues of science believed they could eventually encompass, but in bringing home even this measure of demographic diversity immigration joined science as a force for the destabilization of a public culture grounded in Protestantism.

For the history of the nation's academic and literary elites, however, the most relevant connection between demographic diversification and cognitive demystification is highly specific. Jews who managed to find a place for themselves in the public intellectual life of the nation—rather than speaking to a distinctly Jewish constituency—reinforced the most de-Christianized of the perspectives already current among the Anglo-Protestants. If lapsed Congregationalists like Dewey did not need immigrants to inspire them to press against the boundaries of even the most liberal of Protestant sensibilities, Dewey's kind were resoundingly encouraged in that direction by the Jewish intellectuals they encountered in urban academic and literary communities. Franz Boas was among the earliest of these Jewish intellectuals to achieve prominence. He founded a tradition of relativist anthropology that exercised enormous deprovincializing influence through both Gentile (Margaret Mead, Ruth Benedict) and Jewish (Edward Sapir, Melville Herskovitz) followers.[22] Boas himself was the only prestigious American scientist to campaign actively against the ostensibly scientific racism used to justify the immigration exclusion act of 1924.[23] The biologist Jacques Loeb also became a celebrity well before World War I. Loeb was a forthright atheist whose rejection by New York's Century Association led the Columbia psychologist J. McKeen Cattell to mount a public protest.[24] Loeb became a symbol for the ethical austerity of science and served as a model for Max Gottlieb, the Jewish scientist-hero Sinclair Lewis contrasted to the priggishly moralistic Reverend Ira Hinkey in Lewis's most acclaimed novel, *Arrowsmith*.[25] A third academic Jew who became an animating presence in the second decade of the century was the literary critic Joel Spingarn. He proclaimed a radical aestheticism that violated the prevailing literary culture of moral uplift. After speaking in defense of a colleague being fired when love letters to a secretary were made public, Spingarn himself was dismissed from Columbia University in 1911 by the authoritarian President Nicholas Murray Butler. Spingarn is most remembered today for having helped to found the National Association for the Advancement of Colored People, and for having served for many years as chair of its board.[26]

Boas, Loeb, and Spingarn were all based primarily in New York, as was the editor and novelist Abraham Cahan.[27] Gentiles in the New York of this era produced a number of testimonies to the cosmopolitan influence of Jewish intellectuals.[28] The most famous of these testimonials is "The Intellectual Preeminence of Jews in Modern Europe," written by Thorstein Veblen shortly after his 1918 arrival in New York. Veblen treated Jewish intellectuals—with whom the "rootless" and "marginal"

Veblen, a son of Norwegian immigrants, clearly identified—as "the vanguard of modern inquiry."[29] But if Veblen's essay on the pains as well as the benefits of marginality was in part the product of his Chicago years and of his energetic reading, Randolph Bourne's more romantic "Transnational America" and "The Jew and Transnational America"[30] were full of New York and were openly grounded in Bourne's personal experiences at Columbia and in Greenwich Village. Bourne named Justice Brandeis as an obvious example of a Jewish presence serving to undercut the old Anglo-Protestant provincialism, but he also mentioned four men of Bourne's own generation: Felix Frankfurter, Horace M. Kallen, Morris R. Cohen, and Walter Lippmann.[31] It is a mark of Bourne's astonishing prescience that he was able, on the basis of their very earliest work, to identify these four as the major agents of cultural change that each, in fact, became.

One of Bourne's four young Jewish intellectuals, Cohen, wrote with special eloquence then and later about the passion with which Jewish youth on the Lower East Side were determined to absorb all of the benefits of "the Age of Reason" and to commit themselves fully to its exploration and development.[32] The frustrations men like Cohen experienced while trying to act on these ambitions affected the character of their gradual impact on the old Protestant culture. The obstacles faced by Jews trying to obtain first-rate educations and to make academic careers are well known. Although Harvard's president emeritus Charles W. Eliot and some other liberals within the establishment opposed the quotas that capped Jewish enrollment in the early 1920s at a number of prominent eastern schools, these quotas did operate and were deeply resented by their victims.[33] Equally enraging was the shunning of prospective Jewish faculty, evidence of which is known to anyone who has read academic correspondence from the period 1910–1945.[34]

At issue was more than religion. Jews were suspect in academia partly because many Anglo-Protestants thought them socially crude and aggressive, and politically radical. But religion was a very large part of it, as is revealed by patterns in the location and intensity of suspicion of a Jewish presence. The barriers to Jews in business, engineering, medicine, and law—where technical skills rather than responsibility for constituting and transferring culture were central—were not as high, nor as entrenched. Intellectually ambitious Jewish undergraduates of the teens, twenties, and thirties were routinely counseled to give up on the idea of becoming philosophers or historians and were encouraged to pursue, instead, a career in one of the service professions. Economics, in keeping with the prevailing stereotypes, was the one academic field Jews were regularly encouraged to enter. Psychology, too, was understood to be potentially appropriate for Jews, especially when psychology was viewed as a branch of medicine or of physiology. The social snobbery that victimized Jews was thus the most potent when allied with the defense of a generic, if theologically inconspicuous, Protestantism. As late as 1929, there were in New York City alone twenty-eight "home missions" designed to convert Jews to the Christian faith.[35]

These aspects of the American scene help give meaning to the specific ways in which the Jewish intellectuals began to make a difference, even while still held largely at bay during the quarter-century prior to World War II. An example is Jewish leadership of the movement to make Oliver Wendell Holmes, Jr., into an iconic representative of the American spirit.[36] Holmes's greatness was hailed by American intellectuals of a variety of backgrounds, but Jews did the most to establish Holmes in the public mind as more than just a great judge and scholar.[37] Responsibility for effectively promoting Holmes as a cultural hero is often assigned above all to Frankfurter and Harold J. Laski. Grant Gilmore has argued that these two "concocted the picture of the tolerant aristocrat, the great liberal, the eloquent defender of our liberties, the Yankee from Olympus."[38] From his strategic position at the Harvard Law School, Frankfurter affirmed his reverence for Holmes repeatedly, declaring in 1927 that Holmes had "built himself into the structure of our national life" and "written himself into the slender volume of the literature of all time."[39] It was Frankfurter's recruit to the Harvard faculty, Laski, who took responsibility for the edition of Holmes's *Collected Legal Papers* in 1920. The representation of Holmes as the Complete American Liberal was carried on by Cohen,[40] and later by Jerome Frank[41] and Max Lerner. In Lerner's 1943 rendition, Holmes was "perhaps the most complete personality in the history of American thought." Holmes had always stood by "faith in social reason and in the competition of ideas" and a "belief in the steady, if slow march of social progress." Holmes "was a great man," emphasized Lerner, "regardless of whether he was a great justice."[42]

Holmes was a good choice. His influence promised to help release American culture from a Christian bias that most Jewish intellectuals found provincial at best, and at worst a basis for continued discrimination against Jews and other non-Christians. The old Brahmin was about as "American" as it was possible to get, but he had put great distance between himself and exactly those parts of Protestant culture most oppressive to Jews. Holmes was aloof from Anglo-Saxon nativism and from the genteel tradition in literature for which his father remained an enduring symbol. Moreover, the Olympian Holmes had actually befriended Frankfurter, Laski, and Cohen at a time when Jews felt deeply the sting of social and professional rejection by most men and women of Holmes's milieu.[43] Holmes was not noticeably Christian, and what echoes of heroic Calvinism he carried were easily detached from quotas for Jews at Harvard and Columbia. Jewish intellectuals had a real enemy to fight, and they knew Holmes was no part of it. Hence it is not surprising that of the various specific projects moving the public culture of the United States more decisively in a secular, cosmopolitan direction, the particular project of managing the reputation of Holmes should become one in which Jewish intellectuals took the lead. The making of the agnostic Holmes into an emblem for American life was one step in the construction of a secular vision of American culture—a vision de-emphasizing that culture's historically Protestant components. And this secular vision became a common possession of the American academic and literary intelligentsia during the middle decades of the century.[44]

The men and women who made up this intelligentsia were cultural products of a process of accommodation that left both Jews and Gentiles different from what they would have been had they not interacted with one another. To refer to certain of these intellectuals as Jews, or as Anglo-Protestants, need not imply an ethnic essentialism according to which each party to this historical engagement brought to it a static and monolithic inventory of traits and dispositions. On the contrary, individuals identified ethnically as Jews or as Anglo-Protestants displayed a great range of characteristics, yielding a sometimes anxious discourse over assimilation (were Jews becoming too "anglicized"?) and liberalization (were Anglo-Protestants of this or that particular persuasion giving up a precious heritage in order to participate in a polyglot and secular modernity?).

By the midcentury mark, intellectuals of Jewish origin were no longer systematically excluded from even the teaching of English and philosophy. It is not easy to separate cause from effect in the ethnodemographic transformation of American academia during the midcentury decades. Did Jews find their way into this sector of American life because of a prior de-Christianization well advanced among intellectuals of Anglo-Protestant origin, or because these Jews, themselves, had helped by their very presence and by their pressure against the old exclusionary system to de-Christianize the space they were gradually entering? Both were surely true, but there was an additional factor, more easily isolated.

Hitler was a major agent of this transformation in two respects. His example—horrifying to many Americans even before the full dimensions of the "Final Solution" became known—rendered anti-Semitism of even the genteel sort more difficult to defend. If this helped American Jews beginning careers in the late 1940s and early 1950s, a second of Hitler's acts made a more dramatic and immediate impact: he pushed from Central Europe to a relatively welcoming[45] America a distinctive cohort of Jewish scholars, scientists, and artists that attracted extensive notice within the American academic and literary worlds. This cohort included not only Albert Einstein and a substantial percentage of the physicists who built the atomic bomb, but a galaxy of distinguished humanists and social scientists.[46] The fame and prestige of some of these men and women enabled this migration to have a symbolic impact far beyond the specific, local communities into which these refugee intellectuals were absorbed.[47]

American academia expanded rapidly in the postwar era, and a larger and larger portion of faculties turned out to be Jews, the descendants, in most cases, of the East European Jewish immigration of 1880–1924. In the process, the critical debates conducted in the *Partisan Review*—since the 1930s the central organ of the largely Jewish group known as "the New York intellectuals"—were absorbed into academic departments of English and comparative literature.[48] As this ethnodemographic transformation of several major academic disciplines proceeded during the 1950s and 1960s, the argument was not that these disciplines needed "a Jewish perspective"; these faculty appointments were made on the basis of prevailing professional standards as understood by the disciplines' leaders. As with Cohen and Spingarn a half-century before, but now on a huge scale, Jews were entering communities of discourse on the "universal" terms proclaimed by these communities themselves. By the early 1960s the large number of Jews in sociology led to faculty-club banter to the effect that sociology had become a Jewish discipline. In the literary world the triumphs of Norman Mailer, Saul Bellow, and J. D. Salinger led Leslie Fiedler to hail "the great take-over by Jewish-American writers" of a task "inherited from certain Gentile predecessors, urban Anglo-Saxons and midwestern provincials of North European origin"—the task of "dreaming aloud the dreams of the whole American people."[49]

The de-Christianization that accompanied these changes in the ethnodemographic base of American intellectual life was indirect but not necessarily trivial. Gentiles could take pride in the creation of a collegial environment in which Jewish colleagues would not feel marginalized. Religion was increasingly private, and public discussion was increasingly secular. It is worth considering, in juxtaposition to one another, two widespread perceptions concerning the elite college and university faculties of the last quarter-century. One perception is that the prevailing culture of these faculties is more secular than is the rest of the society and even the rest of the American academy, and that within these faculties the open profession of Christian belief in the course of one's professional work is uniquely discouraged. Most investigators trying to answer the question "Why is there so much Christianity in the United States?" would squander little time interviewing the citizens of Cambridge, New Haven, Ann Arbor, Hyde Park, Madison, and Berkeley.[50] The second perception is that these same faculties are disproportionately Jewish. The first of these two perceptions may be impressionistic in foundation, but the second has been confirmed by a report of the Carnegie Commission on Higher Education. This 1969 study found that while Jews constituted only about 3 percent of the American population, they accounted for 17 percent of the combined faculties of the seventeen most highly ranked universities.[51]

No doubt the culture of elite universities would be more secular than it used to be even had there been no change in their ethnodemographic composition. But I hope it is not unwarranted to suggest that we get some insight into the weakening of the old Protestant cultural hegemony if we attend closely to the settings in which it was once the strongest and was then weakened the most decisively. Such a setting was the elite university. This major American institution was created by people who were, among their other vital identities, Protestants—that fact is surely indisputable and applies even to the era's nonpareil theologian-baiter, Andrew Dickson White—who gradually yielded control of it to people who were either less public about their Protestantism, less fully Protestant, or not Protestant at all, indeed, not even Christian. An informal alliance among liberal Protestants, ex-Protestants, religious Jews, and freethinking Jews did much to bring about this transformation. The role of Jews in the story has rarely been addressed as directly as I address it here.[52] Perhaps this dimension has been avoided because many who have thought about the transition from Protestant culture to religious pluralism have continued to honor an old suspicion that America would be better off today were it somehow more Christian than it is. Given this presumption, any account of how Jews contributed to the diminution of Christianity's influence could be construed as a criticism of Jews, and as grist for the mill of T. S. Eliot's ideological descendants. But this historiographical inhibition disappears if we believe, instead, that whatever may be wrong with American universities, and with America, it is not that they are insufficiently Christian.

This decisive removal from our historiographical presuppositions of the ideal of a Christian America can also have a liberating effect on our treatments of the historical significance of liberal Protestantism in modern United States history. That liberal Protestantism is still much maligned in many circles reflects, I believe, an uncritical acceptance of the most popularly disseminated and polemical of the constructions of Reinhold Niebuhr.[53] What secular followers of Niebuhr sometimes fail to understand is the extent to which Niebuhr's constructions of liberal Protestantism derived from his own affirmations of Christianity: Niebuhr thought the liberals had sold out. Hence many of the "atheists for Niebuhr"[54] disparaged and even effaced the liberal Protestants who facilitated the de-Christianized discursive space the atheists themselves were delighted to inhabit. The religious "integrity" the liberals were said to have abandoned was easy to admire from the safe distance the secularists owed, in part, to the liberals who presided over the decline of Protestant hegemony. Efforts to develop a more fair-minded and nuanced interpretation of liberal Protestantism have been advanced within the circle of "church historians,"[55] but in the larger profession of American historians these have attracted little notice. A promising turn is the recent work of Niebuhr's most convincing interpreter, Richard Fox.[56]

The widespread acceptance of "pluralism" has left a matter for ongoing debate the exact character and implications of this idea for American religious life. Among the unresolved issues is the relation between religious pluralism and the various ideas put forth in the name of "multiculturalism." Although we have been awash in discussions of multiculturalism for several years now, a persistent deficiency in the multiculturalist debate is the relative silence of almost all of its major participants concerning the place of religious affiliation amid other kinds of affiliation. The building and maintaining of communities does involve the drawing of boundaries, and even a measure of exclusion, but where and how to draw the lines that enclose and exclude, and how to assign different weights and roles to the national community as opposed to ethnoracial, religious, and other communities remains a matter of persistent confusion and contention. Some of the ingredients and tensions within the multiculturalist controversy are displayed in the accompanying cartoon. Here, a Bible-carrying and cross-wearing family of presumably Evangelical Protestants is positioned alongside an orthodox Jewish family and in front of a Muslim couple. Religious categories are thus at the center of this multicultural scene, but the cartoonist understandably situates religious identity within a panorama of dress-coded identities defined by race, sexual orientation, and "lifestyles" ranging from straights and yuppies through Deadheads and bikers.

This is not the place to try to provide a sketch of the multiculturalist controversy,[57] but by way of epilogue I do want to identify and comment briefly upon three closely related initiatives in this ongoing discussion as it regards religious pluralism. I select these three because they indicate the dynamism of the struggle to clarify the implications of pluralism, reveal the resentments that some Protestants continue to feel over the loss of their hegemonic position, and raise issues that I believe should concern anyone committed to building or maintaining communities in which both non-Christians and Christians can function in an atmosphere of mutual respect.

One such initiative is to resist the trend toward the "privatization" of religion that has accompanied the transition from Protestant culture to

Reprinted by permission of the *Colorado Springs Gazette Telegraph.*

pluralism. Is not religious commitment trivialized, some ask, by the understanding that one should voice these commitments primarily within one's community of faith and not abroad? This query may carry specifically Evangelical notions of religious authenticity that are uniquely threatened by the transition from Protestant culture to pluralism. Another model of religious authenticity is that of Judaism, as practiced, for example, by the many Jewish politicians and Jewish professors who display very little eagerness to project their own particular religion into American law or into the classrooms of American universities. It may be that as a corollary of the recognition that the United States is not a Christian Israel, Christians will eventually come to accept a model for religious authenticity that owes less to Saint Paul than to the Judaism of the Diaspora.

A second initiative visible in these same, searching discussions concerns the status of science. The salient move is to diminish the cultural authority of science by construing it as but one of many parties to a pluralism the implicit rules of which can then reduce science's cognitive reach to a size manageable by those threatened by it. The enhancing of religion's claims through delimitation of science's scope is a venerable strategy, employed with some skill by Poincaré and Eddington, and advanced in our time in settings ranging from the theology of the Yale

School to the creationism of local school boards. Gadamerian, Kuhnian, and Foucaultian critiques of "the myth of objectivity" have been invoked in the cause. This initiative, too, seems to bespeak a residual resistance to the historic fact that the Enlightenment has essentially won in the cognitive realm, as Schleiermacher sensed it would, and as neither Gadamer, Kuhn, nor Foucault has actually doubted. This initiative also risks treating "science" as an all-or-nothing proposition, silencing, in the manner of many of today's self-styled postmodernists, the hermeneutically self-aware variations on "objectivity" developed by pragmatists and realists. It will be a challenge for defenders of Christianity to direct the more radically postmodernist theories of knowledge and of the human self against the authority of science without, at the same time, undercutting the authority of Christianity, about which Nietzsche, the fountainhead of postmodernist theory, had a lot to say.

A third initiative is to present Christians as victims, to appropriate for Christianity—in its newly adopted role as a beleaguered minority—the arguments developed by feminists, gays, and ethnoracial minorities seeking full participation in the society and the polity. The complaint of Christians as "the newest minority" insists that Christians are discriminated against, and that their opinions are not taken seriously. Everyone but traditional Christians, it seems, gets the chance to speak out. The attitude to which I refer is neatly encapsuled in a remark recently quoted by George Marsden. "Christians," said Mark R. Schwehn, "are now treated in a manner rather like women were treated in the pre-feminist era. Women could be hired, promoted, and retained, so long as their feminism did not figure prominently in their research interests, their scholarly perspectives, and their manner of life generally."[58] Such sentiments invite curiosity as to whether Christianity is generating a number of exciting new research programs, as feminism has proved able to do. Feminism gets attention in the academy partly because its voice is relatively new, and the questions it asks often redirect old discourses in novel and fruitful directions. Women, moreover, have been truly excluded from public and academic life, and are now being included on a large scale for the first time. Hence the appropriation by Christians of the moral standing of a constituency so long victimized invites the suspicion that some of these Protestant appropriators are slow to shed the expectations and psychological habits of hegemony. The universities are, after all, among the few locations in American society in which ideas identified as Christian are not uncritically accepted, and in which feminism is actively encouraged as an intellectual program. Obviously, Christians should not be denied the basic rights owed to any member of the society or of the academy, and the history of Christianity needs to be taught like any other aspect of the American past, no matter what some of us today may think of Christianity's substantive merit.[59] But if some auditors withdraw when religious testimony begins, it may be less a violation of a Christian speaker's rights than an expression of the feeling that this particular message has been heard before and has already contributed most of what it has to offer. If any party to the conversation has had an abundance of opportunities to be heard, it is surely Christianity.

Christianity marched into the modern era as the strongest, most institutionally endowed cultural program in the Western world. The people in charge of this program tried through a variety of methods, some more coercive than others, to implant Christian doctrines and practices in as much of the globe as they could. Yet, as the centuries went forward, this extraordinary empire of power/knowledge lost some of the ground it had once held. Christianity at the end of the twentieth century—the "Christian Century," prophesied by the Protestant hegemonists at its start—is less triumphant in the North Atlantic West than it was in 1500 or 1700 or 1900. Whether what has happened in this part of the world amounts to "secularization" or, as Hans Blumenberg insists, "reoccupation," something has certainly changed.[60] Whether or not other agencies have become vehicles for values that Christianity carried, plenty of other chariots are at hand. The story of the fate of Protestant culture in the United States in the twentieth century is but a fragment of this larger drama of the transformation of the North Atlantic West from a society heavily invested in the cultural program of Christianity to a society in which Christianity found it harder and harder to retain the spiritual capital of its most thoughtful and learned members. If Christianity's continuing adherents include some of the most thoughtful and learned men and women in the world—as I believe they do—the trend is nonetheless real, and the historian's obligation to understand it is no less compelling.

NOTES

1. Eliot signed the preface to *After Strange Gods: A Primer of Modern Heresy* (London, 1934) in January of the year in which it was published. The text was composed of lectures Eliot had delivered in 1933 at the University of Virginia. See especially 14–21. It should be pointed out that this book, so often maligned and dismissed as an anomaly in the Eliot canon, is distinguished by many of the same virtues that helped make Eliot one of the finest critical essayists of the twentieth century. Hence his construction in these pages of an ideal society is all the more important a document of its time and place. The manifesto of the "Nashville Agrarians," *I'll Take My Stand* (New York, 1930) was not overtly anti-Semitic but, of course, displayed a commitment to particularity of people and place that Eliot endorsed.

2. Hence this essay seeks to build upon, and to supplement, existing accounts of this important event in modern American history. Of these accounts, I want

especially to acknowledge the relevant portions of three very recent books: William R. Hutchison, ed., *Between the Times: The Travail of the Protestant Establishment in America, 1900–1960* (New York, 1989); George M. Marsden and Bradley J. Longfield, eds., *The Secularization of the Academy* (New York, 1992); and Martin Marty, *Modern American Religion*, vol. 2, *The Noise of Conflict 1919–1941* (Chicago, 1991), although Marty has put much of his telling of this particular story aside in order to focus more directly on it in the third, and forthcoming, volume of this trilogy. An earlier, classic study is Robert T. Handy, *A Christian America: Protestant Hopes and Historical Realities* (New York, 1971).

3. Some historians would say that there did emerge, by the midcentury decades, a small cohort of dissenting Catholic and ex-Catholic intellectuals who constituted a distinctive, radical presence in American intellectual life. Among these were Dorothy Day, Mary McCarthy, C. Wright Mills, and Jack Kerouac. A beginning in the study of this phenomenon has been made by James T. Fisher, *The Catholic Counterculture in America, 1933–1962* (Chapel Hill, N.C., 1989).

4. Yet when historians of Christianity address the role of Jews in American society, they almost always do so within the fairly narrow frame of "religious history," thus confining their attention to religious Jews. See, for example, Gordon Tucker's "A Half-Century of Jewish-Christian Relations," in *Altered Landscapes: Christianity in America, 1935–1985*, ed. David W. Lotz (Grand Rapids, Mich., 1989), 140–154.

5. For an excellent study of this change in the role of Catholics in American intellectual life, and for a compelling interpretation of Murray, see Patrick Allitt, *Catholic Intellectuals and Conservative Politics in America: 1950–1985* (Ithaca, N.Y., 1993). See also the informative essay by Philip Gleason, "American Catholic Higher Education, 1940–1990: The Ideological Context," in Marsden and Longfield, *Secularization of the Academy*, 234–258.

6. What accounts for the decline, *within American Protestantism*, of the relative influence of the old Protestant Establishment's classical denominations, and the simultaneous growth in the relative influence of groups distinguished by Evangelical, fundamentalist, and Pentecostal tendencies largely avoided by the "mainline" churches? This more narrowly situated question does need to be distinguished from the major concern of this essay.

7. For a vivid invocation of the taken-for-granted status of Protestantism in 1900, see the opening pages of Robert T. Handy, *Undermined Establishment: Church-State Relations in America, 1880–1920* (Princeton, N.J., 1991), esp. 7–8. For a broader account of the generically Protestant public culture of the United States in this era, see the ethnographic portrait of America in 1912 presented in part 1 of Henry F. May, *The End of American Innocence: A Study of the First Years of Our Own Time* (New York, 1959), 3–117.

8. A major occasion for, and indicator of, this acceptance of religious "pluralism" was the enormously favorable reception Protestant leaders gave to Will Herberg's *Protestant-Catholic-Jew* (New York, 1955). This book took specific issue with attacks on pluralism found even within liberal journals such as the *Christian Century* as late as 1950. As the acceptance of pluralism was more and more widely articulated during the 1960s, in the wake of the election of the Catholic John F. Kennedy as president, it became clear that some had in mind a pluralism flour-

ishing within a broadly conceived Judeo-Christian tradition, while others were willing to accept as legitimate a greater variety of religious persuasions, including principled unbelief. An example of the former, Protestant-Catholic-Jew perspective is Franklin Hamlin Littell, *From State Church to Pluralism: A Protestant Interpretation of Religion in American History* (New York, 1962); while an example of the latter, more cosmopolitan vision is Harvey Cox, *The Secular City: Secularization and Urbanization in Theological Perspective* (New York, 1965). By the 1990s the acceptance of the idea of pluralism—however much its exact meaning remained a matter for debate—had reached the point that even some evangelically committed voices were urging Christians to "recognize that they are part of an unpopular sect" in a society populated by a vast diversity of voices on religious issues; see George Marsden, "The Soul of the American University: A Historical Overview," in Marsden and Longfield, *Secularization of the Academy*, 41.

9. That these conditions would militate against the perpetuation of the American religious status quo of 1900 is an implication of the bulk of our sociological and historical literature on "secularization." For a recent sampling and critical reconsideration of this formidable literature, see Steve Bruce, ed., *Religion and Modernization: Sociologists and Historians Debate the Secularization Thesis* (Oxford, 1992), especially the judicious concluding remarks of Bryan R. Wilson, "Reflections on a Many Sided Controversy," 195–210.

10. A recent, controversial example is Roger Finke and Rodney Stark, *The Churching of America, 1776–1990: Winners and Losers in Our Religious Economy* (New Brunswick, N.J., 1992).

11. The closest approach to this parallel I have seen is Leo Ribuffo's reference to "American exceptionalism" at the end of "God and Contemporary Politics," *Journal of American History* 79 (1993): 1533. This perspicacious essay is the best summary treatment of the historiography of politics and religion in the twentieth-century United States.

12. Harold Bloom, *The American Religion: The Emergence of the Post-Christian Nation* (New York, 1992). For a discerning critique of this book, see Henry F. May's review in *Reviews in American History* 21 (June 1993): 185–189.

13. I believe that a sound answer to this question would emphasize the absence of a formal ecclesiastical establishment in the American constitutional order and the consequent availability of voluntary religious affiliation as a device for the formation and maintenance of communities that mediate between the individual and the apparatus of the modern state. In this view, the flourishing of religious groups is largely an "ethnic" phenomenon responsive to a need for social solidarity in units of manageable size authorized by cultural symbols whose spiritual authority derives from accessible traditions. Being "religious" can thus be a way of being "American" in an America understood to be constituted by a dispersal of subgroup identities compatible with American national identity itself. This understanding renders explicable the tendency of immigrants from Mexico and other Latin American countries to become more Catholic as part of their engagement with American society. One work highly relevant to this line of analysis, sadly underexploited by both "church historians" and the larger historical profession, is R. Laurence Moore, *Religious Outsiders and the Making of Americans* (New York, 1986).

14. Consider Royce's *The Religious Aspect of Philosophy* (New York, 1885) and *The Problem of Christianity* (New York, 1913), and James's *The Will to Believe* (New York, 1897).

15. James Turner, *Without God, without Creed: The Origins of Unbelief in America* (Baltimore, Md., 1985), helps us understand the complexity of this process by revealing the precise nature of the decisions made along the way by Protestant intellectuals, but it does not render less real the historical forces with which Turner's cast of characters were obliged to deal. Historians enthusiastic about Turner's provocative claim that "religion caused unbelief" (xii) have sometimes paid insufficient attention to the vital qualifiers Turner attached to his argument—for example, "Unbelievers appeared most often in intellectual locations exposed to science, economic locations shaped by new means of production and distribution, geographic locations unsettled by industrialization and urbanization" (260).

16. Indeed, a striking fact about the multiculturalism of our own time is the relative lack of awareness its earliest adherents displayed of the "cultural pluralism" of Kallen's generation. Kallen himself lost interest in cultural pluralism shortly after he gave this doctrine its name in 1924. So lost from sight was Kallen's cultural pluralism even by 1955 that Herberg made no reference to Kallen when discussing pluralism; when Herberg did cite Kallen, it was in the latter's capacity as a commentator on secular religiosity. Finally in the 1990s Kallen became a major reference point in the multiculturalist debates; see, for example, Michael Walzer, "What Does It Mean to Be an American?" *Social Research* 57 (1990): 591–614.

17. It was in the 1960s, most students of the old Protestant Establishment's history seem to agree, that the public authority of the "mainstream" denominations' combined leadership finally collapsed; see, e.g., Robert S. Michaelsen and Wade Clark Roof, eds., *Liberal Protestantism: Realities and Possibilities* (New York, 1986), esp. 6; Wade Clark Roof and William McKinney, *American Mainline Religion: Its Changing Shape and Future* (New Brunswick, N.J., 1987), esp. 10–39; and the essays collected in Hutchison, *Travail.*

18. On the popularization of this concept in the midcentury decades, see Mark Silk, "Notes on the Judeo-Christian Tradition in America," *American Quarterly* 36 (1984): 65–85.

19. "Typically," Grant Wacker tells us, "the missionaries' perceptions moved from abhorrence to grudging admiration to varying degrees of approval of the ethical and religious ideals of the peoples among whom they worked." Grant Wacker, "A Plural World: The Protestant Awakening to World Religions," in Hutchison, *Travail,* 256. Concerning the cognitive security of small towns, however, one of the finest novels ever written about small-town Protestant culture is organized around the diversifying forces present even in the Burned Over District at the end of the century: Harold Frederic, *The Damnation of Theron Ware* (New York, 1896). Theron Ware's experiences with the freethinking Dr. Ledsmar, the urbane priest Father Forbes, the aesthete Celia Madden, and the realistic, diversity-accepting Sister Soulsby prefigure much of the next century's transition from Protestant culture to pluralism.

20. Charles Peirce, "The Fixation of Belief," *Popular Science Monthly* 12 (1877): 1–15.

21. Conway MacMillan, "The Scientific Method and Modern Intellectual Life," *Science*, n.s., 1 (1895): 541.

22. Boas and his students and their collective impact on American culture have been the subject of a number of studies, perhaps the most pointed of which is Richard Handler, "Boasian Anthropology and the Critique of American Culture," *American Quarterly* 42 (1990): 252–273.

23. The singularity of Boas's leadership in this respect is emphasized in Kenneth M. Ludmerer, *Genetics and American Society: An Historical Appraisal* (Baltimore, Md., 1972), esp. 25.

24. This episode is described in Philip Pauly, *Controlling Life: Jacques Loeb and the Engineering Ideal in Biology* (New York, 1987), 142–144.

25. Sinclair Lewis, *Arrowsmith* (New York, 1925).

26. For an overview of Spingarn's career in the specific context of the academy's response to Jewish intellectuals, see Susanne Klingenstein, *Jews in the American Academy, 1900–1940: The Dynamics of Intellectual Assimilation* (New Haven, Conn., 1991), 104–111. This is a helpful, if sketchy introduction to the topic of its title, but Klingenstein speaks only about professors of philosophy and literature. An adequate treatment of the topic, even for the period Klingenstein addresses, would be obliged to deal extensively with natural scientists (e.g., Samuel Goudsmidt, J. Robert Oppenheimer) and social scientists (e.g., E.R.A. Seligman, Simon Kuznets).

27. Although Cahan edited the leading Yiddish-language newspaper in New York, the *Forward*, he was widely appreciated by Anglophone intellectuals well before the publication of his *The Rise of David Levinsky* in 1917.

28. And not only in New York. When the New York Jew Emma Goldman lectured in St. Louis, the young Roger Baldwin—soon to establish the American Civil Liberties Union—found his life transformed. This incident is discussed in Candace Serena Falk, *Love, Anarchy, and Emma Goldman* (New Brunswick, N.J., 1984), 9–10.

29. Thorstein Veblen, "The Intellectual Preeminence of Jews in Modern Europe," *Political Science Quarterly* 39 (1919): 33–42.

30. Both of these essays of 1916 are reprinted in Randolph Bourne, *War and the Intellectuals: Collected Essays, 1915–1919*, ed. Carl Resek (New York, 1964), 107–133. For additional examples of Anglo-Protestant declarations concerning the culturally liberating effect of contact with immigrant Jews, see the cases cited in my essay "Ethnic Diversity, Cosmopolitanism, and the Emergence of the American Liberal Intelligentsia," reprinted in *In the American Province: Studies in the History and Historiography of Ideas* (Bloomington, Ind., 1985), esp. 39–40.

31. Bourne, "Jew and Transnational America," 132.

32. Morris R. Cohen, "The East Side," *Alliance Review* 2 (1902): 451–454; Morris R. Cohen, *A Dreamer's Journey* (New York, 1949), esp. 98. For another memoir of Jewish-Protestant interaction from the Jewish side in early twentieth-century New York City, see Joseph Freeman, *An American Testament* (New York, 1936).

33. See, e.g., Marcia Graham Synott, *The Half-Open Door: Discrimination and Admissions at Harvard, Yale, and Princeton, 1900–1970* (Westport, Conn., 1979).

34. The difficulties faced by Jewish historians in the historical profession, for example, have recently been documented by Peter Novick, *That Noble Dream: The "Objectivity Question" and the American Historical Association* (New York, 1988), esp. 172–173.

35. See Benny Kraut, "A Wary Collaboration: Jews, Catholics, and the Protestant Goodwill Movement," in Hutchison, *Travail,* 207. Kraut reports that over half of these missions were operated by the established, "mainline" denominations. See also Egal Feldman, *Dual Destinies: The Jewish Encounter with Protestant America* (Urbana, Ill., 1990), which concludes that Protestant efforts to "witness to Jews" were "unrelenting" until the middle of the twentieth century (243).

36. In this paragraph and the next, I draw upon my own study of this episode, "The 'Tough-Minded' Justice Holmes, Jewish Intellectuals, and the Making of an American Icon," in *The Legacy of Oliver Wendell Holmes, Jr.*, ed. Robert W. Gordon (Stanford, Calif., 1992), 216–228, 307–313. The study is reprinted as chapter 3 of the present volume.

37. This ethnodemographic fact is rendered all the more striking by another one: among the earliest and loudest voices to express puzzlement at the liberals' adulation of Holmes was H. L. Mencken, perhaps the era's most vociferous opponent of the established culture of Protestantism, but one without any Jewish connections (and not lacking anti-Semitic prejudices of his own). Mencken understood the antiliberal strains in Holmes that now dominate studies of the jurist but seems not to have grasped Holmes's utility for Mencken's Jewish allies in the fight against the genteel tradition. See Mencken's discussions in *American Mercury* in 1930 and 1932, reprinted in *The Vintage Mencken*, ed. Alastair Cooke (New York, 1955), 189.

38. Grant Gilmore, *The Ages of American Law* (New Haven, Conn., 1977), 48.

39. Felix Frankfurter, *Mr. Justice Holmes and the Constitution* (Cambridge, Mass., 1927), 44.

40. Cohen's *New Republic* essay on the occasion of Holmes's death in 1935 was reprinted in Morris R. Cohen, *Faith of a Liberal* (New York, 1946); see esp. 30.

41. Jerome Frank, *Law and the Modern Mind* (1930; reprint, New York, 1963), 270–277.

42. See Lerner's extensive introduction in *The Mind and Faith of Justice Holmes,* ed. Max Lerner (Boston, 1943), esp. vii, xix, xlvii, xlix–l.

43. This was true even in the century's second decade, but it was more dramatically manifest in 1934, when, just at the moment Eliot was warning against freethinking Jews, the ninety-three-year-old, freethinking Holmes represented himself to Cohen as being of partly Jewish ancestry. See Leonora Cohen Rosenfield, *Portrait of a Philosopher: Morris R. Cohen in Life and Letters* (New York, 1962), 443.

44. See, for example, Henry Steele Commager, *The American Mind: An Interpretation of American Thought and Culture since the 1880's* (New Haven, Conn., 1950), 385–390, which includes a lyric appreciation to Holmes, climaxing with the application to Holmes of Stephen Spender's "I Think Continually of Those Who Were Truly Great."

45. Although America became a permanent or temporary home for refugees from Hitler's Europe possessed of strong connections in the United States and of international reputations in the arts, science, or scholarship, it cannot be repeated often enough that American authorities rejected multiple opportunities to receive or otherwise save Jews who looked to the United States for help. From 1933 to 1945, the United States accepted 132,000 refugees from the Third Reich, scarcely more than the equivalent of the 1940 population of Spokane, Washington. The overwhelming majority of these, moreover, were able to enter the United States only after *Kristallnacht* (November 9–10, 1938). For a helpful demographic and political overview of the migration, see Herbert A. Strauss, "The Movement of People in a Time of Crisis," in *The Muses Flee Hitler: Cultural Transfer and Adaptation, 1930–1945* (Washington, D.C., 1983), 45–59.

46. In order that we be reminded of the scope and character of this influx of Jewish intellectuals, it may be well to list here the names of some of them: Hannah Arendt, Leo Strauss, Erik Erikson, Bruno Bettelheim, Erich Fromm, Kurt Lewin, Kurt Gödel, Paul Lazarsfeld, Leo Lowenthal, Theodor Adorno, Alexander Gerschenkrohn, Albert O. Hirschman, Erwin Panofsky, Ludwig von Mises, Herbert Marcuse, and Erich Auerbach. The deprovincializing effect of Gentile intellectuals from Central Europe was also strong; these ranged from principled atheists like the logical positivist Rudolf Carnap to theologians like Paul Tillich and Jacques Maritain. Their numbers also included Ernst Cassirer, Vladimir Nabokov, and Werner Jaeger.

47. This episode in American intellectual history surely deserves more rigorous study than it has received. Of the studies that have been completed, an especially readable and informative one is H. Stuart Hughes, *Sea Change: The Migration of Social Thought, 1930–1965* (New York, 1975). Hughes points out (18–19, e.g.) that the particular segment of European intellectual life which came to the United States was the most abrasively critical, skeptical, and cosmopolitan within German-speaking Europe.

48. Of the many studies of the *Partisan Review* and its circle, the most detailed, comprehensive, and convincing is Terry A. Cooney, *The Rise of the New York Intellectuals: Partisan Review and Its Circle, 1934–1945* (Madison, Wis., 1986). See also Fred Matthews, "Role Models? The Continuing Relevance of the 'New York Intellectuals,'" *Canadian Review of American Studies* 11 (1988): 69–88.

49. Leslie Fiedler, "Master of Dreams: The Jew in the Gentile World," *Partisan Review* 34 (1967): 347.

50. As one of the most respected and well-informed commentators on the contemporary American religious scene has summarized the situation in regard to the scientific and social scientific segments of these faculties: "Evidence suggests that rationality, natural science, and the social sciences have all exercised a negative effect on traditional religious beliefs and practices. Not only do scientists—and especially social scientists—demonstrate radically low levels of religious commitment, but scientific and social scientific meaning systems also appear to operate as functional alternatives to traditional theistic ideas for a number of people." See Robert Wuthnow, *The Restructuring of American Religion: Society and Faith since World War II* (Princeton, N.J., 1988), 301–302. Wuthnow also notes, concerning the society as a whole, that "the United States may well

be an exception among industrialized countries in the extent of its religious activities" (309).

51. Stephen Steinberg, *The Academic Melting Pot: Catholics and Jews in American Higher Education* (New York, 1974), 103. I have not been able to locate comparable figures for the leadership of the American Civil Liberties Union, or for other groups often said to have played a large role in construing the constitutional church-state separation in terms that have diminished the public space in which Christian belief was once proclaimed with explicit or tacit support of governments. A useful study of the tradition of Jewish devotion to "separationism" is Naomi W. Cohen, *Jews in Contemporary America: The Pursuit of Religious Equality* (New York, 1992).

52. Only the slightest notice of this aspect of the story is taken even by the ultraliberal Harvey Cox; see *Secular City*, 99. The new Evangelical historians have also been remarkably silent in this regard, even down to the present; see, for example, the scant treatment of Jews in George Marsden, *The Soul of the American University* (New York, 1994), one of the most comprehensive analyses ever written of the "secularization" of American academic life. For an affectionate but mildly skeptical portrait of Marsden and other newly prominent, evangelically committed historians, see Leonard I. Sweet, "Wise as Serpents, Innocent as Doves: The New Evangelical Historiography," *Journal of the American Academy of Religion* 56 (1988): 397–416. Sweet is especially sensitive in describing how these historians have dealt with their own awareness that many of their fundamentalist forebears were "on the tracks of their souls," as Sweet puts it, "creeps" (402).

53. Responsibility for this uncritical acceptance within the historical profession rests largely, I believe, with Perry Miller.

54. This phrase was coined and popularized by Morton White, especially in *Social Thought in America: The Revolt against Formalism*, 2d ed. (New York, 1957), 257.

55. I have in mind especially the many contributions of Martin A. Marty and William R. Hutchison and some of their students. See, for example, Hutchison's "Past Imperfect: History and the Prospect for Liberalism," in Michaelsen and Roof, *Liberal Protestantism*, 65–82.

56. See Fox's "The Culture of Liberal Protestant Progressivism, 1875–1925," *Journal of Interdisciplinary History* 23 (1993): 639–660, esp. the two central paragraphs on 640.

57. I have addressed the multiculturalist debate in my "How Wide the Circle of the We? American Intellectuals and the Problem of the Ethnos since World War II," *American Historical Review* 98 (1993): 317–337, and in my *Postethnic America: Beyond Multiculturalism* (New York, 1995).

58. Mark R. Schwehn to George M. Marsden, June 4, 1990, quoted in Marsden, "The Soul of the American University," in Marsden and Longfield, *Secularization of the Academy*, 45.

59. I share Leo Ribuffo's lament that the "editors of the standard volumes surveying historiographical trends" do not "consider religious history worthy of much mention, let alone a separate essay." See Ribuffo, "God and Contemporary Politics," 1533.

60. For my understanding of the character and import of Hans Blumenberg's *The Legitimacy of the Modern Age,* brought out in an English translation in 1983, I am largely indebted to Martin Jay, "Blumenberg and Modernism," in Jay's *Fin-de-Siècle Socialism* (New York, 1988), 149–164. I prefer "de-Christianization" to "secularization" partly because the former specifies the decline of a particular cultural program, while the latter has become more deeply mired in contentious disputes over its meaning in relation to what is and is not "religious." A lucid survey of the problem, although couched in the terms of one major thinker's agendas, is Thomas Luckmann, "Shrinking Transcendence, Expanding Religion?" *Sociological Analysis* 30 (1990): 127–136. For a more detailed study of an episode in the Protestant-culture-to-pluralism story that is informed by an understanding of these semantical ambiguities, see Henry C. Johnson, Jr., "'Down from the Mountain': Secularization and the Higher Learning in America," *Review of Politics* 54 (1992): 551–588.

CHAPTER THREE

The "Tough-Minded" Justice Holmes, Jewish Intellectuals, and the Making of an American Icon

This essay addresses in relation to one particular, indisputably major career both the cognitive and the ethnodemographic dimensions of the process of de-Christianization as experienced by American intellectuals. Although I incorporated a brief section of this essay into "Jewish Intellectuals and the De-Christianization of American Public Culture in the Twentieth Century," which appears just previously in these pages, here the question of Oliver Wendell Holmes, Jr.'s appeal to Jewish intellectuals of the twentieth century is set in the context of the particular version of "scientific," secular culture Holmes had adopted in his Victorian youth and continued to display, in many respects, in his maturity.

This piece was first published in The Legacy of Oliver Wendell Holmes, Jr., *ed. Robert W. Gordon (Stanford, Calif., 1992), 216–228, 307–313.*

WHEN A correspondent less than half his age asked the seventy-eight-year-old Justice Oliver Wendell Holmes, Jr., to place himself in the history of ideas, Holmes identified himself with "the scientific way of looking at the world." The influence of this "scientific" perspective sharply separated Holmes and his generational peers from Holmes's father and the men around him, the justice informed Morris R. Cohen.[1] This exchange of 1919 is a convenient point of access to two related issues in the study of Holmes and of his place in American intellectual history. One issue is just what "the scientific way of looking at the world" meant for Holmes. By clarifying this, we might advance our understanding of Holmes's work as a public moralist and perhaps even as a theorist of law. The second issue is what significance there may be in the fact that intellectuals of Jewish origin played a demographically disproportionate—even within the population of American academic intellectuals interested in law and philosophy—role in making Holmes into an American icon, an emblem for the "American character." By attending to the needs and aspirations of Cohen, Felix Frankfurter, Harold Laski, and other Jewish admirers of Holmes we might add an ethnic dimension to our understanding of a much-discussed paradox: that a major folk hero for the liberal intelligentsia is a man who has been plausibly described by Grant Gilmore as "savage, harsh, and cruel, a bitter and lifelong pessimist who saw in the course of human life nothing but a continuing struggle in which the rich and powerful impose their will on the poor and weak."[2] The two issues are largely distinct from one another, but they do connect through the utility a "scientific" persona held for proponents of a genuinely secular, de-Christianized liberalism for the public culture of the United States.

Commentators on Holmes have described his "scientific" proclivities as "Darwinist," "positivist," "pragmatist," "skeptical," "historicist," "empiricist," and "naturalist." None of these characterizations are mistaken. The obvious potential of each for misleading and confusing students of Holmes can be neutralized by clear and careful use. Yet we can get a firmer and less ambiguous sense of the center of intellectual gravity in Holmes if we focus instead on what Holmes's friend and almost exact contemporary, William James, called "tough-mindedness."[3]

"Tough-mindedness" was introduced by James in the first chapter of his pivotal work of 1907, *Pragmatism*, when he sought to clarify "The Present Dilemma of Philosophy." That dilemma, explained James, was the appalling choice the average, philosophically concerned soul was asked to make between two obviously inadequate competing parties: there were the deterministic, pluralistic, pessimistic, tough-minded empiricist skeptics on the one hand, and the voluntaristic, monistic, optimistic, tender-minded religious idealists on the other.[4] Scholarship on James himself has been needlessly trapped by these two ideal types and has gotten embroiled in arguments over whether James was not really more tender—or more tough—than this or that other scholar has alleged, sometimes ignoring the fact that a major point of James's career was to insist that one does not have to limit one's basic philosophic choices to these two alternatives.[5] But the case of Holmes was different. Nothing was more important to Holmes, philosophically, than to insist that the very choice James wanted to transcend was the choice demanded by the age.

It is easy to see Holmes in the terms proposed by James. Holmes was eager to focus on contingent historical forces rather than on timeless, rational structures; he was persistently fatalistic rather than voluntaristic; and he attributed to the objective order of experience supreme authority at the expense of the subjective. Holmes was relentless in upholding the real over the ideal and the factual over the fanciful. He was irreligious. Holmes was unequaled among American intellectuals of his generation in successfully projecting for himself an image of "toughness" over "tenderness." Although James's famous categories have often been dismissed as a pair of straw men designed to render more attractive James's own worldview, Holmes actually espoused one of these sets of values, and to the proud exclusion of the other. Although he sometimes concluded his after-dinner speeches with a dash of Emersonian idealism, his preferred sensibility was one of True Grit. It is ironic that Holmes is often counted a "pragmatist," when he had no sympathy whatsoever for the dilemma to which James proposed pragmatism as a solution. Holmes thought James's pragmatism an "amusing humbug," according to which one hoped to "modify the multiplication table" by "yearning." Similarly, Holmes found James's solicitousness toward religious sensibilities an effort to "turn down the lights so as to give miracle a chance."[6] Indeed, from a Jamesean viewpoint, Holmes was part of the problem. Holmes understood this very plainly. "You would say that I am too hard or tough-minded," Holmes wrote to James when the latter sent him a copy of *Pragmatism*.[7]

This is not to claim that James developed his categories with Holmes in mind, but there is no doubt that this particular map of intellectual alternatives was suggested to James by a circle of mid-nineteenth-century British secular intellectuals with whom Holmes strongly identified himself and against whom James's own career as a philosopher was directed. The members of this circle were often called "scientific naturalists" or, less helpfully, "positivists"; they included Herbert Spencer, G. H. Lewes, T. H. Huxley, John Tyndall, W. K. Clifford, Henry Buckle, and—although his reticence in philosophical and religious matters made his position in this movement ambiguous—the great Charles Darwin himself.[8] To James, these "knights of the razor," as he called them sardonically,[9] were anathema on account of their parochial misunderstanding of science and their extraordinary ability to intimidate people who would prefer to take a more generous view of religious experience and individual volition. While James mocked the pretensions of *Popular Science Monthly*—the major American medium for the dissemination of the views of this circle—Holmes so rejoiced in its influence that he sent a fan letter to its militant editor, E. L. Youmans.[10] Holmes celebrated the triumphs of this truly "scientific," reality-facing, ostentatiously stoic cadre over the sentimentalism he associated with his own father. While James thought his friend Holmes was making rather a spectacle of himself by representing as marks of toughness the scars worn by the sword-fighting duelists in German universities, Holmes seemed convinced that the battle against sentimentalism was never won.

Holmes's invocation of "the influence of the scientific way of looking at the world" thus served to identify himself with a highly specific historical moment. Mark DeWolfe Howe has detailed Holmes's participation in this moment as a young man: Holmes read Spencer, J. S. Mill's commentary on Auguste Comte, and was especially engaged by Lewes.[11] Holmes mentioned to Cohen the names of Darwin, Spencer, and Buckle. Lest there be any doubt about just what it was for which these names were a code, Holmes listed the traits of his own father that he found incompatible with the "scientific" outlook for which these men stood. He alluded to the old poet's softness of attitude, his apparent yearning for things spiritual, and his interest in such purely literary issues as whether Shakespeare's plays were really written by Francis Bacon.[12] Holmes in this same letter countered Cohen's speculation that Enlightenment rationalism had been a barrier between himself and his father. Holmes was firm: "No, it was not Voltaire." Holmes distinguished the relevant "scientific" outlook from two things with which it might be confused, the rationalistic skepticism of the eighteenth century and the philosophically mute natural knowledge one could derive from the study of medicine. Such things were available even to his father.[13]

The claims of the tough over the tender largely encompass the most widely discussed of Holmes's ideas about the law, especially as expressed in his attacks on the "theology" of Christopher Columbus Langdell and in his famous aphorism of 1881, "The life of the law has not been logic; it has been experience."[14] The standard virtues of toughness are also expressed throughout Holmes's career-long effort, as Robert W. Gordon has phrased it, "to treat the law as a cultural expression of the felt necessities, power struggles, and ideals of actual human beings in social life."[15] Certainly Holmes's "external standard" for tort liability, often said to be the central and most important single idea in his jurisprudence, sought to mark off as decisively as possible an order of objective, public fact from an order of subjective motivation and to make the law responsive primarily to the first of these two orders.[16] The doctrine of "objective causation" has a tough-minded sound, but Holmes's much-discussed rejection of it served, rather than betrayed, his vision of true science. According to this doctrine, any social event had to have—for the purposes of private law—a single and proximate cause. This counted as "objective" in the highly geometric world of Langdell's orthodox "legal science," but this orderly, rationalistic world was, from a Holmesian perspective, incontrovertibly "tender." Holmes, in the name of a more empirical science, would have none of this obviously fictional account of human behavior.[17] Although recent scholarship is no doubt correct to insist that Holmes actually incorporated more of the Langedellian jurisprudential world than has often been acknowledged, the innovations for which Holmes is remembered do depart from the geometric foundation of that world.

That world has recently been clarified by Thomas C. Grey in ways that better enable us to see how Holmes worked his way out of the orthodox system with which he actually shared so many premises. Especially illuminating in this respect is Grey's explication of classical orthodoxy in terms of the five goals of an ideal theory of law: comprehensiveness, completeness, formality, conceptual order, and acceptability. The last of these goals, acceptability, was the least ably defended by Langdell and his followers, Grey points out.[18] "Acceptability" here refers to the acceptability of a legal system as judged by extralegal values, as judged by the ideals and desires of the people under the system's jurisdiction. Holmes's deepest misgivings about classical legal science were concentrated here, on the question of that science's ability to meet the appropriate standard of social acceptability. It is no wonder that a judge who once called himself "a supple tool of power"[19] should lead a jurisprudential reform keyed by respect for the desires of the community as determined by political struggle.

Here in his construction of "acceptability"—in his vision, that is, of law as the instrument of an external, superior, yet thoroughly social force—is the cardinal jurisprudential expression of Holmes's tough-mindedness: public life, according to Holmes, is a competitive struggle for material resources and power among a number of historic social blocs, one or another of which will at a given time control the polity and thereby place on the shoulders of other classes and groups the risks and other disagreeable burdens attendant upon the life of the community as a whole. To this "will of the de facto supreme power of the community," as Holmes described it in his 1873 commentary on the gas stokers' strike, the legal system must be acceptable.[20]

Holmes's prescriptions for a "scientific" approach to the making as well as the study of the law are sometimes taken to mitigate this deference to what Holmes liked to call "the crowd." Surely, these prescriptions imply a role for human reason in improving the law and suggest a less fatalistic perspective? No doubt they do, but to a degree rendered low in the extreme by Holmes's most explicit and systematic discussion of the issues, "Law in Science and Science in Law." There, Holmes was at pains to remind his readers of how small is the practical relevance of the scientific-historical study of law, an enterprise he praised in terms of the Cambridge mathematician's boast that a particular theorem could "never by any possibility be made of the slightest use to anybody for anything." Such study could have the "negative and skeptical" value of showing certain rules to be mere "survivals," no longer responsive to contemporary social needs, Holmes granted. When he turned from the historical dimension of the "science" of law to the practical, Holmes invoked, without identifying it as such, the old Benthamite project of measurement. To establish the postulates of law "upon accurately measured social desires instead of tradition" was the mission of this second dimension of legal science. Here, Holmes spoke repeatedly about our "ultimate dependence upon science" in determining the "worth" of the social ends competing for control of the law's direction, but "worth" meant "strength" and "intensity," while "science" meant "quantitative comparison by means of whatever measure we command." Hence the deference remains: the warrant for the reform of the law is the prior existence of measurable social force. That the critical intellect might actively instruct, in a Deweyite mode, rather than passively register, was not suggested here. Holmes's ideal of "a commonwealth in which science is everywhere supreme" was unattainable, he admitted, but what matters more for the purposes of this analysis is Holmes's sense of exactly what would make such a commonwealth scientific: "statistics" and "modern appliance[s]."[21] Holmes later endorsed the notion that our "desires" ought to be more "intelligent," but precious little of his work developed that classically Deweyan notion.[22] Grey is correct to characterize Holmes as "an instrumentalist without an adequate system of ends."[23]

To orient our interpretations of Holmes in terms of his preference for the values of "toughness" need not reduce the diversity and depth of his intellectual achievement to a handful of extremely general preferences. Nor need such attention to Holmes's grounding in Victorian scientific naturalism impede our understanding of other influences on his intellectual development, including his much-discussed experiences in the Civil War. Nor need we abandon altogether the notion that Holmes was a "pragmatist," much as this term portends anachronism when applied to a person who disavowed the name and sometimes explicitly resisted the doctrines he associated with it.

Holmes was distinctive, after all, in developing theories of law that were "situated in and reflective of practice," as Grey has observed: "Holmes was the first writer to base a jurisprudential theory in a perspective derived from the practice of law."[24] Moreover, Holmes's vision of the law as a set of ever-changing, practical, social instruments obviously paralleled the antifoundationalist accounts of human knowledge developed by James, C. S. Peirce, and John Dewey.[25] He once professed to believe that success in a free market was the best test of an idea's truth.[26] While often scornful of the notion that the "creative intelligence" celebrated by the pragmatists could improve the world, he did voice with genuine eloquence the ideal of making habits and desires "intelligent."[27] But what little he said about the character of the scientific enterprise itself—concerning which the classic pragmatist philosophers made their most distinctive contributions to modern thought—was old-fashioned Victorian scientific naturalism. The characteristic pragmatist concern with the nature of human cognitive equipment was utterly alien to Holmes, who perpetuated instead a mid-Victorian acquiescence in the unquestioned dominance of the physical world. Some of his aphorisms suggested the pragmatic notion that all thought was connected to action, but when he spoke with the most feeling about the glories of the human intellect he made commandingly clear a distinction between thought and action, between "science" and "the fight."[28]

In addition the historicism Holmes displayed the most consistently was only incidentally "pragmatic": Holmes was conventionally "tough" in holding that law was socially situated and instrumental as "the will of the sovereign," and he actually out-toughed his legal-positivist predecessors and contemporaries by stressing the historical contingency of sovereignty itself. Holmes denied to received political arrangements the legitimacy others sought to perpetuate and was willing instead to accept unflinchingly the legislative authority of the newly empowered working class. He claimed to disagree with exactly those ideas of James's that he understood James to defend in the book called *Pragmatism*. Most of Holmes's pragmatism fit neatly within the perimeter of his "tough-mindedness." *Holmes was a pragmatist incidentally; he was a Victorian scientific naturalist by persistent, purposive exertion.* Holmes was "in many respects an Englishman," observed Howe; his "commitment to the English tradition" served to "set him out of the central stream of American life."[29]

The practice of playing up Holmes's pragmatism and playing down his affinities with the British savants of the 1850s and 1860s has served to make him seem all the more American. Hence the issue of his pragmatism is an appropriate point at which to turn to the second of the issues to which these brief comments are addressed: the matter of Holmes's becoming an American icon. To speak of his having been made into an icon need not imply that Americans have had no defensible basis for admiring Holmes, nor for seeing in him traits that other admirable Americans have shared. But behind the persistent speculation about the dynamics of Holmes's reputation has been a perceived incongruity between the particular qualities attributed to him and the illiberal, if not reactionary, character of many of his actual social values and some of his judicial acts.[30] How could the author of "The Soldier's Faith"—a celebration of an unthinking and unquestioning obedience to orders and a vindication of violence for its role in "the breeding of a race fit for headship and command"—come to be a special darling of egalitarian, anti-imperialist intellectuals devoted to the life of the mind and to its politically progressive uses?[31]

The paradox is solved, we are sometimes told, by the fact that liberals were able to exploit the Lochner dissent, some free-speech opinions, a few of Holmes's other judicial acts, and certain themes in his theoretical writings. Since Holmes was inclined to defer to legislatures and since legislatures in the Progressive Era tended to enact progressive legislation, Holmes looked liberal by disagreeing with court colleagues who wanted to invalidate that legislation on constitutional principles. Jan Vetter has recently provided an incisive account of the ups and downs of Holmes's reputation in relation to the political and jurisprudential needs of successive generations of American lawyers and intellectuals.[32] No doubt these jurisprudential and political dimensions were central to the process by which Holmes became the kind of hero he did become. This standard explanation probably explains most of what needs to be explained. Yet there remains to be explored an ethnic dimension to the process by which Holmes became an icon for American liberal intellectuals. This ethnic dimension consists largely in the selective appreciation and use of Holmes's "tough-mindedness" by young Jewish intellectuals.

Many Boston Brahmins of Holmes's generation displayed anti-Semitic tendencies. This is true of Henry Adams, for example, and Henry James.[33] Whatever anti-Semitism Holmes may have harbored was well concealed. His friendships with Felix Frankfurter, Harold Laski, and Louis Brandeis are common knowledge, although almost nothing has been written about his openness to Jewish intellectuals or about the intense engagement some of them felt with him. Edmund Wilson is one of very few commentators on Holmes to have taken an interest in his conspicuous responsiveness, during his old age, to Jewish intellectuals.[34] To one of the latter, Holmes even claimed to have himself been of partly Jewish origin: in 1934, he represented himself to Cohen as the descendant of a Dutch Jewish family, the Vondells.[35] Holmes complained more than once to Sir Frederick Pollock about "the wide-spread prejudice against the Jews," lamented its victimization of Laski and Frankfurter, and professed his own social indifference as to who was Jewish and who was not.[36]

Holmes's greatness was hailed by American intellectuals of a variety of backgrounds, but those of immigrant Jewish origin were especially prominent in the ranks of those who did the most to establish Holmes in the public mind as more than just a great judge and scholar.[37] Responsibility for effectively promoting Holmes as a cultural hero is often assigned above all to Frankfurter and Laski. These two largely "concocted," according to Grant Gilmore in 1977, "the picture of the tolerant aristocrat, the great liberal, the eloquent defender of our liberties, the Yankee from Olympus."[38] From his strategic position at the Harvard Law School, the enterprising and often eloquent Frankfurter affirmed his reverence for Holmes repeatedly during the 1910s and 1920s. In 1927, he could say that Holmes had "built himself into the structure of our national life" and "written himself into the slender volume of the literature of all time."[39] When Frankfurter recruited Laski to the Harvard faculty in 1916, the latter took up the cause immediately and with all his legendary animation. Laski was so involved with the Holmes project that he ended up with the responsibility for putting together *Collected Legal Papers* in 1920.[40]

The representation of Holmes by Frankfurter and Laski as more than an eminent professional jurist—as a Great Man—was also carried on by Cohen, Frankfurter's onetime roommate, and later by Jerome Frank and Max Lerner. When Cohen thought Holmes was wrong, he was capable of expressing the thought with lines from *Hyperion:* "But . . . thou art the King, and only blind from sheer supremacy."[41] Frank's 1930 characterization of Holmes as the truly "adult" jurist was an accolade of special significance since Frank chose to analyze the entire legal profession in terms of personality development; most judges, according to Frank, had the emotions of children.[42] In 1943 Lerner declared Holmes to be "perhaps the most complete personality in the history of American thought." Holmes's life had a "wholeness" produced by "the New England aristocracy at its best." By 1943 some doubts had surfaced about Holmes's adequacy as the Complete American Liberal, but Lerner would not suffer the possibility that Holmes was only a fragment of the desired whole. The qualities Holmes did lack, suggested Lerner, were not so obviously desirable in an American hero: Holmes did not partake of "the pattern of torture and complexity," the "darker urges of the Dionysian" expected of "the modern hero" by followers of Dostoevsky and Nietzsche. Holmes, it would seem, was a child of light. He possessed what we now need, Lerner averred: the stuff to inspire "militant democracy." Holmes was one who, "at the high tide of capitalist materialism," stood by "faith in social reason and in the competition of ideas" and held to a "belief in the steady, if slow march of social progress." To be certain that his readers placed Holmes in a sufficiently broad cultural frame of reference, Lerner minimized the jurist and focused on the personality: "Holmes is a great man regardless of whether he was a great justice."[43]

The characterizations of Holmes offered by Frankfurter, Laski, Cohen, Frank, and Lerner gain part of their significance from the development—in which all five were agents—of an ethnically diverse, secular intelligentsia in the United States. The intellectual community for which Holmes became a hero was formed by the amalgamation of two anti-provincial revolts, one manifest especially among well-to-do WASPs of native stock, directed against the constraints of "Puritanism," and the other manifest especially among the sons of immigrants, directed against the constraints of Jewish parochialism, particularly as identified with Eastern Europe. The two antiprovincial movements reinforced one another and espoused in common a cosmopolitan ideal in keeping with which intellectuals of both backgrounds sought to carry out the intellectual work of their generation, including the developing of a satisfying interpretation of America itself.[44]

Although it is often said that the quarter-century between the late

1910s and the early 1940s is a period in which Jewish intellectuals were, on a significant scale, "assimilated" into American life, less notice has been taken of the extent to which these Jewish intellectuals themselves helped to reconstitute American intellectual life and helped to construct, in the process, the particular, liberal vision of American culture that became a common possession of the American intelligentsia during the middle decades of the twentieth century.[45] The building of Holmes into the "structure of national life" was one step in this construction. He was to be an emblem for America.[46]

Holmes had a lot to offer. To begin with, he was, after all, a man of the *law*, an element of secular culture especially congenial to intellectuals coming out of the culture of Judaism. Moreover, his background and experience made him about as "American" as it was possible to get, and his sheer age reinforced this fact. By 1930, Holmes was probably the only man or woman alive who could remember having had conversations with John Quincy Adams.[47] Juxtaposed with this primordial Americanness for all to see was the peculiar distance Holmes put between himself and the old WASP tradition, partly on "tough-minded" grounds. He had rejected as trivial the literary culture of his father—"build thee more stately mansions, O my soul"[48]—long before the rest of educated society had done so. He had given up on the idea of necessary progress and on the notion that William McKinley was its culmination when many of his contemporaries had still believed such nonsense. Holmes was not noticeably Christian. He was not an idealist and a sentimentalist, but a realist and a skeptic. His "tough-mindedness" seemed directed against the notorious "genteel tradition." He could be seen as an enemy of exactly those aspects of the New England WASP tradition most threatening to young Jewish intellectuals in the 1910s, 1920s, and 1930s. He kept his distance from the cultural provincialism of Boston and was aloof from Anglo-Saxon nativism. If he was not "a traitor to his class," he had certainly shown himself open to the entrance of new social groups into the mainstream of American life.

Holmes's influence promised, then, to help release American culture from a Christian bias that most Jewish intellectuals found provincial at best and that at worst provided a basis for continued prejudice against Jews and other non-Christians. Whatever echoes of heroic Calvinism one could find in Holmes were, like those found in Melville—whose genius was being discovered in the early 1920s—easily detached from the stuffy and snobbish Protestantism that favored quotas for Jews at Harvard and Columbia. Moreover, Holmes had looked Darwinism in the face, it was said, while others flinched on account of their loyalty to Christian theology. The aristocrat Holmes was a refreshing countermodel to "the genteel tradition," against which the likes of Frankfurter and Cohen were allied with a substantial minority of WASP intellectuals of humble social origins, including John Dewey and Malcolm Cowley.[49]

Hence it is not surprising that of the various specific projects that went into the effort to move the public culture of the United States more decisively in a secular, cosmopolitan direction, the particular project of managing the reputation of Holmes should become one in which Jewish intellectuals took a conspicuous lead. Holmes's "tough-mindedness" itself required some managing; it could be a liability as well as an asset. The keepers of "the liberal Holmes" were obliged to diminish his pessimism, his fatalism, his respect for brute force, and indeed most of the traits that have given rise to the doubt that he was "liberal." As if to neutralize the mystification of war found in "The Soldier's Faith," Lerner placed immediately following it in *The Mind and Faith of Justice Holmes* a brief speech featuring one of the most idealistic of the rhetorical flourishes with which Holmes concluded his public performances.[50]

While Holmes's distinctive appeal to Jewish intellectuals of Frankfurter's generation is thus explained, in part, by the considerations noted above, there was an additional, more personal foundation for this appeal: the warm response Holmes made to some of his young admirers, just at a time when intellectuals of Jewish origin were subject to exclusion and insult on the part of other men and women of Holmes's social milieu. The most Olympian of the living Brahmins left the impression that he cared about them. He even answered their letters.

Laski wrote a thank-you note to Holmes after having been received at Beverly Farms through the good offices of Frankfurter ("You teach our generation how to live," said Laski; "I want badly to come again"), and Holmes's immediate, extremely cordial reply set in motion the correspondence that ultimately filled two lengthy volumes of small type.[51] Cohen had cause for pride when Holmes had bound for his private convenience the several reprints of his philosophical papers Cohen had sent to the justice.[52] Holmes chose to cite one of these papers as a major source of inspiration for his "Ideals and Doubts" in 1915.[53] The anti-Semitism of other "old Americans" had been damaging his academic career, but suddenly the thirty-five-year-old Cohen found himself in correspondence with, and being cited appreciatively by, a justice of the Supreme Court who had fought for the Union in a Massachusetts regiment almost twenty years prior to Cohen's birth in Russia.[54]

Holmes had no children, and it has often been suggested that his relationships with these bright, vigorous younger men derived in part from his feeling for them as surrogate sons.[55] He valued and responded to young intellectuals of various backgrounds, including the clerks sent to him from Harvard by Frankfurter. Since he apparently had no particular preference for Jews, the number and intensity of his relationships with Jewish intellectuals was probably a function of the greater need these immigrants and sons of immigrants had for Holmes. They persisted. It is not implausible to suppose that they had more to gain from a relationship with Holmes than did their less marginal Gentile contemporaries. Frankfurter "placed his faith," as Michael Parrish has explained, "in the good sense, the educability, and the benevolence of the country's old elite, represented by Holmes, Henry Stimson, and Franklin D. Roosevelt."[56] There may also have been a deeper psychological dynamic in their attraction to Holmes. If he was aware of having no son, were they—as Edmund Wilson has speculated—looking for a fully American father? Some of them had left their own fathers behind as they crossed cultural and religious boundaries. Laski told his Orthodox father in Manchester, "I am English, not Polish; an agnostic, not a Jew." At eighteen, Laski married a Gentile woman and, being then threatened with disinheritance, broke with his family. Cohen's case was less dramatic, but he, too, was aware of the inability of his East European Jewish father to help him survive and prosper in the secular American world in which he had chosen to make his difficult way.[57]

Whatever the merit of these speculations about the psychology of fatherhood, there is no doubt that just as the position of Holmes in the American pantheon was being consolidated in the era of World War II, the great hero came under attack. It was said that Holmes was not really a good American after all, that he had betrayed American ideals, that he was a crypto-fascist, that his adulation by the likes of Lerner betrayed something sick in American life. And who led this attack? A group very far removed from Frankfurter's circle: Jesuits. Speaking from Catholic law schools, Christian "absolutists" were then reacting against secular liberalism; they exhibited Holmes as the enemy of a true, spiritually healthy Americanism.[58] Simultaneously, milder criticisms of Holmes were developed in a more purely jurisprudential context by Lon L. Fuller and Walton H. Hamilton without advancing any obvious political, religious, or ethnic agendas,[59] but the Catholic critique of Holmes bore directly on the larger cultural concerns that animated Lerner and his predecessors in the enterprise of promoting Holmes as an American icon.

The contrasting images of Holmes offered during World War II by Lerner and the Jesuit law professors were among the last to gain any significance from ethnic and religious distinctions between American intellectuals. By the 1950s, the academic and literary life of the United States had incorporated—and had been in part transformed by—numerous Jewish intellectuals. Neither in the discussion of Holmes nor in the discussion of most other topics were the participants remotely as conscious as the previous generation had been of who was Jewish and who was not. Contests over the meaning of Holmes's career would continue, but the issues at stake would be more narrowly jurisprudential. To be the subject of such contests, large or small, to be claimed by rival parties, to have one's historical significance at risk in the push and pull of doctrinal disputes, to be "in the fight" . . . Holmes would be happy with his fate.

NOTES

1. Holmes to Cohen, February 5, 1919, in Leonora Cohen Rosenfield, *Portrait of a Philosopher: Morris R. Cohen in Life and Letters* (New York, 1962), 321.

2. Grant Gilmore, *The Ages of American Law* (New Haven, Conn., 1977), 49.

3. Holmes was born in 1841; James in 1842. The relationship between the two men is a prominent theme in the intellectual history of their generation. See, e.g., George M. Fredrickson, *The Inner Civil War: Northern Intellectuals and the Crisis of the Union* (New York, 1965), 217–238.

4. William James, *Pragmatism: A New Name for Some Old Ways of Thinking* (Cambridge, Mass., 1978), 13.

5. See David A. Hollinger, "William James and the Culture of Inquiry," in Hollinger, *In the American Province: Studies in the History and Historiography of Ideas* (Bloomington, Ind., 1985), 3–22.

6. Holmes to Laski, March 29, 1917, in *The Holmes-Laski Letters: The Correspondence of Mr. Justice Holmes and Harold J. Laski, 1916–1935*, ed. Mark DeWolfe Howe, 2 vols. (Cambridge, Mass., 1953), 1:70; Holmes to Pollock, September 1, 1910, in *The Holmes-Pollock Letters: The Correspondence of Mr. Justice Holmes and Sir Frederick Pollock, 1874–1932*, ed. Mark DeWolfe Howe, 2 vols. (Cambridge, Mass., 1941, 1946), 1:167.

7. Holmes's note to James is quoted in Ralph Perry, *The Thought and Character of William James*, vol. 2 (Boston, 1935), 462. Holmes appears to have better understood the religious character of James's pragmatism than have many of James's defenders: "I now see," Holmes wrote to Sir Frederick Pollock, "that the aim and end of the whole business is religious"; Howe, ed., *Holmes-Pollock Letters*, 1:140. I owe this last reference to Thomas C. Grey.

8. On "Victorian scientific naturalism," see Frank Miller Turner, *Between Science and Religion: The Reaction to Scientific Naturalism in Late-Victorian England* (New Haven, Conn., 1974), 8–37.

9. William James, *The Will to Believe* (Cambridge, Mass., 1979), 105.

10. James identifies this magazine as a symbol for overbearing scientism in two essays, "The Teaching of Philosophy in our Colleges" (1876) and "Remarks on Spencer's Definition of Mind as Correspondence" (1878), as reprinted in James, *Essays in Philosophy* (Cambridge, Mass., 1978), 4, 7. Holmes's letter to Youmans, May 3, 1874, is reprinted in John Fiske, *Edward Livingston Youmans: Interpreter of Science for the People* (New York, 1894), 315: the magazine "comes to me like the air they send down to the people in a diving bell."

11. Mark DeWolfe Howe, *Justice Oliver Wendell Holmes*, vol. 1, *The Shaping Years, 1841–1870* (Cambridge, Mass., 1957), 209–222. See also H. L. Pohlmann, *Justice*

Oliver Wendell Holmes and Utilitarian Jurisprudence (Cambridge, Mass., 1984), 117–139, which interprets Holmes in relation to this English milieu, especially as dominated by Mill's ideas about science.

12. The dangers of taking at face value Holmes's representation of his father's mind are only now being identified; see Peter Gibian, "Opening and Closing the Conversation: Style and Stance from Holmes Senior to Holmes Junior," in *The Legacy of Oliver Wendell Holmes, Jr.*, ed. Robert W. Gordon (Stanford, Calif., 1992), 186–215. It is a measure of the junior Holmes's authority in twentieth-century American intellectual life that his libels against the senior Holmes have so often been accepted as true.

13. Holmes to Cohen, February 5, 1919, in Rosenfield, *Portrait of a Philosopher*, 321.

14. OWH, *The Common Law*, ed. Mark DeWolfe Howe (Cambridge, Mass., 1963), 5.

15. Robert W. Gordon, "Holmes' *Common Law* as Legal and Social Science," *Hofstra Law Review* 10 (1982): 719, 746. Gordon rightly interprets Holmes in the context of a scientific naturalism more distinctively Victorian and more crude, philosophically, than the "positivism," "Darwinism," and "pragmatism" that other scholars have found in *Common Law*.

16. See OWH, *The Common Law*, chaps. 2, 3, and 4; OWH, "Privilege, Malice, and Intent," in *Collected Legal Papers* (New York, 1920), 117 (orig. pub. *Harvard Law Review* 8 [1894]: 1).

17. For Holmes's role in the undermining of this particular doctrine, see Morton J. Horwitz, "The Doctrine of Objective Causation," in *The Politics of Law: A Progressive Critique*, ed. David Kairys (New York, 1982), 201, 213.

18. Thomas C. Grey, "Langdell's Orthodoxy," *University of Pittsburgh Law Review* 45 (1983): 1, 6, 10, 13, 42, 44.

19. Quoted in Yosal Rogat, "The Judge as Spectator," *University of Chicago Law Review* 31 (1964): 213, 249–250.

20. OWH, unsigned, "Summary of Events: The Gas-Stokers' Strike," *American Law Review* 7 (1873): 582, 583. Gordon points out the continuity between this early statement of Holmes's and his more famous "liberal" Lochner dissent of 1905; see Gordon, "Holmes' *Common Law*," 734, 740.

21. OWH, "Law in Science and Science in Law," in *Collected Legal Papers*, 211, 225, 231–232, 239, 242.

22. OWH, "Ideals and Doubts," in *Collected Legal Papers*, 305 (orig. pub. *Illinois Law Review* 10 [1915]: 1).

23. Thomas C. Grey, "Holmes and Legal Pragmatism," *Stanford Law Review* 41 (1989): 787.

24. Ibid., 836. Grey's is the most comprehensive and persuasive case yet made for Holmes as a "pragmatist" in the mode of Peirce, James, and Dewey, although I believe the strongest contribution of the essay is in its extracting from Holmes's work the rudiments of a "legal pragmatism" suitable for development in our own time. In so doing, Grey deals extensively and accurately with Holmes's antipathy toward many of the dispositions of the classic pragmatists. This forthright approach to the difficulties in interpreting Holmes as a "pragmatist" is unusual even in the most recent of the law review literature on the subject. See, for exam-

ple, the mechanical application of "positivist" and "pragmatist" models to Holmes in the learned but pedestrian study by Catharine Wells Hantzis, "Legal Innovation within the Wider Intellectual Tradition: The Pragmatism of Oliver Wendell Holmes, Jr.," *Northwestern University Law Review* 81 (1988): 541. Representative of the earlier literature on Holmes as "pragmatist" are the following studies: Max Fisch, "Justice Holmes, the Prediction Theory of Law, and Pragmatism," *Journal of Philosophy* 39 (1942): 85; Philip P. Wiener, *Evolution and the Founders of Pragmatism* (New York, 1949); "Holmes, Peirce, and Legal Pragmatism," *Yale Law Journal* 84 (1975): 1123. This unsigned piece is a striking instance of a common tendency to stretch the concept of pragmatism to cover apparently any doctrine of one or another of pragmatism's acknowledged exemplars; various of Peirce's ideas are formalistically compared to Holmes's, and the latter are discovered to be "pragmatic" simply because they are shared with Peirce!

25. Holmes's historicist conception of law is most cogently set forth in his "The Path of the Law," *Collected Legal Papers*, 167.

26. See *Abrams v. New York*, 250 U.S. 616 (1919) (Holmes, J. dissenting).

27. OWH, "Ideals and Doubts," in *Collected Legal Papers*, 305.

28. OWH, "Law in Science," in *Collected Legal Papers*, 224: "I doubt if there is any more exalted form of life than that of a great abstract thinker, wrapt in the successful study of problems to which he devotes himself, for an end which is . . . simply to feed the deepest hunger and to use the greatest gifts of the soul. But after all the place for a man who is complete in all his powers is in the fight. The professor, the man of letters, gives up one-half of life that his protected talent may grow and flower in peace."

29. Howe, *Justice Holmes: The Shaping Years*, 243.

30. This speculation has been sufficiently widespread to generate an anthology designed to guide classroom discussions. See David H. Burton, ed., *Oliver Wendell Holmes, Jr.—What Manner of Liberal?* (Huntington, N.Y., 1979). By far the most compelling attack on the notion that Holmes was a liberal has been made in Rogat, "The Judge as Spectator."

31. "The Soldier's Faith," a Memorial Day address of 1895, was the most vividly etched of the popular speeches Holmes delivered in the 1880s and 1890s; it is reprinted in *The Mind and Faith of Justice Holmes: His Speeches, Essays, Letters and Judicial Opinions*, ed. Max Lerner (Boston, 1943), 18.

32. Jan Vetter, "The Evolution of Holmes: Holmes on Evolution," *Occasional Pamphlet Number Ten of the Harvard Law School* (Cambridge, Mass., 1983), 75. See also the earlier, more comprehensive study by G. Edward White, "The Rise and Fall of Justice Holmes," *University of Chicago Law Review* 39 (1971): 51.

33. This striking difference between Holmes and these two Brahmin contemporaries is not mentioned by Rogat in his extensive comparison of the three men. See Rogat, "The Judge as Spectator," 230.

34. See Edmund Wilson, "The Holmes-Laski Correspondence," in Wilson, *The Bit between My Teeth* (New York, 1965), 78, 98–100; see also Edmund Wilson, *Patriotic Gore: Studies in the Literature of the American Civil War* (New York, 1965), 785.

35. Rosenfield, *Portrait of a Philosopher*, 443. This comment on Holmes's part may help distinguish his receptiveness to Jewish correspondents as opposed to

others of "outsider" status, such as the Asian John Wu and the Catholic priest Patrick Sheehan. G. Edward White has warned against the attribution of too much social significance to Holmes's letter writing to the socially marginal: "He was willing to write to anyone whose ideas he found interesting, so long as he did not have to entertain the correspondent at home": White, "Looking at Holmes in the Mirror," *Law and History Review* 4 (1986): 439, 462.

36. Holmes to Pollock, April 5, 1919, in Howe, ed., *Holmes-Pollock Letters*, 2:8; Holmes to Pollock, October 31, 1926, in ibid., 2:191. Although Holmes told Pollock he could easily get to be friendly with someone and not know whether the person was Jewish, he seems to have been very much aware of Laski's Jewishness. The day after Holmes first met Laski, he referred to him in a letter to Pollock as "an astonishing young Jew"; Holmes to Pollock, July 12, 1916, in ibid., 1:238. See also Holmes to Pollock, February 18, 1917, in ibid., 1:243.

37. By contrast, one of the earliest and loudest voices to express puzzlement and dismay at the adulation of Holmes by liberal intellectuals was a critic with no Jewish connections, H. L. Mencken. See H. L. Mencken, "Mr. Justice Holmes," in *The Vintage Mencken*, ed. Alistair Cooke (New York, 1955), 189 (orig. pub. *American Mercury*, May 1930, a review of Alfred Lief, comp., *The Dissenting Opinions of Mr. Justice Holmes* [New York, 1930], and as remarks in *American Mercury*, May 1932).

38. Gilmore, *Ages of American Law*, 48.

39. Felix Frankfurter, *Mr. Justice Holmes and the Constitution* (Cambridge, Mass., 1927), 44; and see Felix Frankfurter, "The Constitutional Opinions of Justice Holmes," *Harvard Law Review* 29 (1916): 683.

40. OWH, "Preface," *Collected Legal Papers*.

41. Morris R. Cohen, *Faith of a Liberal* (New York, 1946), 30, where Cohen reprinted an essay of 1935, written for the *New Republic* on the occasion of Holmes's death. This essay is, from today's perspective, one of the most discerning of the appreciations of Holmes written from the Holmes-as-liberal-hero perspective. While Cohen's identification of Holmes with J. S. Mill, and with faith in reason, is characteristic of the genre, he is explicitly critical of Holmes's militaristic sympathies, his extravagant fatalism, and his Malthusian-Darwinian conception of social life.

42. Jerome Frank, *Law and the Modern Mind* (1930; reprint, New York, 1963), 270.

43. Lerner, ed., *Mind and Faith of Justice Holmes*, vii, xix, xlvii, xlix–l.

44. For the developments summarized in this paragraph, see Hollinger, *In the American Province*, chap. 4, "Ethnic Diversity, Cosmopolitanism, and the Emergence of the American Liberal Intelligentsia." See also David A. Hollinger, *Morris R. Cohen and the Scientific Ideal* (Cambridge, Mass., 1975).

45. As manifest, for example, in a number of major works by Jewish and WASP scholars published between 1940 and the mid-1950s. See Alfred Kazin, *On Native Grounds* (New York, 1942); Lionel Trilling, *The Liberal Imagination* (New York, 1950); F. 0. Matthiessen, *American Renaissance* (New York, 1940); Morris R. Cohen, *American Thought: A Critical Sketch* (New York, 1954); Daniel J. Boorstin, *The Genius of American Politics* (Chicago, 1953); Henry Steele Commager, *The American Mind: An Interpretation of American Thought and Character since the 1880's*

(New Haven, Conn., 1950). The growth of "American Studies" in the ethnic, religious, and ideological settings of the World War II era has been helpfully illuminated by Philip Gleason in three articles; see "Americans All: World War II and the Shaping of American Identity," *Review of Politics* 43 (1981): 483; "World War II and the Development of American Studies," *American Quarterly* 36 (1984): 343; "Pluralism, Democracy, and Catholicism in the Era of World War II," *Review of Politics* 49 (1987): 208.

46. For the account of Holmes in Commager's classic synthesis of the midcentury liberal intelligentsia's vision of American culture, see Commager, *The American Mind*, 385–390. Commager signs off the relevant chapter by eulogizing Holmes with Stephen Spender's "I Think Continually of Those Who Were Truly Great."

47. For this striking thought I am indebted to Morton Keller, who illustrates the length and diversity of Holmes's life by observing, at the outset of his *Affairs of State* (Cambridge, Mass., 1977), that Holmes could count among his personal acquaintances both John Quincy Adams and Alger Hiss.

48. This line from the senior Holmes's "Chambered Nautilus" was often cited as an example of the vacancy of his "uplifting" poetry.

49. Indeed, the prevailing public culture of American colleges and universities as late as the early 1930s retained many of the traits that gave the "genteel tradition" its name, and inspired many plays on the word "Gentile." For a discussion of one prominent example, New York University, see David A. Hollinger, "Two NYUs and 'The Obligation of Universities to the Social Order' in the Great Depression," in *The University and the City*, ed. Thomas Bender (New York, 1988), 249. This essay is reprinted as chapter 4 of the present volume. Young Jewish intellectuals of the period had a real enemy to fight, and they knew Holmes was no part of it.

50. At the heart of life "there rises a mystic spiritual tone that gives meaning to the whole. . . . It suggests that even while we think that we are egoists we are living to ends outside ourselves"; OWH, "Parts of the Unimaginable Whole," in Lerner, ed., *Mind and Faith of Justice Holmes*, 27.

51. Laski to Holmes, July 11, 1916, and Holmes to Laski, July 14, 1916, in Howe, ed., *Holmes-Laski Letters*, 1:3–4. Striking personal testimony concerning the authenticity of Holmes's respect and affection for Laski is offered by Kingsley Martin, *Harold Laski, 1893–1950: A Biographical Memoir* (London, 1953), 44–45.

52. Holmes to Cohen, March 9, 1916, in Rosenfield, *Portrait of a Philosopher*, 315.

53. OWH, "Ideals and Doubts," in *Collected Legal Papers*, 303.

54. A few years later, when Cohen wanted a break from full-time teaching at the City College of New York, Holmes personally contributed part of the money on which Cohen and his family lived during a privately arranged "sabbatical." The book on which Cohen was then working, *Reason and Nature: The Meaning of Scientific Method* (New York, 1931), was in turn dedicated to Holmes.

55. Wilson, *The Bit between My Teeth*, 91.

56. Michael Parrish, *Felix Frankfurter and His Times: The Reform Years* (New York, 1982), 3.

57. Martin, *Harold Laski*, 9; Morris R. Cohen, *A Dreamers' Journey* (New York, 1949), 69; Wilson, *The Bit between My Teeth*, 91.

58. See Francis E. Lucey, "Natural Law and American Legal Realism: Their Respective Contributions to a Theory of Law in a Democratic Society," *Georgetown Law Journal* 30 (1942): 493. My sense of the Jesuit attack on Holmes, and upon the liberal-realist milieu for which he was a symbol, derives from White, "The Rise and Fall of Justice Holmes."

59. Lon L. Fuller, *The Law in Quest of Itself* (Chicago, 1940), 92–95; Walton H. Hamilton, "On Dating Mr. Justice Holmes," *University of Chicago Law Review* 9 (1941): 1.

CHAPTER FOUR

Two NYUs and "The Obligation of Universities to the Social Order" in the Great Depression

The conference of 1932 analyzed here introduced no new ideas and inspired no imitators. Some of today's intellectuals may feel sympathy for one or another of the enduring doctrinal persuasions expressed at the conference—the need for "values" in higher education, perhaps, or the need for a more "rational" approach to public affairs—but are likely embarrassed by the tone of the argumentation and will probably prefer to remember from history more attractive advocates of these ideas. Many conferences are forgettable, and this would seem to be one of them. But when what was said at this meeting of academic intellectuals and their allies outside academia is considered in relation to what was not said, and in relation to the ethnoreligious and political context of the event, the proceedings can be seen as a splendid "period piece." Examining it is an opportunity to confront a number of preoccupations, tensions, and enthusiasms characteristic of the period.

What "Christianity" was then understood to mean in universities and colleges not affiliated religiously is prominent among the historical realities to which we gain access by studying this event. Recovering this reality makes it easier for us to comprehend the desire of so many intellectuals of the midcentury decades to create an academic culture free of it. The muted character of what we can recognize today as a conflict between "religious conservatives" and "technocratic progressives" can remind us, in turn, that "culture wars," like other kinds of warfare in the midcentury decades, were cold as well as hot.

I undertook this study at the invitation of New York University in relation to the centennial of that institution's graduate school. It was originally published in The University and the City, *ed. Thomas Bender (New York, 1988), 249–266.*

THE GREAT DEPRESSION happened along at a uniquely inconvenient time for the leaders of New York University. NYU was ready to celebrate its centennial, but what kind of celebration would be appropriate amid "the disorganized economic conditions" and the "widespread personal distress and social confusion" to which NYU leaders professed to be sensitive in 1932? Finding the right tone for a big party at the Waldorf-Astoria was far from the most serious challenge created for academic administrators by the Great Depression, but the problem was a delicate one.

The solution, explained the editor of the published proceedings of the centennial event, was to select a theme suitably responsive to the times: "The Obligation of Universities to the Social Order." NYU would project no ivory-tower aloofness, no complacent self-absorption; it would instead confront society head-on. It would convene at the Waldorf an ambitious conference on the social responsibilities of higher education.[1]

Twentieth-century universities routinely produce symposiums, but this gathering of American intellectual leaders invites our attention for several reasons, only one of which is the opportunity to watch a private university struggle for a credible public identity amid the pressures of the Great Depression. The conference was a peculiar episode in the history of urban consciousness: NYU was, of course, an urban university, but it chose in 1932 to address its social obligations in terms that ignored this fact. In both the content and the style of its centennial celebrations NYU revealed a wish to escape altogether from its own city of New York and from urban life in general. This wish was not countered even by the dozens of guests who were invited to address the social obligations of the academy. That there might be a distinctly urban role for universities was not even suggested by these speakers and discussants, whose obliviousness toward this notion—such a commonplace today—shows how easily NYU found contemporary support for its exercise in urban denial. NYU's invited guests also cooperated with the university's use of the conference to associate itself with a conservative, genteel culture increasingly on the defensive in metropolitan New York. The NYU centennial conference was a modest event but one at which the unique circumstances of a single university served to focus the commitments and uncertainties of a larger, depression-shocked community.

That larger community was represented at the conference by a number of individuals whose contemporary prominence lends historical significance to the event. These included the era's most influential political scientist (Charles E. Merriam of Chicago), economist (Wesley Clair Mitchell of Columbia), and political commentator (Walter Lippmann of the *New York Herald Tribune*), as well as the presidents of Yale (James Rowland Angell), Columbia (Nicholas Murray Butler), Union Theological Seminary (Henry Sloane Coffin), and the University of California (Robert Gordon Sproul). The heads of the Brookings Institution (Harold G. Moulton) and the Carnegie Institution (John C. Merriam) also participated, as did George Soule of the *New Republic*, Harvard's eminent philosopher William Ernest Hocking, and the financial titan Thomas W. Lamont of J. P. Morgan and Company. The conferees also included a handful of European dignitaries, a few government officials, the then-famous poet Alfred Noyes, and several dozen garden-variety college presidents, deans, and senior professors.

The wish to escape the city was expressed not only through shared silence about cities. NYU chancellor Elmer Ellsworth Brown revealed at the outset his own social ideal: he opened the conference by urging his guests to think of themselves as, in effect, farmers. Universities are like "pioneer institutions," Brown explained, ready to help one another perform tasks of construction. In "olden days" when "a barn was to be built, or a new roadway made through the forest" amid "widely scattered plantations," neighbors assembled to carry out the task cooperatively.[2] Brown's casual characterization of the conferees as rural barn raisers was perhaps a trivial aside, but it betrayed with unconscious eloquence an ambivalence about modernity that Chancellor Brown brought to the task of organizing the conference. This ambivalence served to structure the discourse in terms that make the event all the more revealing an indicator of the convictions and uncertainties of NYU's loquacious guests. Before scrutinizing Brown and his university any further, however, we must attend to the intellectual content of the conference itself.

The conference was dominated by two strong intellectual impulses. One was resoundingly technocratic and progressive: social engineering, it was said, must go forward immediately, casting aside anachronistic traditions. Our universities must more aggressively supply experts and trained statesmen to bring society's chaos under rational and, it is hoped, democratic control. The social sciences must be developed more extensively, following in the footsteps of the physical and biological sciences, in order to produce more and better knowledge, and this social-scientific knowledge must be put to concrete use by managers and officials at all levels of social organization.[3] This first, technocratic-progressive impulse was, of course, merely an intensification of the talk about social engineering that social scientists and many other liberal intellectuals had been promoting off and on throughout the 1920s and the Progressive Era.[4]

The second impulse was adamantly religious and conservative: "spiritual values," it was said, must be reaffirmed lest a godless materialism take over the world. Our universities must teach the insights of traditional religious faith in order that the new generation not lose sight of the "eternal verities" wrongly rejected by inexplicably popular "pseudointellectuals" and cynics claiming to speak on behalf of modern science and modern art. What we really need on our campuses are mechanisms that will somehow re-create the atmosphere that we once maintained with chapel services.[5] This second, religious-conservative impulse possessed an even longer ancestry than technocratic-progressivism, but it was by 1932 self-consciously reactionary, protesting against contemporary culture in the name of a timeless wisdom ostensibly institutionalized the most perfectly in the old-fashioned Christian college of nineteenth-century America.[6] Yet a sign of its strength was the praise the *New York Times* offered for the conference's emphasis on "spiritual values."[7]

The technocratic-progressive impulse was predictably the most evident in two symposiums addressed to the relation of universities to the political and economic changes then being experienced by industrial societies. Merriam, Soule, Mitchell, Moulton, Lamont, and their colleagues in both social science and business management sang the praises of scientific method, of intelligence, of knowledge, of expertise, of planning; indeed, these terms were virtually incanted amid expressions of the faith that social science would soon produce its Newtons and its Pasteurs. But the social obligation of the university in this connection was not simply to sustain research; universities were to train experts for government and industry and to educate citizens so that the electorate could respond appropriately to the initiatives of the experts. The Depression simply made these services of the university all the more imperative. A very large proportion of the conference was given over to the earnest articulation in persistently general terms of this familiar technocratic-progressive vision.

The elitist character of this vision was expressed by Sir Arthur Salter, a British delegate and longtime official of the League of Nations. What we need, Salter explained, is "a few central leaders, a great number of specialized and local leaders, and an informed and receptive public opinion."[8] What could be more "technocratic" than this notion of informed public opinion as ideally "receptive" rather than as the proper, ultimate agent of political change? Many of the conferees understood that such ideas stood in tension with classical "democratic" ideology. None renounced democracy by name, but many referred guardedly to the "experiments" in centralized planning being carried out by Mussolini and Stalin. Even Charles E. Merriam, the most persistent and self-conscious of democracy's defenders at the conference, spoke in a realistic idiom about "propaganda" and "mass manipulation." But Merriam believed that such techniques as used by democratic leaders in conjunction with an aggressive program of "civic education" would consolidate a polity based on knowledge, not arbitrary will. "The heart of modern power," he insisted, "is not brutality but intelligence and organization for the purpose of putting that intelligence into effective operation."[9]

It was fitting that Merriam's address, the conference's most pointed and carefully formulated expression of faith in the political efficacy of knowledge and education, should end with an impassioned vindication of science as a broad, cultural ideal. "I have seen the red tide flowing down the streets of Moscow," he testified, and in Berlin "the 100,000 shouting 'Heil, Hitler' with shining faces." But here at home, "Who will supply the great idealisms that sweep men's souls from time to time and stir their hearts?" Merriam's answer was highly cognitive. He called his audience to look to "science," and he charged the university with the mission of spreading a sympathetic understanding of science as "not a cold figure of stone" but an agent of "life and light."[10]

Merriam's peroration was but one of a number of signs that the technocratic progressives at the NYU conference were in possession of a rudimentary program for *culture*. Yet the conference provided an altogether separate symposium for cultural issues, and in it Merriam's secular-liberal ideas were not voiced. The cultural symposium, entitled "The University and Spiritual Values," was a religious-conservative monolith to which we will turn in a moment. Amid the political and economic talk and in Lippmann's address at the conference's final banquet there was heard a plea for a culture organized around the scientific enterprise. Education was to foster a critical attitude, a capacity for discerning judgment, a disposition to base one's beliefs on evidence, a willingness to consider new ideas, a commitment to look empirical realities in the face, and a suspicion of partisanship. If modern society was to be increasingly dependent on knowledge, then the citizens of that society needed themselves to be knowers, to be comfortable with what the conferees again and again called the spirit of science. When they spoke in this vein the conferees quite clearly hoped for the spreading throughout society of a distinctly cognitive ethic, a cluster of commitments to such classically "scientific" ideals as objectivity, rationality, disinterestedness, and veracity; and they saw the university as an agency of the spreading of such a cognitive, scientific ethic.[11] The type of mind an ideal university ought to produce, suggested NYU economist Walter E. Spahr, was the mind of Francis Bacon: discursive, discerning, searching, patient, experimental, skeptical, and independent.[12]

The explicit cultural program advanced in the "spiritual values" symposium was far indeed from Francis Bacon and the Enlightenment, far from John Dewey and the ethic of science, and far from the implicit, if not illicit, cultural program hinted at by the technocratic progressives at other symposiums within the conference. The constant theme was not the potential of scientific culture but the inability of science to provide any culture at all and the imperative to make universities more like churches. "One of the most essential functions . . . of the university today," said Aurelia H. Reinhardt, the president of Mills College, is the opportunity it can provide "for group worship."[13]

Although Union's Coffin projected a nondefensive attitude toward the modern, scientific intellect and directed prophetic religion instead against the values of "Main Street," his colleagues were less troubled by commercial culture than by the encroachments of science on the sphere of old-time religion.[14] Speaker after speaker protested that the secular trend had gone too far, that the commendable idea of academic autonomy had been taken so far that our colleges and universities were losing their religious roots. Philosophy, one speaker suggested, ought to be taught only by positive believers, never by a skeptic.[15] The mode celebrated the most consistently was not knowledge but inspiration. The president of Lafayette College, William Mather Lewis, declared that more "than any other influences of the university," the one most beneficial "to the social order" was probably the inspiration provided by the paintings and statues past which a student walks while going to and from class.[16]

The antagonism toward science and secularism manifest in the religious-conservative impulse was most cogently expressed in the biblical phrase one speaker attributed to a sincere university student confronted with academic life: "They have taken away the Lord . . . and we know not where they have laid Him." The phrase was picked up and quoted by other speakers, just as Salter's words about "leaders" and a "receptive public" were quoted repeatedly. If Salter voiced the political consensus of the conference, this plaintive cry of the spiritually searching undergraduate voiced the consensus of the cultural symposium. The speaker who introduced this anxiety about the missing Jesus Christ was the poet Alfred Noyes, author of "The Highwayman" and other popular, neo-Romantic works of verse. Noyes was introduced as one who had wisely recognized the limitations of "scientific philosophy" and who saw to "those deeper things which we call religion."[17]

Noyes's speech was decidedly the most polemical and contentious in the entire conference. It condemned materialists in philosophy and science, agnostics in religion, and modernists in the arts. Although the failure to keep science in its place was annoying enough to Noyes, nothing was more anathema to him than modernist literature. The "pseudo-intellectuals" who wrote and celebrated such literature too often mocked and discredited the structure of religious belief which has so long energized, stabilized, and unified "the civilized world." These modernists, complained Noyes, have taken away "our dogmas, creeds, and traditions." The young, Noyes continued, are being "robbed of their birthright in Christendom by the jaded cynicism" of irresponsible men of letters, and their allies in philosophy who exalt mere knowledge over religious insight. As if to counter the demystifying tendencies of the age, Noyes quoted at some length from his own mystical verse about nature and nature's God:

> There's many a proud wizard in Araby and Egypt
> Can read the silver writings of the stars as they run;
> . . . But *I* know a Wizardry can take a buried acorn
> And whisper forests out of it, to tower against the sun.[18]

The frank mystifications of the religious-conservative impulse are all the more noticeable since historians remember the year 1932 for so many efforts at demystification made around that time, especially in New York City. About two weeks after the conference a young professor at Union Theological Seminary published *Moral Man and Immoral Society*. In that famous attack on Protestant idealism Reinhold Niebuhr offered a largely materialist explanation of and a revolutionary solution for the problems of the Depression. Almost simultaneous with the conference there appeared another legendary work of 1932, by two young professors from Columbia, Adolph Berle and Gardner Means: *The Modern Corporation and Private Property*, the most influential deflation of capitalist ideology published in the United States during the 1930s. Six weeks before the conference there appeared the notorious manifesto *Culture and Crisis*, in which a host of intellectuals, mostly New Yorkers, announced that the established culture was serving to obfuscate a corrupt capitalist system. The signers of this manifesto, including Edmund Wilson, John Dos Passos, Malcolm Cowley, James Rorty, Lincoln Steffens, Sherwood Anderson, and Sidney Hook, declared their support for the Communist candidates in the election of 1932.[19]

These enterprises of polemical demystification may help to place the "spiritual values" symposium in bold relief, but for this effect one need not look beyond the conference itself. The very titles assigned to the several symposiums by conference organizers carried the implication that politics and the economy are subject to change, but culture is not. "The University and Governmental Changes" and "The University and Economic Changes" were juxtaposed not to "The University and Cultural Changes" but to "The University and Spiritual Values."

The emphasis on timeless, "spiritual" values was fully consistent with the mission Chancellor Brown had been pursuing during his two decades as head of NYU. That mission, as described respectfully in the NYU centennial history published in 1933 by NYU historian Theodore Francis Jones, was to "spiritualize the machine created by an earlier age."[20] Jones did not make any connection between Brown and George Santayana's concept of the "genteel tradition," but it is an apt coincidence for our purposes that exactly during the summer Brown had taken office as chancellor of NYU in 1911 Santayana was delivering at Berkeley his sardonic lecture on the idealistic academic culture of the United States. No doubt historians have made too much of Santayana's invidious contrast: a cloyingly wholesome, flaccid, narrowly Protestant idealism mocked by the vigor and authenticity of an aggressive, earthy, modern civilization. This contrast has long since become a cliché, but its terms do speak very directly to what was going on at NYU in 1932, especially to the obvious use of "spiritual values" to keep the polyglot, contingent cultural life of the metropolis at a distance. Santayana identified urban life as the concentration of everything with which the genteel tradition was not prepared to cope: "the American Will inhabits the skyscraper," he said, while the American Intellect continues to reside in a colonial mansion.[21]

NYU leaders sometimes celebrated the colonial mansion as the ideal setting for a university. The NYU campus in the Bronx, "University Heights," was praised by the dean of its principal unit, University College of Arts and Pure Science, as a form of country life: "a retired hill-top," "quiet" and "secluded." There was explicit talk of "walling in" this campus in order to "shut out the city." The history of "the Heights" throughout the 1910s and 1920s had been, according to historian Jones, largely an effort to protect this stately cloister "from the overwhelming forces of the new city."[22]

By far the most disturbing of these urban forces were, of course, immigrant Jews. As more and more Jewish students had sought and gained entry into the "retired hill-top" during the 1910s, NYU leaders worried that this institution would be overrun by "aliens."[23] Such worries were common to many universities of the northeastern United States during the 1920s.[24] The "problem," as it was termed at the time, was more acute for New York City institutions as a result of the high concentration of immigrant Jews in that city. Alumni and student groups at "the Heights" were sometimes stridently anti-Semitic. Jewish organizations were systematically discriminated against in campus life, especially during World War I and the subsequent Red Scare, when East European Jewish immigrants were linked in the popular mind with Bolshevism. In 1919, shortly after undergraduate leaders had formally petitioned Chancellor Brown to limit Jewish enrollment to 20 percent, NYU introduced into its admission procedures "a personal and psychological examination." Although Brown denied publicly that this test was designed to enable NYU to more easily reject Jewish applicants, the nature of the examination itself and the private correspondence surrounding it leave no doubt whatsoever as to its purpose.[25] And it worked, at least for a few years: Jewish enrollment at the Bronx campus dropped during the early and mid-1920s from nearly 50 percent to less than 30 percent.

This infamous test was still in use in 1932, although Jones speculated that it might soon be dropped because the problem to which it was addressed had been dealt with at the source: immigration from eastern

Europe had been restricted.[26] No one had more reason to feel triumphant about this restriction than Brown's chief aide in the matter of the
conference and editor of the published proceedings, NYU sociologist
Henry Pratt Fairchild. During the debates over immigration restriction
in the 1920s Fairchild had proven to be one of the most intellectually
able and influential nativists in the United States. His greatest claim to
fame was his book of 1926, *The Melting Pot Mistake.* At the time of the
centennial celebration itself, Fairchild had just finished his term as
president of the American Eugenics Society.[27] Although Fairchild's own
editorial comments in *The Obligation of Universities to the Social Order* did
not address eugenicist issues, his prominent involvement in the centennial is a reminder of the nativist heritage brought to the centennial by
NYU leadership.

Yet during the same thirteen years since NYU had formally institutionalized admissions discrimination against Jews on the Bronx campus,
NYU had been developing an antithetical response to New York City and
to immigrant Jews which renders all the more striking the centennial
conference's studied aloofness from urban life. Beginning in 1919 NYU
developed its downtown Washington Square facilities to meet the educational needs of exactly those New York City young people who would not
or could not attend college outside the city yet were prevented by cost or
discrimination from attending Columbia or the Bronx campus of NYU.
Only the City College of New York served this constituency on a large
scale before the development of NYU's Washington Square College.
While this venture in self-consciously urban education appealed to NYU
leadership in part as a survival measure—a way to pick up revenue from
an expanding and imperfectly addressed educational market—it soon
generated a certain pride in its own mission.[28] Nowhere was this pride
more evident than in the person of its dean, James Buell Munn, during
the four years immediately prior to the centennial.

Dean Munn's frank enthusiasm for Washington Square's service to
urban Jews is worth dwelling on because it prefigures NYU's subsequent
forthright acceptance of an urban mission and because it helps to identify voices silenced, in effect, by Brown's design of the events of 1932.
Munn exalted the city as a setting for education with the same intensity
that other NYU deans held forth on the virtues of cloistered hilltops and
regular chapel. While his colleagues treated the city as culturally unnatu-
ral, as a menace to true culture, Munn steadfastly defended it as filled
with "natural cultural opportunities" and as a "laboratory." While Jewish
students had no difficulty gauging the limits of their welcome at the
Bronx campus, they were similarly quick to understand the eagerness of
this wealthy Mayflower descendant—Munn traced his lineage to William
Bradford himself—to see that they got a good education. Toward this

end Munn devoted not only his pedagogic and administrative energies but money from his private inheritance as well. The personal correspondence between Washington Square students and the patrician Munn now fills twenty-eight substantial folders in the NYU archives.[29]

The friendly interaction between Munn and Jewish students is of some historical significance: it was an episode in the emergence of an ethnically diverse, cosmopolitan, largely urban intelligentsia in the United States.[30] Such episodes are easy to overlook amid today's proper eagerness to confront honestly the anti-Semitism and snobbish exclusivity we now find so striking when we scrutinize the era between about 1910 and World War II. Yet it was during these same years that there took place—especially in New York City—a historic transformation in the ethnic foundation of American intellectual life: intellectuals of East European Jewish origin did make their way into the academic and literary professions and, in so doing, altered the culture of these professions in secular, cosmopolitan directions. If this de-Christianization did not become fully visible until the 1950s, when so many of its leading agents became prominent writers and professors, the basic steps in the transformation were made earlier, when the careers of these Jewish writers and professors were begun. The beginnings of these careers, in turn, depended in part on measures of support—small from our perspective today but substantial in their context—offered by established intellectuals of Protestant Anglo-Saxon stock. Randolph Bourne and Justice Oliver Wendell Holmes, Jr., are among the most famous of these "old WASPs" who celebrated and helped to sponsor the enlivening of American intellectual life by immigrant Jews and their offspring.[31] In the company of these influential WASP Semitophiles belongs NYU's Dean Munn.

If Munn represents the coming of a "new" NYU—the institution that has now developed from Washington Square College into the proudly urban, ethnically diverse university that celebrates Munn's memory and finds it natural to convene a conference on "universities and cities"—the centennial celebrations of 1932 were a studied affirmation of an "old" NYU.[32] A few months before the centennial celebrations Munn left NYU to join the English department at Harvard University. His perspective on urban education was detailed in the chapter on Washington Square College that he wrote for Jones's centennial history,[33] but Brown's conference proceeded as though Munn and his Washington Square skyscraper never existed. The official culture of NYU as displayed at the centennial celebrations remained that of the colonial mansion in the Bronx.[34]

How different the conference would have looked had the cultural symposium been a forum for the articulation and defense of the liberal-secular program so obviously consistent with the technocratic-progressive impulse. Where was John Dewey? If the technocratic-progressive impulse had a philosopher, one ready to state what might be the cultural dimensions of technocratic-progressivism, such a philosopher was, of course, Dewey himself. And Dewey was close at hand, uptown at Columbia University. But Dewey was not involved in the NYU conference.[35] Other secular-liberal philosophers were easy to find in New York but seem not to have been invited. Prominent among these were Morris R. Cohen of CCNY, Horace Kallen of the New School for Social Research, and NYU's own Sidney Hook, who, although still very young, had already become a prominent controversialist in the intellectual life of New York City.[36]

Brown seems to have wanted something very different from Deweyite secular liberalism, whether emanating from Dewey himself—a lapsed Protestant—or from Dewey's Jewish as well as Gentile followers in New York City academia. The first indication in the archival sources of Brown's intentions concerning the cultural segment of the conference is Brown's decision to turn this whole segment over to John C. Merriam, president of the Carnegie Institution of Washington and elder brother of the Chicago political scientist Charles E. Merriam, one of the conference's leading technocratic progressives. This sibling connection played little role in the conference, but Brown approached Charles Merriam only after obtaining John Merriam's commitment to participate.[37] John Merriam, then aged sixty-three, was a paleontologist of some note and a journeyman convocation speaker specializing in inspirational talks on vaguely scientific themes.[38] We are left to guess just how calculating was Brown's decision to involve John Merriam in the conference. In the earliest relevant written correspondence between the two men they refer to a prior agreement—first reached by telephone, or at a January 15 luncheon at the Century Club—that "spiritual values and the university" should be the topic of the symposium over which John Merriam was to preside.[39] Although Brown and his staff left copious records of the centennial, they left very little of what a historian would now most like to have: a record of the grounds on which they asked certain individuals and not others to participate in the conference.[40] One thing we do not have to guess about is the degree of enthusiasm Brown felt toward John Merriam's approach. Brown allowed Merriam to invite whomever he wished to hold forth on "spiritual values." Thus, Brown managed to keep his conference free of "scientific," classically "New York" philosophers such as Dewey and Cohen, who were always eager for an opportunity to criticize the genteel tradition.

That Brown himself bears major responsibility for the character of the conference is rendered more plausible by what may be the earliest surviving planning document for the centennial celebration. "Tentative

Suggestions Relating to the Centennial Celebration of New York University" was apparently written by Vice President Harold O. Voorhis or a member of his staff. This memorandum offers, as its very first proposal, the theme of NYU as an "exponent of the City of New York." The "central features of the celebration should be three convocations" addressed to higher education: first as "a concern of the City," second as a concern of "the Nation," and third as a "world concern."[41] How the conference was transformed from this into what actually took place is now lost in Brown's private conversations with John Merriam and perhaps Yale's James Rowland Angell, whom Brown consulted frequently while planning the conference.

Whatever may have been Brown's designs, the religious conservatives and the technocratic progressives remained remarkably oblivious to one another throughout the conference. Fairchild hinted in his editorial afterword that he, at least, was troubled by the failure of the conference's two major intellectual directions to connect up with one another. "How," Fairchild asked, are "spiritual values" to be related to "specialized scientific expertise"? Fairchild did not pretend to have an answer to this question. He merely raised it as an afterthought, an example of an issue not resolved by the conference[42]—not even formulated, it would have been more accurate to say. Yet the conference did contain one setting in which one might expect to find this issue formulated and addressed: a fourth symposium, on the "Aims and Province of the University Today." Here technocratic-progressivism might actually confront religious-conservatism. But at this symposium, organized for Brown by Angell, very little was heard of the religious-conservative impulse.[43]

Technocratic-progressivism was on the defensive at this fourth symposium, but against an antiutilitarian disposition whose spokesmen did not directly challenge the liberal-secular orientation of the technocratic progressives. Might applied social science and the training of experts and professionals diminish the university's commitment to basic research and to liberal arts education? Was the obligation of universities to the social order proudly nonutilitarian, simply to search for truth, and to share it with the world, especially with students, or was this obligation broader, requiring schools of engineering and business? Cardinal Newman figured prominently in these debates, but not as the champion of religion; he was quoted rather as a defender of a nonutilitarian ideal of higher education. Many of the symposiasts regarded themselves as bold iconoclasts for finding the educational ideals of Newman too narrow. President Angell, playing the role of liberal innovator, declared in a spirit of great magnanimity that engineering was not necessarily incompatible with intellectual excellence.[44]

The symposium on the aims and province of the university was the liveliest, frankest, most spontaneous within the entire conference, yet the upshot was easily predictable: universities ought to be pluralistic communities, striving for excellence in the three classic modes of the American university—research, teaching, and service. What cultural talk there was paralleled that of the political and economic symposiums. A life of discerning inquiry was said to be of great moral worth. Einstein was quoted to the effect that civilization depended on its moral forces, and Sir James Irvine of St. Andrews University, Scotland, offered the ethic of science as exactly such a force. Cosmopolitanism was endorsed against the claims of provincial traditions.[45]

The failure of Charles Merriam and other proponents of "scientific culture" to challenge the religious conservatives on the floor is at first glance the most surprising feature of the discourse of the conference, but this lack of contentiousness has a certain logic. They were the guests, after all, of Chancellor Brown, whose center of cultural gravity was no secret. And in the absence of more argumentative champions of secular liberalism such as Dewey and Cohen, the obvious leader of that persuasion was Charles Merriam, younger brother of the man who presided over and dominated the conference's conservative-religious element. The Merriams, moreover, were on friendly terms with each other. Indeed, Charles Merriam had emulated his older sibling since childhood and continued to rely on John Merriam's influence in support of his various projects.[46]

The live-and-let-live attitude of the technocratic progressives toward the religious conservatives was consistent, moreover, with the tone of most of the conference, which was an exceedingly circumspect affair. It avoided all mention of the presidential election of two weeks before, was guarded in its response to the crisis of the Depression, remained altogether aloof from New York City, proved to be conventional in the issues it framed, and was fastidious in its concern for propriety.[47] Brown's summary of the conference reduced it to a list of fifteen platitudes.[48] Fairchild was somewhat more bold. In his afterword to *The Obligation of Universities to the Social Order* Fairchild observed that the conference really did not provide much guidance for how universities should deal with the future.

Fairchild also offered his own piece of social analysis which, had it been prominent on the agenda of the conference itself, might have made the affair more exciting than it had been. "In the era that is dawning," he suggested, "in every department and interest of life, the producer's philosophy must be supplanted by a consumer's philosophy." In the realm of knowledge, for example, the point would be not so much to get more of it but to make more active and extensive application of the knowledge already in existence.[49] Here was the basis for a real argument within the technocratic-progressive tradition: should the priority be the finding of new truth or the more effective application and distribution of what we now know? Do our society's problems endure and worsen because we lack knowledge or because we have failed to reform our economic practices and political institutions in the light of truths we now possess? At ultimate issue, of course, was the extent to which society's health could be achieved and maintained through purely cognitive as opposed to overtly political measures. A number of speakers and discussants did express what can be fairly characterized as conflicting dispositions on this issue. Soule, Salter, Charles Merriam, and University of Minnesota president Lotus Delta Coffman placed more emphasis on "application," while Irvine and University of Pennsylvania economist Thomas Gates came down more strongly on the side of "pure" science.[50] Yet none formulated Fairchild's issue as sharply as Fairchild did, and none made an argument as sustained as his for one side or the other. A *New York Times* article claimed the conferees had significantly differed over the question of seeking new truths as opposed to applying existing truths, but the *Times*—prompted, one wonders, by Fairchild himself?—made the conflict seem more vivid than it had been.[51]

It would be a mistake, however, to exaggerate Fairchild's departure from the circumspect tone of the NYU centennial conference. He concluded *The Obligation of Universities to the Social Order* very generally: "there must be," on the part of universities, "an immediate and practical translation" of the ideal of social obligation "into terms of direct social guidance and participation."[52] Fairchild was perhaps the most confident and forthright of the conference's technocratic progressives, but even he did not claim to know just how the university ought to involve itself in what he took to be a new consumer's world.

The intellectual perimeter within which the technocratic progressives operated at the NYU conference was no doubt determined more by the genuine uncertainties of the conferees than by an excess of deference for their religious-conservative host. These uncertainties were felt, moreover, by people who had been accustomed to living with religious-conservatism in American universities throughout the 1920s and the Progressive Era. As late as 1932 virtually all American universities continued to display in their official culture a strong religious-conservative aspect. This was true even of the great secular, state universities: Robert Gordon Sproul of the University of California explicitly identified himself with Noyes, Hocking, and John Merriam, and concluded his own contribution to the "spiritual values" symposium by quoting his Victorian predecessor, Benjamin Ide Wheeler. Wheeler's call to "nobler living" might have been grist for Santayana's irreverence, but according to Sproul, Wheeler had said it all. There was no need to revise or even to reformulate inherited ideas about universities and values.[53] Hence Chancellor Brown's technocratic-progressive guests were not thrown so sharply on the defensive as one might suppose. They were accustomed to such talk. From the magnates of higher education it was to be expected.

Such expectations were soon to change. By the time of the "Harvard Red Book" in 1945 the secular-liberal program for culture voiced intermittently at NYU in 1932 had supplanted the religious-conservative program in more and more of the academic space of the United States.[54] This program drew its share of critics, but Robert Hutchins, Mortimer Adler, and their allies developed educational models more classical than Christian and less given to the justification of ethnocentric policies and practices than were the preachments of Noyes, Hocking, and John Merriam.[55] But 1932 was very distant from 1945 in the history of American higher education's public ideologies. Speeches that could be hooted at as anachronistic if delivered in the 1940s or 1950s were still, in 1932, blandly conventional.

The genteel tradition in the culture of American universities declined at different speeds and in response to different pressures from one institution to another. Nothing threatened that tradition more directly than did polyglot cities, especially the city of New York. The challenge presented by New York City was uniquely acute at NYU, moreover, as a result of NYU's peculiar position as a private university forced to find its student market in what Columbia counted as its leftovers.[56] NYU tried for years to be a junior Columbia but found itself increasingly dependent on a student clientele drawn from the city. The nativist Fairchild did not see the irony, but his "consumerist" vision of the modern political economy was being vindicated all around him in the transformation of NYU by Jewish consumer-students. The university was forced to allow its Jewish enrollment to climb again. Even before the added financial pressures of the Depression, Jewish enrollment at "the Heights" had returned in 1929 to the 1919 levels of more than 50 percent. Yet in that same year of 1929 an effort was made to build a chapel there and to endow a department of religion "to counteract," as Dean Archibald L. Boulton phrased it, "the manifold influences of the city." No donor could be found.[57] Three years later, at the centennial conference, the genteel tradition made what was, in effect, its last stand at NYU. That institution's future social obligations were defined not by Dean Boulton and Chancellor Brown but by the recently departed Dean Munn, and by the city of New York.

NOTES

1. Henry Pratt Fairchild, ed., *The Obligation of Universities to the Social Order: Addresses and Discussion at a Conference of Universities under the Auspices of New York University at the Waldorf-Astoria in New York, November 15–17, 1932* (New York, 1933), xiii. Hereafter this volume will be cited as *OUSO*.

2. Brown, in *OUSO*, 203.

3. For examples of the sentiment that social science must now produce the triumphs earlier wrought by physical and biological sciences, see *OUSO*, 188–189, 194–195 (Thomas S. Gates), 200 (Osward W. Knauth), 207 (Walter E. Spahr), 234 (Harold G. Moulton), and 310 (C.E.A. Winslow).

4. The tradition of technocratic-progressivism is the subject of an extensive secondary literature, much of which has been influenced by Morton G. White, *Social Thought in America: The Revolt against Formalism*, 2d ed. (New York, 1957); and Robert Wiebe, *The Search for Order, 1877–1920* (New York, 1967). The aspects of this tradition most manifest at the NYU centennial conference are helpfully addressed in two more narrowly focused studies: James A. Nuechterlein, "The Dream of Scientific Liberalism: *The New Republic* and American Progressive Thought, 1914–1920," *Review of Politics* 42 (1980): 167–190; and Donald T. Critchlow, *The Brookings Institution, 1916–1952: Expertise and the Public Interest in a Democratic Society* (De Kalb, Ill., 1985).

5. For an unironic plea for attention to "eternal verities," see *OUSO*, 397 (William Mather Lewis); for an attack on the "Pseudo-intelligentsia of modern literature," see 358 (Alfred Noyes); for celebrations of chapel, see 349–350 (William Ernest Hocking), 405 (Frederick C. Ferry), and 414–416 (James L. McConaughy).

6. For this religious-conservative tradition in American universities between the Civil War and 1910, see the section on "Discipline and Piety" in Laurence R. Veysey, *The Emergence of the American University* (Chicago, 1965), 21–56.

7. The *Times* gave extensive coverage to the conference but editorialized the most enthusiastically about defenses of "spiritual values" against the pretensions of science; see the issue of November 20, 1932, sec. 2, 1.

8. Sir Arthur Salter, in *OUSO*, 161. This phrase was quoted by others as the essence of the matter; see, e.g., 197 (John T. Madden) and 446 (Chancellor Brown).

9. Charles E. Merriam, in *OUSO*, 240, 248. Soule's contribution to the proceedings was strongly supportive of Merriam's; see George Soule, in *OUSO*, 288–295.

10. Merriam, in *OUSO*, 255–257. On Merriam's career, see Barry Karl, *Charles E. Merriam and the Study of Politics* (Chicago, 1975).

11. This faith in the cultural capabilities of men and women in their capacities as scientific "knowers" is a major presence in modern American and European intellectual history, yet we do not have an accepted term for addressing it. I have proposed that we call it cognitivism; see David A. Hollinger, "The Knower and the Artificer," *American Quarterly* 39 (1987): 37–55, esp. 42–43.

12. Walter E. Spahr, in *OUSO*, 209.

13. Aurelia H. Reinhardt, in *OUSO*, 421. For the explicit complaint that the modern technical mind "lacks culture," see Angel Guido, in *OUSO*, 437.

14. Henry Sloane Coffin, in *OUSO*, 457–465.

15. Philip M. Brown, in *OUSO*, 425.

16. *OUSO*, 403 (Lewis).

17. Noyes, in *OUSO*, 363; see also *OUSO*, 350 (John C. Merriam).

18. Noyes, in *OUSO*, 355–356, 361–363.

19. Reinhold Niebuhr, *Moral Man and Immoral Society* (New York, 1932); Adolph Berle and Gardner Means, *The Modern Corporation and Private Property* (New York, 1932); *Culture and Crisis: An Open Letter to the Writers, Artists, Teachers, Physicians, Engineers, Scientists and Other Professional Workers of America* (New York, 1932). See also three other works of polemical demystification receiving widespread attention at the same moment: Jerome Frank, *Law and the Modern Mind* (New York, 1930); Lincoln Steffens, *The Autobiography of Lincoln Steffens* (New York, 1931); and John Chamberlin, *Farewell to Reform: The Rise, Life and Decay of the Progressive Mind in America* (New York, 1932). The spate of recent studies of "the New York intellectuals" can serve to remind us how much of the intellectual life of New York City in the 1930s remained outside academic institutions. See, e.g., Terry A. Cooney, *The Rise of the New York Intellectuals: Partisan Review and Its Circle, 1934–1945* (Madison, Wis., 1986); and Alan M. Wald, *The New York Intellectuals: The Rise and Decline of the Anti-Stalinist Left from the 1930s to the 1980s* (Chapel Hill, N.C., 1987).

20. Theodore Francis Jones, *New York University 1832–1932* (New York, 1933), 193.

21. George Santayana, "The Genteel Tradition in American Philosophy," in *Winds of Doctrine* (New York, 1913), 186–215, esp. 188.

22. Jones, *New York University*, 220–221.

23. For a guarded account of this concern on the part of NYU administrators of the period, see ibid., 234–235.

24. The controversy over "quotas" for Jewish students at Harvard is perhaps the most famous of these episodes. For a recent study of the leading Ivy League universities in this connection, see Marcia Graham Synott, *The Half-Open Door: Discrimination and Admissions at Harvard, Yale, and Princeton, 1900–1970* (Westport, Conn., 1979). NYU's case was addressed briefly and critically in a popular book published shortly before the conference, Heywood Broun and George Britt, *Christians Only: A Study in Prejudice* (New York, 1931), 106–111.

25. A detailed and well-documented account of these develments is in Robert Shaffer, "Jews, Reds, and Violets: Anti-Semitism and Anti-Radicalism at New York University, 1916–1933" (master's essay, New York University, 1985); copy in NYU Archives. Of special interest are the letters of 1922, quoted by Shaffer, between President Emeritus Charles W. Eliot of Harvard and Chancellor Brown. In this correspondence Eliot deftly destroys Brown's claim that the admissions tests were for purposes other than the exclusion of Jews from NYU. These letters can be found in the Chancellor Elmer E. Brown Papers. Box 52, Folder 4, NYU Archives.

26. Jones, *New York University*, 235. Jones's reference was to the congressional legislation in 1924.

27. Fairchild's view on the "melting pot" fit comfortably with the general outlook of the NYU leadership, but his politics were decidedly to the left. While Brown was supporting Herbert Hoover for reelection in 1932, the socialist Fairchild published a sweeping attack on the "profit motive" in the pages of *Harper's*. The following year he visited the Soviet Union. When he died in 1956 he was the subject of a warm memorial essay by two of the nation's leading socialist intellectuals: Leo Huberman and Paul Sweezy, "In Affectionate Memory of Henry Pratt Fairchild, 1880–1956," *Monthly Review* 8 (1956): 242–243. For Fairchild's political analysis in 1932, see "The Fallacy of Profits," reprinted as "Profits vs. Prosperity" in Henry Pratt Fairchild, *Versus: Reflections of a Sociologist* (New York, 1950), 21–44. The relevant holdings in the NYU Archives do not indicate how and why Brown entrusted Fairchild with the responsibility of editing the proceedings of the conference; see Centennial Conference Records, Box 2, Folder 13, "Henry P. Fairchild." For information on Fairchild's career, I am indebted to Robert C. Bannister.

28. For a very helpful account of the relationships between Columbia, NYU, and CCNY in the demographic and cultural context of metropolitan New York during the early decades of the twentieth century, see Thomas Bender, *New York Intellect: A History of Intellectual Life in New York City, from 1750 to the Beginning of Our Own Time* (New York, 1987), 266–293, esp. 286–292.

29. James B. Munn, "The Washington Square College," in Jones, *New York University*, 386–387. For a sketch of Munn's career, see the pamphlet by Bayrd Still, *James Buell Munn, 1890–1967* (New York, 1979). Munn's correspondence with Washington Square students, during and after the years these students spent in college, are in the James Buell Munn Estate Collection, Series II, subseries C, Folders 8 through 36, NYU Archives. I have not studied these letters, but it is clear that they constitute an important source for clarifying the dynamics of interaction between Jews and Anglo-Saxon Protestant patricians during Munn's generation.

30. I have addressed this historic transition in "Ethnic Diversity, Cosmopolitanism, and the Emergence of the American Liberal Intelligentsia," in David A. Hollinger, *In the American Province: Studies in the History and Historiography of Ideas* (Bloomington, Ind., 1985), 56–73. For a more detailed study on the basis of a single but pivotal career, see David A. Hollinger, *Morris R. Cohen and the Scientific Ideal* (Cambridge, Mass., 1975).

31. The locus classicus in the literary record of this celebration is Randolph Bourne, "Trans-National America," *Atlantic* 118 (1916): 86–97. Holmes's intense engagement with young Jewish intellectuals is addressed in David A. Hollinger, "The 'Tough-Minded' Justice Holmes, Jewish Intellectuals, and the Making of an American Icon," in *The Legacy of Oliver Wendall Holmes, Jr.*, ed. Robert W. Gordon (Stanford, Calif., 1992). This essay is reprinted as chapter 3 of the present volume.

32. The notion of two NYUs was sometimes suggested even at the time; for example, Broun and Britt, *Christians Only*, 107.

33. Munn, "The Washington Square College," 379–390.

34. There is some irony in the fact that this "Heights campus," once a symbolic bastion of genteel WASP exclusivity, has become in our time a campus of

the City University of New York devoted especially to the education of black and Hispanic citizens of the city.

35. As far as I have been able to determine, the records of the conference contain no evidence that Dewey was invited or that his appropriateness as a speaker was ever discussed.

36. For Hook's troubles with NYU administrators at this time (he was a candidate for promotion in 1932), see his recently published memoirs, *Out of Step: An Unquiet Life in the Twentieth Century* (New York, 1987), 529–532. In his account of NYU in 1932 Hook is explicit in distinguishing Munn's style from other faculty and administrative personnel with whom Hook had to deal. For the development elsewhere in New York of an academic culture at variance with prevailing norms, see Peter M. Rutkoff and William B. Scott, *The New School: A History of the New School for Social Research* (New York, 1986), esp. 19–64.

37. John Merriam was authorized by Brown to approach his brother Charles for ideas about the political symposium. See Elmer E. Brown to John C. Merriam, February 20 and March 2, 1932, in NYU Archives, Centennial Conference Records, Box 6, Folder 1.

38. John C. Merriam's relevant work is reprinted in *Published Papers and Addresses of John Campbell Merriam*, 4 vols. (Washington, 1938), vol. 4.

39. John C. Merriam to Elmer E. Brown, January 4 and February 27, 1932, NYU Archives, Centennial Conference Records, Box 6, Folder 1.

40. My search for information of this sort has been greatly assisted by Thomas J. Frusciano, university archivist at NYU.

41. "Tentative Suggestions Relating to the Centennial Celebration of New York University," Records of the Office of Vice President and Secretary (Harold O. Voorhis), Box 4, Folder 6, NYU Archives.

42. Fairchild, in *OUSO*, 491.

43. For hints of religious-conservatism in this symposium, see *OUSO*, 87 (Daniel L. Marsh), 92 (Philip M. Brown), and 97 (Edgar Dawson).

44. James Rowland Angell, in *OUSO*, 21.

45. *OUSO*, 25, 28 (Lotus Delta Coffman), 56 (Irvine), and 58–59 (Samuel P. Capen).

46. Karl, *Charles E. Merriam*, 13, 207, 263.

47. *OUSO* is ostentatious in its ceremonial display, squandering twenty-one pages of large type on a listing of the universities who sent representatives, even though some of these were simply the New York consul-general for this or that foreign nation. Pains were taken to impress the reader with how exclusive was the list of men and women invited to the conference. A "high society" tone was suggested; Fairchild thought it worth mentioning (xvii) that "the wives of those invited were included in the invitation."

48. Brown, in *OUSO*, 443–450.

49. Fairchild, in *OUSO*, 484–486. The notion that early-twentieth-century America experienced a basic transition from an economy and culture of production to an economy and culture of consumption has recently become very popular among historians; see, for example, Warren I. Susman, *Culture as History: The Transformation of American Society in the Twentieth Century* (New York, 1984), esp. xix–xxx.

50. *OUSO*, 24–38 (Coffman), 40–56 (Irvine), 150–168 (Salter), 184–195 (Gates), 239–257 (C. Merriam), 288–295 (Soule).

51. *New York Times*, November 20, 1932, sec. 8, 1.

52. Fairchild, in *OUSO*, 492.

53. Robert Gordon Sproul, in *OUSO*, 376–386, esp. 386.

54. Paul H. Buck et al., *General Education in a Free Society: Report of the Harvard Committee* (Cambridge, Mass., 1945), popularly known as the "Red Book" on account of its crimson dust jacket, became a prominent referent point in the consolidation during the 1940s and 1950s of a more secular and liberal ideal for the cultural functions of American universities.

55. The Hutchins-Adler attack on technocratic-progressivism and "the cult of science" began to alter the discourse about higher education as early as 1936, with the publication of Hutchins's *The Higher Learning in America* (New Haven, Conn., 1936). For a cogent account of the controversy in the late 1930s and early 1940s, see Edward A. Purcell, Jr., *The Crisis of Democratic Theory* (Lexington, Ky., 1973), 147–152.

56. Columbia's President Butler (who served from 1901 to 1945) envisioned a hierarchical division of educational labor, Thomas Bender has explained, according to which Columbia "educated Wall Street lawyers and city and state school administrators," while "NYU and CCNY could supply neighborhood lawyers and public school teachers." Butler used the prestige of the Columbia presidency to support the growth of CCNY and the creation of Brooklyn College in 1932, "hoping to divert immigrant students" from Columbia. See Bender, *New York Intellect*, 288.

57. Evidence of the financial calculations behind the relaxation of anti-Jewish admissions practices is presented in Shaffer, "Jews, Reds, and Violets," 43–47. Dean Boulton's remarks in a letter of April 4, 1929, are cited by Shaffer, 43.

CHAPTER FIVE

The Defense of Democracy and Robert K. Merton's Formulation of the Scientific Ethos

Disciplinary discourses often contain versions of their own history that historians, when they bother to look, find too narrow. These self-contained narratives of a discipline's past emphasize the analytic power of the specific, creative works that have shaped the discipline, and pay little attention to whatever extradisciplinary engagments may have helped to inspire these acts of creativity. But historians rarely bother to look. They are usually content to leave to the discipline's own chroniclers the task of assigning historical meaning to pivotal innovations and classic texts. Robert K. Merton's contributions to sociology have long been subject to this pattern of attention and neglect. Sociologists have developed and reproduced a disciplinary memory recalling Merton's having established or transformed one research program after another, while historians writing the transdisciplinary history of Merton's generation have largely bypassed his work. These historians have taken account of sociological work more openly addressed to the concerns of a nonprofessional audience, such as David Reisman's The Lonely Crowd *(1950), but rarely of the more "narrowly professional" work of Talcott Parsons or Merton. This was the historiographical context in which I became interested in Merton's contributions to the subdiscipline of sociology of science.*

In the essay reprinted here, I try to show that one need not diminish in the slightest Merton's contributions to sociology by discovering and analyzing the function these same ideas performed in the cultural wars of the era of World War II. I argue that Merton's formulation of the "ethos" of science—its prevailing ideals for cognitive behavior—constituted a distinctive contribution to the ideology of liberal democracy as that ideological cause was being developed by Anglophone intellectuals in the West during the late 1930s and early 1940s. I also try to identify the specific features of Merton's formulation of the scientific ethos that enabled this formulation to play a disciplinary role never attained by the bulk of those contemporaries of Merton's who shared his belief that democracy and science belonged together. Indeed, these features are the same: the points of Merton's that were the most ideologically effective in 1942 were exactly the ones that most faciliated the building of sociology of science as a professional discipline a quarter-century later.

Long after completing this study I became aware of an aspect of Merton's life relevant to the themes of this volume, to which I want to call attention here: his Jewish upbringing. In his Charles Homer Haskins Lecture of 1994 for the

American Council of Learned Societies, Merton has described his childhood in Philadelphia as Meyer H. Schkolnick, and the process by which he took on the very English name by which he has been known throughout his career. See Robert K. Merton, "A Life of Learning," ACLS Occasional Paper No. 25 *(New York, 1994), esp. 9.*

"The Defense of Democracy and Robert K. Merton's Formulation of the Scientific Ethos" was written in 1980 but not published until three years later in Knowledge and Society *4 (1983): 1–15.*

THE FAITH THAT science and democracy are indissolubly bound up in a single cultural mode had enjoyed a long history before it was passionately reaffirmed in the late 1930s and early 1940s by enemies of the Third Reich. Hitler's repudiation of democracy and his effort to endow German science with a distinctly Nazi orientation seemed to confirm once again the naturalness of the connection between democracy and science, and to demand a defense of both. Especially in the English-speaking world did antifascist intellectuals insist that the scientific enterprise was an expression of democratic political culture, and that the autonomy of science depended upon the strength of democracy. The ranks of democracy's defenders did include some persons aloof from science, and eager to oppose fascism in the name of religious and philosophical principles that antedated modern science. But democracy's link with science was addressed by a host of academic intellectuals in the United States and Great Britain who thereby entered into what one of their number, the young sociologist Robert K. Merton, called "realistic participation in the revolutionary conflict of cultures."[1]

Merton made this observation in an essay of 1942 entitled "A Note on Science and Democracy." The paper was to become in later decades, under a succession of different titles, one of the most widely discussed papers in a discipline that Merton helped to found: the sociology of science. What gave this paper its role in the discipline's development during the 1960s and 1970s was, of course, its formulation of the "scientific ethos": Merton's attribution to science of the four norms, "universalism," "disinterestedness," "communism," and "organized skepticism." Not all sociologists of science have found Merton's formulation adequate, but it has dominated their efforts to explicate the governing values of scientific communities, and has been at the center of the controversy over whether such values actually affect the behavior of scientists and the course of scientific development. These sociologists, however, have not typically been interested in the relation of science to democracy.[2] This once exciting topic has long since been dropped as naive or uninteresting.[3] Moreover, the few scholars who have taken up this question recently are more often than not aloof from Merton's entire approach to it, as they tend to regard science as part of a system of domination and a "threat," in philosopher Paul Feyerabend's phrase, "to democracy."[4]

The more well-defined has become the sociological study of science done in Merton's name, the more detached has Merton's formulation of the scientific ethos become from a context in which the practice of sociology and the defense of democracy went comfortably together. Merton himself has aided in this process of separation. What was once "A Note on Science and Democracy" turned up in *Social Theory and Social Structure* (1949, 1957, and 1968) as the somewhat more sociological "Science and Democratic Social Structure." The same essay had altogether escaped a democratic title by 1973, when it was billed, in *The Sociology of Science*, as "The Normative Structure of Science." By 1977, Merton's perspective on his early contribution had become so controlled by the ability of that contribution to speak to an ongoing, technical discipline that he allowed himself to express apparently genuine puzzlement that he had somehow failed, in 1942, to invent the method of "citation analysis."[5] The antifascist setting of Merton's formulation was almost an embarrassment to Merton's editor of 1973, Norman W. Storer, who implied that the vulnerability to criticism of the 1942 piece derived from the peculiar circumstances of its publication. "It was originally written at the request of Georges Gurvitch, then a refugee from Nazi-occupied France, for the first issue of his ill-fated *Journal of Political and Legal Sociology*, which expired soon after it was born," explains Storer, who adds that on account of the needs of Gurvitch's journal "the paper was saddled" with its "rather misleading title."[6]

"A Note on Science and Democracy" is an entirely appropriate title for what Merton wrote in 1942. If its bluntness as an instrument for performing more than the most rudimentary work in sociology is too obvious for even so devoted a Mertonian as Storer to deny, the essay stands as one of the most robust and firmly grounded of its era's contributions to the intellectual defense of science and democracy. Merton's formulation of the scientific ethos is a benchmark in the emergence of social definitions of the scientific enterprise and in the development of ideological self-consciousness on the part of apologists for science. It is also an intelligent and revealing artifact of the effort made by a generation of intellectuals to vindicate a set of social values identified with the liberal political tradition.

Gurvitch's journal, moreover, was an undertaking of some consequence. During its five years of operation it served as a forum for some of the period's most creative and energetic young scholars; the issue on "Democracy and Social Structure" to which Merton contributed also drew articles from Robert M. McIver, Karl N. Llewellyn, David Riesman,

Talcott Parsons, and Kingsley Davis, as well as a book review from Claude Lévi-Strauss. Merton shared with these men a willingness to commit his scholarship to Gurvitch's endeavor in social science and antifascism.

What Merton contributed to that endeavor is all the more striking an episode in intellectual history when we recognize an irony in it: the same aspects of Merton's formulation that rendered it distinctive and effective as a vindication of democracy also rendered it susceptible to use by a professional academic discipline oblivious to its political matrix. To see how this ironic turn came about, we must begin by recognizing the political as well as the sociological matrix of Merton's work leading up to his "Note."

During the mid-1930s, Merton worked on his important dissertation, *Science, Technology, and Society in Seventeenth-Century England*, which was published in 1938, the same year in which he brought out an article on "Science and the Social Order." This article includes several references to the "scientific ethos," and is often cited as a kind of warm-up for "A Note on Science and Democracy";[7] the latter could just as well be seen as an afterthought to "Science and the Social Order." The essay of 1938 carries on from Merton's dissertation a Weber-inspired interest in "cultural conditions" that assure the "support of science," and takes as its specific starting point the sober recognition that these conditions are sometimes terminated. Although "Science and the Social Order" seeks to explicate in a general way Weber's aphorism that "the belief in the value of scientific truth is not derived from nature but is a product of definite cultures," Merton's particular focus is on the conspicuous hostility to science manifest in "Nazi Germany since 1933." He reviews the increased demands made upon science by the totalitarian Nazi state, and contrasts these demands to the relative autonomy allowed scientists in liberal, democratic societies. Amidst quotations from several Nazi spokesmen condemning liberalism and cosmopolitanism, Merton explains that the conflict between Nazism and science amounts to an incompatibility of ethos: "The sentiments embodied in the ethos of science—characterized by such terms as intellectual honesty, integrity, organized skepticism, disinterestedness, impersonality—are outraged by the set of new sentiments that the State would impose in the sphere of scientific research."[8] Merton's notion of scientific ethos was thus developed in the course of an explicit consideration of the relation of Nazism to science. This consideration was continued in the "Note on Science and Democracy," which includes a number of passages taken from the essay of 1938.[9]

The "Note" itself begins by alluding to the widespread "revolt against science" that has "led scientists to recognize their dependence upon particular types of social structure," and has compelled them "to vindicate the ways of science to man." In response to this pressure there has emerged "a clarification and reaffirmation of the ethos of modern science." This ethos, Merton explains, is a "complex of values and norms which is held to be binding on the man of science." Examination of this complex can introduce the larger problem Merton wants to put on the academic agenda: "the comparative study of the institutional structure of science." Comparative work of this sort had only begun, Merton acknowledged, but he found "some basis for the provisional assumption that science is afforded opportunity for development in a democratic order which is integrated with the ethos of science." The pursuit of science has not been "confined to democracies," Merton granted, but he was quick to follow up his suspicion that democracy is peculiarly conducive to the advancement of science; he launched into an account of "universalism," the norm to which he devotes the most attention and to which he most pointedly contrasts Nazism. Merton was anything but evasive on the political significance of his analysis of scientists' professed determination to ignore "race, nationality, religion, class and personal qualities"; his conclusion about the norm of universalism bears quoting because it manifests the concern in this essay that was as vital to the antifascist preoccupations of 1942 as it was trivial to the cause of sociology of science three and four decades later:

> However inadequately it may be put into practice, the ethos of democracy includes universalism as a dominant guiding principle. Democratization is tantamount to the progressive elimination of restraints upon the exercise and development of socially valued capacities. Impersonal criteria of accomplishment and not fixation of status characterize the democratic society. Insofar as such restraints do persist, they are viewed as obstacles in the path of full democratization. . . . To the extent that a society is democratic, it provides scope for the exercise of universalistic criteria in science.[10]

Merton's discussions of his other three norms were brief and less explicitly directed to the contrast between Nazi Germany and democratic states. The second norm, "communism," Merton linked to societies with opportunity for free discussion. "Secrecy is the antithesis of the norm; full and open communication is its enactment." Merton's "communism" was the belief in the "common ownership" of the results of science. In potential conflict with this norm was "the definition of technology as 'private property' in a capitalist economy." To get around this, scientists were either "advocating socialism," Merton pointed out, or were taking out patents on their own work in order "to ensure its being made available for public use."[11]

This public dimension of science is also addressed in Merton's account of "disinterestedness," his third norm. What matters to Merton here is science's institutionalized aloofness from personal self-aggrandizement; the "public and testable character of science" demands the "exacting scrutiny" of one's peers, with the result that "fraud" is virtually absent "in the annals of science." Individuals and interest groups are prevented from shaping in their own interest what the society accepts as truth. Such abuses increase, however, "when the structure of control exercised by qualified compeers is rendered ineffectual," as in Nazi Germany.[12]

"Organized skepticism," Merton's fourth and final norm, entails a refusal to respect the sacred. Science's insistent questioning can create tension within political, religious, or economic spheres of life; conflict can intensify either with the expansion of science or when institutions other than science "extend their area of control." Merton concludes his discussion of organized skepticism, and the entire "Note on Science and Democracy," by observing that in "modern totalitarian society, anti-rationalism and centralization of institutional control both serve to limit the scope provided for scientific activity."[13]

What made the essay of 1942 so striking a contribution to contemporary discourse about "science and democracy" was its claim that democratic values are institutionalized in a concrete, social constituency. Most other contributors lacked Merton's sense that science was a cultural system, a pattern of attitudes actually embodied in a community. Adamantly as they might affirm the link between science and democracy, they tended to depict both in the abstract. In a characteristic affirmation, one patriot pointed out that both science and democracy required "the maintenance of the balanced function of the whole through the balanced coordination of its parts."[14]

Democracy and science, it was commonly noted, shared such qualities as freedom of thought and respect for the dignity of the human race.[15] These qualities were commonly attributed to scientists or to democrats as individuals, or to the general "spirit" of science or of democracy. In one of the most theoretically ambitious discussions of the relationship, the philosopher Abraham Edel compared what he took to be the goals, techniques, and attitudes of science and of democracy, but never spoke about their embodiment in institutions.[16] Sidney Hook, in one of the most energetically argued and widely noted contributions to the cause, treated the era's conflict—between science and democracy on the one hand and their common enemies on the other—as a choice individuals could make between alternative sets of beliefs on behalf of which arguments were to be given. This was not, in itself, a mistake on Hook's part, and there's no doubt that *Reason, Social Myths and Democracy* had more to say about the ideological issues of the moment than did "A Note on Science and Democracy." But Hook's work is an endeavor in conventional political argument, and thus differs from Merton's, despite the fact that Hook begins with the notion of "ethos" and sees his book as a brief in support of the ethos constituted by the social values of science and democracy.[17] Merton, by depicting science in terms of an interlocking set of specific, institutional imperatives, endowed science with a social weight and concreteness that made it seem all the more formidable an extension of any social order with which it could be found to bond, and all the more implacable an enemy of any social order with which it could not.

That Merton could contribute this emphasis to the discussion owed much to the fact that he was, after all, a sociologist. Among American sociologists he was, moreover, unusually conscious of the European tradition of Durkheim, Weber, Pareto, and Mannheim that was conducive to the viewing of science as a social institution.[18] As early as 1937 Merton wrote a critical essay for *Isis* on European work in sociology of knowledge.[19] Merton's social sense of science was also promoted by Merton's familiarity with the Marxist tradition. Merton's work was not explicitly grounded in Marxist theory, but his concerns overlapped with those of J. D. Bernal and the circle of socialist scientists gathered around Bernal in England. Merton made frequent use of the writings of this circle, including Bernal's *Social Function of Science.*[20]

Yet Merton's emphasis was not unique to him, even among American participants in this episode, nor can Merton's formulation of the scientific ethos be traced entirely to the fact that he was practicing sociology rather than political theory or cultural criticism. Attention to some of the contributions most akin to Merton's can illustrate how easily Merton's "Note" blended into the antifascist discussions of the era.

An essay similar to Merton's was presented, for example, at one of the period's most overtly ideological gatherings, the "Conference on the Scientific Spirit and Democratic Faith" held in New York City in April 1943. This conference was designed as an answer both to fascism and to what the conference's leaders saw as a worrisome sort of antifascism: the movement of neo-Thomist and other conservative thinkers for "fixed principles, inflexible rules of morality, and unquestioned acceptance of a supernatural interpretation of human experience." Here Horace Kallen, Herbert Schneider, and a number of other self-styled "radical democrats" lamented the rise of authoritarianism, and celebrated the freedom and open-mindedness of scientific inquiry.[21] Here, too, the director of Yale's Institute of Social Relations, Mark A. May, delivered "The Moral Code of Scientists."

May does not use the term "norms," but he does provide a list of imperatives that make up the "code," and he asserts that these imperatives actually operate within "the fellowship of science." Moreover, May focuses on how this "culture of science" interacts with the "wider culture of society," including "the religious, political and economic beliefs" with which scientific culture may come "into direct conflict." As May formulates the morality of science, it consists of six imperatives. "Absolute honesty" with oneself and with one's fellow scientists is one; "science has no place and no use for misrepresentation, skullduggery . . . or deceitfulness in any form whatsoever." A second obligation for scientists is the fearless acceptance of verified facts regardless of the personal consequences of such acceptance. That the results of science are "common property to men everywhere" is May's third item, which is elaborated in his fourth: the contributors to this common store of knowledge are to be recognized as such, and not victimized by the "pirating" of their ideas. Fifth, controversies among scientists are to be settled by an appeal to facts rather than by ad hominem arguments, personal vituperation, or "an appeal to authority." Finally, the code includes full "freedom of inquiry," and it is here especially, May notes, that "dictators and tyrants" have come into conflict with communities of scientists.[22]

May shares with Merton the recognition that the moral standards of science are only imperfectly enforced. Both provide examples of the violation of these standards, and treat the condemnation of the violators by other scientists as evidence of the vitality of the code. Although May does not point as explicitly as Merton does to the system of review by peers, May has in common with Merton a persistent emphasis on the institutionalized behavior of a social constituency: May contrasts the moral code *"practiced"* within the scientific community with that *"practiced"* even in the "most civilized societies."[23] May is more evangelical than Merton, expressing the hope that the spread of the international "subculture of science" will gradually "change man's attitudes, beliefs, and ways of thinking to conform more and more to those of science,"[24] while Merton is content to outline the points of harmony and strain between the scientific ethos on the one hand and the ethos of democratic and nondemocratic societies on the other. Had May's paper been kept visible through reprintings, it might have been picked up in the 1960s by scholars building the discipline of sociology of science.

The notion of a scientific "ethos" was also advanced explicitly by the British biologist C. H. Waddington, in his polemically antifascist book of 1941, *The Scientific Attitude*. "It is an ethos which allows plenty of scope for individuality," but it insists that individuals support their ideas "by reasons which other people can verify, and that they should be willing to accept the judgment of critical experiments as to whether they have made out their case." Waddington's diffuse account of the scientific ethic included no enumerated list of components, but his sense of these components was consistent with Merton's and with May's. Further, he connected the scientific ethos to the "behavior of scientists in their corporate and professional capacity," and he pointed to the "very remarkable agreement among scientists throughout the world" that Nazism "is incompatible with the scientific temper and is, for that reason among others, to be ethically condemned." Although Waddington was distressed with the state of existing democratic societies and called for their reconstruction along the lines of the values more fully embodied in science, he identified himself as a "democrat" and insisted that it was by democratic standards that the political philosophy of Marxism was to be judged.[25]

Whether the Soviet Union manifested the "democracy" so crucially tied to "science" was, of course, a matter of great disagreement and confusion among antifascist intellectuals in the United States and Britain. That Stalin's government was in the column of democracy was affirmed by Bernal and other Communists as resolutely as it was denied, for example, by Michael Polanyi, whose revulsion at the Soviets as well as the Nazis inspired his own defense of science in terms of the needs of a "scientific community."[26] Merton's 1942 text says nothing about the Soviet Union by name, but his 1949 version adds two footnotes (retained, with some revisions, in later printings) about events in Russia, thereby treating Stalin's regime along with Hitler's as antipathetic to at least the "universalism" of science.[27] The assertion that "our" system and that of the Soviet Union are merely two kinds of democracy was made by the historian Henry E. Sigerist in an article quoted by Merton to support the conclusion that science has generally flourished in democratic periods of history.[28]

About the basic ideals at issue there was less ambiguity. Whether or not individual antifascist intellectuals regarded socialism in general, and even Soviet Communism in particular, as an extension of the democratic political tradition of the West, many rallied around a set of classically liberal values associated with that tradition. The liberty, equality, and fraternity of individuals was to be defended and expanded without regard to race, nationality, or religion; the free march of the human mind was to be obstructed by no sacred cows, vested interests, or other particularisms. Susceptible as these commitments were to divergent political application, they were specific enough to be contrasted to fascism, and it was in the name of these general commitments that English-speaking antifascist intellectuals of the late 1930s and early 1940s affirmed and sought to clarify the bond between science and democracy.

The commitments reinforced in this episode did not, of course, represent the only ways in which the scientific "spirit" had been depicted, nor had these commitments altogether controlled thinking about the relation of science to democracy. Merton and his contemporaries drew selectively upon a sizable inventory of ideas that were accessible through what we can distinguish as two loosely connected traditions in the public discussion of science. The first tradition consisted of explicit characterizations of the relation of science to democracy; the second consisted of characterizations of the scientific "spirit," "attitude," or "habit of mind."

Common values were not the only basis suggested for the connection between science and democracy. J. McKeen Cattell, longtime editor of *Science* and one of the early twentieth century's most indefatigable advocates of public support for science, took a materialist approach; he insisted that democracy was dependent upon the ability of science-based technology to create the abundance that Cattell saw as democracy's prerequisite.[29] Elitist notes were commonly sounded under the rubric of "science and democracy, " as when John C. Merriam warned that democracy's future was in danger unless the public learned "dependence upon those who know."[30] How vacant the notion of "democracy" could become is indicated by the closeness of Merriam's outlook to the view that science and technology had rendered democracy obsolete. Indeed, many affirmations of science's service to "democracy" employed this word as a code for the existing American, and in some cases British, economic and political order; science was depicted, in effect, as a great asset to the *nation* rather than to a distinctive political culture transcending the American national interest.[31] Yet the sense that science and democracy somehow embodied the same antiauthoritarian values was also articulated frequently, if in a less intense manner than was to become typical of the antifascist intellectuals in the late 1930s and early 1940s. John Dewey, Morris R. Cohen, Horace Kallen, and Walter Lippmann were among those who advanced this conviction in the early decades of the twentieth century.[32]

When Merton in 1942 referred wearily to the "countless writings"[33] on the scientific spirit, he identified the second of the two traditions drawn upon by antifascist defenders of science and democracy. Many contributions to this genre were oblivious to democracy. These pronouncements had arisen from a variety of contexts not addressed by Merton, including rivalries between advocates of humanistic and scientific education, and between the scientific profession on the one hand and the elites, on the other, of religion, literature, commerce, and politics. Whatever they said or did not say about democracy, characterizations of the scientific spirit assigned to it a host of qualities which, taken together, were not always compatible. Woodrow Wilson celebrated "calm Science seated—recluse, ascetic, like a nun,"[34] but others rejoiced that science had "no vestige of aged asceticism about it," and that its spirit led people to gaze "at their wholesome, naked selves and out upon a far-flying world."[35] Idle curiosity was essential to Thorstein Veblen's account,[36] while Randolph Bourne stressed an active, omnivorous hunger for experience.[37] Yet the range of attributions to the scientific spirit was not infinite, nor did each quality assigned to the ideal scientist get equal time in public discussion. The qualities emphasized by Merton—and by May—were certainly among those most commonly associated with science during the late nineteenth and early twentieth centuries in the United States and Great Britain.[38] These qualities were emphasized in Sinclair Lewis's romantic novel about the scientific enterprise, *Arrowsmith*,[39] and less explicitly by John Dewey,[40] the foremost of those in whom the tradition of writings about the scientific spirit had overlapped with the tradition of writings about science and democracy.

Dewey himself survived to become perhaps the most eminent of the American intellectual defenders of science and democracy in the late 1930s and early 1940s. Several features of Dewey's own contribution to that defense can help put Merton's formulation of the scientific ethos in perspective. In 1939 Dewey offered an account of the "scientific morale" parallel in basic respects to the contributions of Merton, Waddington, and the New York conferees on "The Scientific Spirit and Democratic Faith." If the similarities between what Dewey offers in an openly prophetic voice and what Merton offers in a more detached voice can remind us of Merton's participation in the conventions of contemporary liberalism, the differences between the two can show us all the more vividly the distinctness of Merton's participation.

Dewey extolled the "morale of fair-mindedness, intellectual integrity, of will to subordinate personal preference to ascertained facts and to share with others what is found out, instead of using it for personal gain," and he depicted this morale as the possession of the "body of scientific inquirers," a small but crucial segment of the population. He hoped this morale would become "a weighty and widespread constituent of culture," and he linked this hope with the "future of democracy." Dewey explicitly called attention to the "disinterestedness" of this morale. He contrasted this morale with the protection from "critical inquiry and test" that religions have sometimes afforded certain doctrines; he noted this morale's commitment to the common possession of knowledge; and he wished for a time when this morale's determination to base belief on evidence would replace "habit, accidents of circumstance, propaganda, personal and class bias" as popular foundations for belief.[41] Yet Dewey's account, even when all four components of Merton's formulation are shown to be part of it, is enmeshed within an ambiguous argument on behalf of science's ability to establish moral ends. It lacks, therefore, the straightforward simplicity of Merton's list of norms. Moreover, Dewey, like so many of his fellows, stopped short of attributing to the morality of science the concreteness of a set of norms enforced within a substantial social institution. Finally, Dewey makes no pretense to the critical distance that gives so much added rhetorical power to Merton's formulation: Dewey simply states what he takes to be the values of science, while Merton purports to subject to sociological analysis statements of the order made by Dewey.

When Merton's formulation of the scientific ethos is examined in the context of the period's efforts to defend the political culture science was felt to share with democracy, it becomes apparent how small were the innovations that enabled Merton to make so distinctive a contribution. Three modest innovations were involved. First, instead of offering as his own the language in which the ideals of the scientific life were commonly prescribed or described, Merton endorsed the language by long distance: He warranted the authenticity of the ideals by describing an objective entity—a body of literature—in which they could undoubtedly be found. Thus Merton was able to reinforce the reigning conventions without becoming an uncritical participant in them. Second, Merton cast to the winds all fear of being thought simplistic and literal-minded; he offered a no-nonsense list of basic ideals that was easy to remember and to employ as a basis for investigating particular cases. Third, he made the deductive leap from the existence of these ideals in the literature to the claim that they actually functioned as norms within the community of science. When Merton declared that "the behavior of scientists" was characterized by "a distinctive pattern of institutional control over a wide range of motives,"[42] he offered no evidence other than the fact that certain ideals were indeed set forth in the literature of prescription and condemnation. Whether or not his deduction is justified is a question in sociological theory about which sociologists can argue; the leap, in any event, was as light a stroke as it was a fateful one for the development of the sociology of science.

At the heart of these innovations, especially of the third, was the notion of a "scientific community." This notion had surfaced a number of times before—in the writings of Charles Peirce,[43] to cite a famous example—but Merton put this notion to a use not previously fashionable. He attributed to the community the role of actively maintaining in its members the imperatives that other commentators had grounded in a less distinctly social understanding of science. The ideals of science had been depicted as imperatives often enough, but such imperatives had generally been assigned either to an unspecified and grandly imperial "science," to individual scientists endowed with the personal character ideally suited to science, or to procedures and methods which, if carried out often enough by an individual, would of necessity make these ideals part of that individual's character.

Merton's formulation of the scientific ethos occupies in the history of ideas about the enterprise of science a place comparable to that of Frederick Jackson Turner's "frontier thesis" in the history of ideas about the American West. Turner, as Henry Nash Smith has shown, codified in 1893 certain elements in a vital tradition of mythological writings about the American West.[44] Turner also responded to what his generation viewed as something of a crisis: the fear that the closure of the frontier— announced in the census of 1890—would transform the character of American life. Turner's voice, like Merton's, was academic; if Turner translated into scholarly terms a range of beliefs about the West generated and perpetuated by a variety of popular interests, anxieties, and aspirations, Merton translated into academic terms a range of beliefs about science that had been similarly generated and perpetuated. Turner's formulation of the "frontier thesis," like Merton's of the scientific ethos, took a while to catch on, and to create its academic industry: the contribution that seemed at first to simply share in the conventions of other writings directed to the present crisis was seen, after a few years, to have distinctively reinvigorated those conventions and given them viability with a more critical discourse.

The expansion of the social space allotted to science in modern times inspired, and was reciprocally encouraged by, the hope that science was a vehicle for values accepted by the social constituencies upon which science depended for support, and which were understood to be the beneficiaries of the advancement of science. As the autonomy of science from external influences and demands was increasingly urged and defended in the nineteenth and twentieth centuries, it became all the more important that the moral qualities for which science was ostensibly a vehicle be seen as *intrinsic* to science: if certain approved imperatives were understood to be endemic to the very enterprise of science, society could rest more comfortably with the expansion of science. Even if the diverse individuals and groups caught up in this dynamic did not always attribute the same values to science, their various accounts of the imperatives of science manifest the same large trust that science possessed both a morality and the effective means to maintain it. A crucial function of Merton's formulation of the scientific ethos was to renew this trust, and to do so in terms of the values his generation of intellectuals was most eager to affirm in the face of fascism.

Was this trust justified? Are we still to regard communities of scientists as vehicles for the classical liberal values? Access to these issues has been limited by the separation of Merton's formulation of the scientific ethos from its original location within the defense of democracy. Students of the scientific enterprise and its historical development will no doubt continue to argue over what role, if any, the Mertonian "norms" play in the actual practice of any given science,[45] but in so doing they will echo a debate in which the stakes were higher.

NOTES

1. Robert K. Merton, "A Note on Science and Democracy," *Journal of Legal and Political Sociology* 1 (1942): 116.

2. The chief exception to this was published in 1952, well before the discipline of sociology of science actually developed; Bernard Barber, *Science and the Social Order* (New York, 1952).

3. In his exhaustive survey of the sociological literature on the scientific ethos, Nico Stehr does not even find cause to mention the relation of science to democracy as an issue under discussion. Stehr distinguishes between two active traditions of research and analysis, one concerned with "cognitive" norms and the other with "social" norms; both study life *within* communities of scientists. See Nico Stehr, "The Ethos of Science Revisited," *Sociological Inquiry* 48 (1978): 172–196, esp. 178.

4. Paul Feyerabend, *Science in a Free Society* (London, 1978), 76.

5. Robert K. Merton, *Social Theory and Social Structure: Toward the Codification of Theory and Research* (Glencoe, Ill., 1949), 307–316 (1957 edition, 550–561; 1968 edition, 604–615); Robert K. Merton, *The Sociology of Science: Theoretical and Empirical Investigations*, ed. Norman W. Storer (Chicago, 1973), 267–278; Robert K. Merton, "The Sociology of Science: An Episodic Memoir," in *The Sociology of Science in Europe*, ed. Robert K. Merton and Jerry Gaston (Carbondale, Ill., 1977), 48–50. It is perfectly reasonable, of course, that sociologists—including Merton, his followers, and his critics—should focus on what this text has done, and can or cannot still do, for the sociology of science; rarely does the sociological literature address as a historian would the historical setting and significance of this text. One very brief but sensible effort to do this, however, has been made in passing by M. D. King, while performing one of the most compelling assessments yet made of the limitations of Merton's work; see M. D. King, "Reason, Tradition, and the Progressiveness of Science," *History and Theory* 10 (1971): 15–16. Another interesting paper appeared too late for me to use: Yaron Ezrahi, "Science and the Problem of Authority in Democracy," in *Science and Social Structure: A Festschrift for Robert K. Merton*, ed. Thomas Gieryn (New York, 1980), 43–60; see esp. 46.

6. Storer, in Merton and Gaston, *Sociology of Science*, 226.

7. Robert K. Merton, "Science, Technology and Society in Seventeenth-Century England," *Osiris* 4 (1938), pt. 2, 360–632; I have used the edition brought out as a book (New York, 1970). See Thomas S. Kuhn's account of this work's significance in Kuhn's "The History of Science," in *International Encyclopedia of the Social Sciences*, ed. David L. Sills, 14 (1968): 79–80.

8. Robert K. Merton, "Science and the Social Order," *Philosophy of Science* 5 (1938): 321–322, 327.

9. Merton, "Note," 126.

10. Ibid., 115–121.

11. Ibid., 121–123.

12. Ibid., 125–126.

13. Ibid., 126.

14. William Galt, "Science and Democracy," *Journal of Psychology* 14 (1942): 155–160.

15. E.g., Harold D. Lasswell, "Science and Democracy: The Search for Perfection," *Vital Speeches* 7 (November 15, 1940): 85; the *New York Times* editorial, "Science and Democracy," quoted in *Science* 86 (October 22, 1937): 375–376; Edgar J. Witzemann, "The So-Called Scientific Method and Its Role as a Process in Democracy," *Scientific Monthly* 43 (1936): 122–129; and Waldemar Kaempffert, "Science, the Machine, and Democracy," in *Science and Man*, ed. Ruth Nanda Anshen (New York, 1942), 149–150. Kaempffert's article also offers a representative paean to the universalism of science.

16. Abraham Edel, "The Relations of Science and Democracy," *Journal of Philosophy* 41 (1944): 701–710.

17. Sidney Hook, *Reason, Social Myths and Democracy* (New York, 1940), esp. 3, 5, 9–11, 291–297.

18. For a helpful account of Merton's relation to this tradition, especially in the 1930s, see Lewis A. Coser, "Merton's Uses of the European Sociological Tradition," in *The Idea of Social Structure: Papers in Honor of Robert K. Merton*, ed. Lewis A. Coser (New York, 1975), 85–100.

19. Robert K. Merton, "The Sociology of Knowledge," *Isis* 27 (1937): 493–500. Even here, Merton referred to the Nazi attack on science (500).

20. Merton's familiarity with the Marxist tradition was revealed, for example, by his attentiveness in *Seventeenth-Century England*, 142–143, 206, to the now legendary paper by the Soviet scholar B. Hessen, "The Social and Economic Roots of Newton's 'Principia,'" in *Science at the Cross-Roads* (London, 1931), 147–212. Cf. Merton, "Note," 124. See also Merton's references to Bernal, Lancelot Hogben, and Hyman Levy in Robert K. Merton, "Science, Population and Society," *Scientific Monthly* 44 (1937): 170; Merton, "Social Order," 328; and Merton, "Note," 122–123. On the activities of Bernal and his circle, see the very helpful monograph by Gary Werskey, *The Visible College: The Collective Biography of British Scientific Socialists* (New York, 1979).

21. Eduard C. Lindeman, ed., *The Scientific Spirit and Democratic Faith* (New York, 1944), ix, xi. Edward A. Purcell, Jr.'s study of American ideas about democracy in this era emphasizes the seriousness with which the New York conference took the outspoken critique of secular liberalism mounted by Catholic intellectuals and other "absolutists"; see Purcell, *The Crisis of Democratic Theory: Scientific Naturalism and the Problem of Value* (Lexington, Ky., 1973), 179–180, 204. The sweeping affirmations of this conference can be contrasted to the more guarded treatment of the same set of issues by the Chicago philosopher Richard McKeon at a similar conference held simultaneously at the New School for Social Research. There, in what was certainly one of the most learned and closely argued contributions to this entire discourse, McKeon warned against the flattening of concepts of "science" and "democracy" fostered by the necessities of the mo-

ment: specifically, he feared that the particular positions taken by John Dewey on problems in ethics and metaphysics would be uncritically accepted because they were so embedded in the amorphous rhetoric of "science and democracy." See Richard McKeon, "Democracy, Scientific Method, and Actions," *Ethics* 55 (1945): 235–286, esp. 236–237, 273, 278, and 280.

22. Mark A. May, "The Moral Code of Scientists," in Lindeman, *Scientific Spirit,* 40–46.

23. Ibid., 44 (emphasis in original).

24. Ibid., 43.

25. C. H. Waddington, *The Scientific Attitude* (London, 1941), 26–27, 84, 85, 92–93. The misleading account of this text in Neal Wood, *Communism and British Intellectuals* (New York, 1959), 132–133, designates it as the "high point of the onslaught on democratic politics." Flippant and unsubtle as Waddington's book is, its political content is considerably more complicated than this.

26. See Michael Polanyi's address to the Manchester Literary and Philosophical Society, February 1942: "Self-Government of Science," reprinted in his *Logic of Liberty* (Chicago, 1951), 49–67, esp. 53. Polanyi has described his reaction to the Lysenko affair and to the Bernalists in a 1963 preface to his *Science, Faith and Society,* 2d ed. (Chicago, 1964), 8–9.

27. Merton, *Social Theory,* 398–399.

28. Merton, "Note," 117. For Sigerist's views of the Soviet Union, see his "Science and Democracy," *Science and Society* 11 (1938): 297.

29. Cattell took this line in 1912, for example, at a convocation address at Indiana University; he printed it twenty-six years later: J. McKeen Cattell, "Science and Democracy," *Scientific Monthly* 46 (1938): 80–88.

30. John C. Merriam, "The Research Spirit in Everyday Life of the Average Man," *Science* 52 (1920): 478.

31. This is an implication of Ronald C. Tobey's study of the promotional activities of several scientists during the 1920s, and seems to apply the most directly to Robert A. Millikan and Michael Pupin; see Tobey, *The American Ideology of National Science, 1919–1930* (Pittsburgh, Pa., 1971).

32. See, as examples, John Dewey, *The Influence of Darwin on Philosophy* (New York, 1910), 59–60; [Morris R. Cohen,] "Liberalism and Irrationalism," *New Republic* 30 (1922): 333; Walter Lippmann, *Drift and Mastery* (New York, 1914), passim; Horace Kallen, "Pragmatism," *Encyclopedia of the Social Sciences* 12 (1934): 311.

33. Merton, "Note," 117.

34. Woodrow Wilson, "Princeton in the Nation's Service," Address of October 31, 1896, in *Papers of Woodrow Wilson,* ed. Arthur S. Link et al. (Princeton, 1971), 10:31.

35. Frederick Barry, *The Scientific Habit of Thought* (New York, 1927), 300.

36. Thorstein Veblen, "The Place of Science in Modern Civilization," *American Journal of Sociology* 11 (1906): 585–609.

37. Randolph Bourne, *Youth and Life* (New York, 1913), 19–20.

38. A useful indicator of popular notions about the scientific spirit is the anthology of writings on that topic designed for use in college classrooms, Leo Saidla and Warren E. Gibbs, eds., *Science and the Scientific Mind* (New York, 1930).

39. Sinclair Lewis, *Arrowsmith* (New York, 1925).

40. E.g., *The Quest for Certainty* (New York, 1929), 100–101, 228.

41. John Dewey, *Freedom and Culture* (New York, 1939), 142, 145, 148, 151.

42. Merton, "Note," 124.

43. See the helpful article by Jacob Lizka, "Community in C. S. Peirce: Science as a Means and as an End," *Transactions of the Charles S. Peirce Society* 14 (1978): 305–321.

44. Henry Nash Smith, *Virgin Land: The American West as Symbol and Myth* (Cambridge, Mass., 1950), 291–305.

45. A substantial portion of the literature criticizing Merton denies that very much of the behavior of scientists within given, specialized disciplines can be explained by reference to any ethos general to science, or by reference to the Mertonian norms in particular. The most widely noted critique of this sort is S. B. Barnes and R.G.A. Dolby, "The Scientific Ethos: A Deviant Viewpoint," *European Journal of Sociology* 11 (1970): 3–25. That such critiques of Merton might lead scholars away from the study of "scientific values" has been suspected by Thomas S. Kuhn, *The Essential Tension: Selected Studies in Scientific Tradition and Change* (Chicago, 1977), xxi–xxii. Correct as Kuhn undoubtedly is to defend the study of values against anyone who thinks it "absurd to conceive the analysis of values as a significant means of illuminating scientific behavior," many of the points made by Barnes and Dolby would serve as sensible cautions to anyone seeking to use Merton's formulation as a basis for pursuing the program endorsed by Kuhn.

CHAPTER SIX

Free Enterprise and Free Inquiry: The Emergence of Laissez-Faire Communitarianism in the Ideology of Science in the United States

An irony in the history of relations between science and culture is that the interests of professional communities of scientists, as understood by the recognized leaders of these communities, are not always identical with the general programs for culture advanced in the name of science. The irony is clear if this study of the politically salient representation of science is read alongside the story told in the essay on Kulturkämpfe *reprinted as chapter 8 of this book.*

"Free Enterprise and Free Inquiry" traces the gradual displacement of individualist by communitarian terms in assertions of scientific autonomy. The basic idea that the work of scientists should go forward with a minimum of interference from society had long been expressed in a political language akin to the classically individualist ideology of free enterprise. But this language served the needs of the scientific establishment imperfectly during the era when the National Science Foundation came into being. A major incentive to employ communitarian terms was the ability of these terms to convey a sense that science was practiced by a community possessed of its own polity, its own system of governance. This sense was relevant to the task of justifying huge expenditures of public funds for activities not directly accountable to the elected representatives of the people. If science was guided by its own democracy, there was less need for Congress to take a hand in running it.

What I call "laissez-faire communitarianism"—let the community of science alone!—could be construed as an elitist doctrine, a means of isolating the institutionalized leadership of the natural sciences from the society's political processes. Among the people alert for signs of this elitism were some followers of John Dewey, including the journalist Waldemar Kaempffert, who were simultaneously eager to see the society as a whole become more scientific. But the very broadness of their notion of what it meant to be "scientific" made it difficult for the Deweyites to clarify the issues over which they disagreed with the defenders of a distinctive professional cohort dominated by physicists, whose high prestige increased at the end of World War II when the role of physics in the making of the atomic bomb became known. Hence as World War II and the early Cold War transformed the political economy of American science, tension grew between the project of building a more scientific culture—addressed more directly in "Science as a Weapon in

Kulturkämpfe *in the United States during and after World War II"—and the project of advancing capital-intensive research in the natural sciences.*

That tension did not prevent leading physicists from extoling the virtues of scientific method as a model for critical thinking on the part of an enlightened citizenry, nor did it prevent cultural reformers from appreciating an apparatus of unprecedented strength for the doing of natural science. But the difference beween the two became harder to miss, and the effort to understand the relationship between them become more of a struggle.

This article first appeared New Literary History *21 (1990): 897–919.*

TWO WEEKS after Albert Einstein took up residence in Princeton at the new Institute for Advanced Study in 1933, Einstein and his wife were invited to the White House by President and Mrs. Franklin D. Roosevelt. The invitation was intercepted by the director of the institute, Abraham Flexner, who took it upon himself to respond on Einstein's behalf. With the patience becoming a person of great responsibility and wisdom, Flexner explained the imperatives of pure science to the well-meaning Roosevelts. "Professor Einstein" had come to Princeton "for the purpose of carrying on his scientific work in seclusion," Flexner wrote. Invitations from politicians and even from learned societies were being declined for him. There was no need for the great scientist even to see such mail. It was "absolutely impossible to make any exception," lest the progress of science be retarded by an unending sequence of political and journalistic interruptions.[1]

Einstein himself was a very political person, and was, of course, eager to see the president. The country's most distinguished émigré scientist was miffed when he found out what Flexner had done. Neither Einstein nor his wife was satisfied when Flexner explained that he had only been performing for the Einsteins the same humble task Flexner's own secretary routinely performed for him: the screening out of bothersome and trivial inquiries from newspapers and the like. But Einstein managed eventually to sneak away from the institute in order to meet the Roosevelts, and to thereby depart, momentarily at least, from the role in which Flexner had sought to install him on Einstein's very first day in Princeton. "As early as 9:30 this morning," Flexner had recorded with evident satisfaction at the end of that great day, Einstein and a colleague "were quietly working at an algebraic problem."[2]

This idealized picture of the life of science—two "quiet" males working undisturbed on something esoteric—was also displayed in the interwar era's most popular fictional account of science, Sinclair Lewis's *Arrowsmith*, a novel so revered that it served as the chief basis on which Lewis became the first American to win the Nobel Prize for literature. In the climax of that book, Lewis sent Martin Arrowsmith and Terry Wickert to the perfect isolation of the Vermont woods, there to pursue the calling of pure science, free from the distractions of politicians, bureaucrats, committees, and women. *Arrowsmith* offers a persistently anti-institutional, indefatigably antisocial (and thoroughly misogynist) account of the life of free inquiry.[3]

The conceits of Flexner and the romanticism of Lewis can make us aware of two closely related assumptions about science and society that were widespread in the United States during the 1920s and 1930s. First, science was altogether a thing apart from the rest of society: the social gulf between the scientist and other people was taken to be prodigious. Second, scientists themselves were individuals, working largely alone, or in the cloistered company of one or two colleagues. Even people who knew better sometimes displayed a pastoral vision of science, according to which one or two individual investigators went off to the woods or to a desert island to think and experiment by themselves.[4]

The representation of the scientific enterprise in American discourse of the period was largely controlled by individualist conventions that militated against the recognition that scientists were inevitably entangled in the life of a larger society, and interacted with that society (and with each other) by means of a substantial and intricate *community*. Yet the concept of the "scientific community" is now so central to our discussion of science that one wonders how any society possessed of large numbers of scientists could ever get along without it. So conscious are we now of the social interaction among scientists, of the obligations they owe to one another, of the system of authority that operates within subdisciplines and within groups of disciplines, and of the place of the scientific community among a virtual infinity of other "communities" within American society that it is easy to overlook how recently this consciousness has been manifest. But only since the early 1960s has the concept of the "scientific community"—which serves to flag this consciousness for us—come into everyday use. To be sure, the concept was anything but new. It had been central to the philosophy of science developed by Charles Peirce in the 1860s and 1870s.[5] What happened in the early 1960s was not the invention of the concept, but an astonishing increase in the frequency of its public use. Where one formerly referred to "scientists," or "the scientist," one now spoke of "the scientific community."

This decisive linguistic change was one of the most striking of the events that distinguish what we can now identify as a watershed in the history of discourse about science, an episode in recent intellectual history constituted by a remarkable collection of books and articles published within the brief period 1962 through 1965. At virtually a single historical moment, there appeared Fritz Machlup's *The Production and Distribution of Knowledge in the United States*, Derek Price's *Little Science, Big*

Science, Don K. Price's *The Scientific Estate,* Karl Hill's *The Management of Scientists,* Warren Hagestrom's *The Scientific Community,* and, most famous of all, Thomas S. Kuhn's *The Structure of Scientific Revolutions.* This little renaissance of "science studies," as we can recognize it from the distance of a quarter-century, also included influential, relevant work by Joseph Agassi, Clark Kerr, Michael Polanyi, and Joseph Ben-David.[6] These writings substantially reshaped our understanding of the relationship between knowledge and society, made the further exploration of this relationship a major commitment of the post-1960s academic generation, and endowed that generation with a set of terms for carrying out this mission.

One can certainly find scattered references to "the scientific community" during the 1940s, and especially during the 1950s. I will be calling attention below to some specific examples. But when one looks for these words in many of the obvious places, the words are simply not there. One place they would seem to belong is in Vannevar Bush's classic of 1945, *Science—The Endless Frontier,* released shortly before the dropping of the atomic bomb, the making of which Bush himself had overseen in his capacity as the American government's chief science advisor.[7] One expects to find explicit reference to "the scientific community" in this text because the concept is central to Bush's argument. Bush's major concern, of course, was to ward off government control of science. Bush wanted massive federal funding of science, but he did not want the specific allocation of these funds to be determined by the government. Scientists themselves knew best how to advance science, he insisted, but Bush was vague on just how they made their decisions, on exactly what was the relevant structure of authority. All you had to do, he seemed to say, was to give the money to the leading universities and private laboratories, and somehow scientists, acting freely, would advance the frontiers of knowledge.

Bush's language was as persistently individualistic[8] as Kuhn's language seventeen years later was to be persistently communitarian. Bush was an adroit administrator of science, and knew perfectly well that scientists worked in groups and together constituted what would later come to be routinely called a "community." Yet the scientists of Bush's prose were a collectivity of heroic individuals, comparable in spirit to Daniel Boone or Davy Crockett, pushing back the frontiers. Kuhn's scientists were team players, organization men who knew how to follow instructions and defend dogmas.

Conventions for representing the scientific enterprise were thus altered significantly between 1945 and 1962. Although the practice of science itself changed in many respects during this postwar era, those changes did not at all amount to the creation of a scientific community (which we now take to be coterminous with the history of science itself). The scientific community has been continuous; it is our public language for talking about it that has been transformed. A comprehensive explanation of this change would try to take into account circumstances apparently fostering the increased popularity of several comparable usages for collectivities defined by occupation or ethnicity, including "the business community" (in place of the earlier "business" or "the businessman"), and "the Negro [or black] community" (in place of "the Negro"). Without pretending to offer such a comprehensive explanation for the popularization of the notion of a "scientific community," I want to identify and analyze one major source of it: the revolutionizing of the political economy of physical science in the wake of World War II. As a result of the Manhattan Project and its several administrative aftermaths, especially the creation of the National Science Foundation in 1950, physical scientists found themselves enmeshed in a system of capital-intensive research funded by a government responsive to popular political pressures and preoccupied with military priorities.[9] Science's new measure of economic dependence upon the public and the military appeared to threaten the political autonomy of science, and thus stimulated a new political consciousness on the part of scientists and others concerned about science's place in society. The more science became a political "constituency" like others, the more explicitly did its leaders in such organizations as the American Association for the Advancement of Science and the National Academy of Sciences regard themselves as spokespersons for a concrete, historical, interacting community rather than for a timeless "science" or an indefinite dispersion of "scientists." Hence the concept of the "scientific community" gained some of its popularity on account of the superior service it offered in the defense of the relative autonomy of a scientific community that had not been previously compelled to declare itself.

The story makes the most sense if we begin with Bush and the immediate political challenge to which *Science—The Endless Frontier* was addressed. Then, I want to turn to the ideological traditions of the 1920s and 1930s to which Bush was heir: traditions according to which the very idea of free inquiry was tied to laissez-faire individualism. After illustrating the power of this traditional link between free enterprise and free inquiry, I will try to show how this traditional connection shaped the debate between Bush and his critics in 1945. Then, I will trace the gradual rise of a more communitarian ideology of science from 1945 through the early 1960s.

Science—The Endless Frontier is deservedly remembered as both a political charter for the massive federal funding of science and a ringing vindication of free inquiry. But Bush's emphasis on the apparent link between intellectual progress and independence from public pressure was not the only perspective available in 1945 to an advocate of federal support for science. Indeed, a very different emphasis had been voiced during the war, and Bush's document was designed—as Daniel Kevles's scholarship[10] has shown in detail—to discredit the growing enthusiasm in some quarters for democratic planning of science in the public interest. This notion was based on the sense that the growth of knowledge, like other human projects, was susceptible to rational, centralized planning. Senator Harley Kilgore of West Virginia suggested that research ought to be organized to serve national needs as formulated by democratically elected representatives of the people. Kilgore and his supporters were fond of pointing out that the doctrine of laissez-faire had been widely discredited in the atmosphere of the New Deal; why should this anachronistic way of thinking continue to control research? The *New York Times* often agreed with Kilgore, editorially, and the *Times* had on its staff a well-known science writer, Waldemar Kaempffert, who wrote extensively and testified before Washington committees in support of Kilgore's ostensibly democratic approach to science policy.[11]

Bush saw two dangers in Kilgore's way of thinking. Basic research would suffer as a result of pressure to do practical, applied work. And freedom of inquiry would be compromised by government control. Hence *Science—The Endless Frontier* aimed to direct federal funds into preexisting universities and research institutes. There, the traditional prerogatives of individual investigators would presumably remain intact, as they might not, according to Bush, if federally sponsored research were instead carried out in government laboratories. To advance this institutional aim, and to keep government scrutiny of sponsored research at a minimum, Bush stressed both the necessity of basic research and the impossibility of planning it. "Scientific capital," Bush explained, was "painstakingly developed by research in the purest realms of science," and could then be drawn upon for various medical, military, and industrial purposes.[12] While the outcome of basic research could never be predicted in particular—and thus could not be planned as a socialist might—the outcome in general of basic research was so wonderfully predictable that society was bound to profit if massive amounts of tax dollars were allocated to it. Bush's document represented society as a potential irritant to, and retardant of, the process of advancing knowledge. Society's contribution to knowledge was as narrow, then, as knowledge's contribution to society was broad.

Bush was merely codifying two popular beliefs that dominated American discourse about science and society in the 1920s and 1930s. First, knowledge advances the most quickly and surely when its pursuers are liberated from social influences of any kind. Second, society's welfare ultimately depends upon advances in scientific knowledge. These two beliefs constitute rudimentary theories concerning the role of society in the advancement of knowledge, and the role of knowledge in the advancement of society.[13] The two theories shared the assumption that knowledge was something autonomous, an entity that could be trusted to shape society since its own shape was produced by truths external to, and somehow above, society. In this view, science was to be left alone just as the market was to be left alone in classical political economy. Individual investigators were best left to do as they wished, for the truth controlled the outcome of inquiry in much the same way that Adam Smith's "invisible hand" controlled the outcome of entrepreneurial activities.[14]

This perspective on knowledge and society was not unique to America, nor to the decades immediately preceding 1945. But there its elements can easily be found, vividly etched in a number of very different contexts. It can be found, for example, among Bush's most immediate ideological predecessors, the scientists who campaigned to obtain funding from private industry. Robert A. Millikan and George Ellery Hale sought corporate endowments for physics and chemistry, arguing not only that industry would ultimately profit from "pure science," but that the very purity and freedom of science would be endangered if scientists were obliged to turn instead to government for support.[15] In an article of 1928 appropriately entitled "Science and the Wealth of Nations," Hale managed to integrate free inquiry and free enterprise on terms designed to please industrialists of the Hoover era.[16] The public relations campaign led by Millikan and Hale popularized extravagant ideas about all the good things pure science could do, if funded, then left alone. Millikan, for example, urged that the public trace back to the beneficence of science what Millikan described as "the thousands of wide-awake, courteous, service-station men" so evident along the highways of the land.[17] Moreover, the activities of Millikan and Hale perpetuated and intensified a tradition according to which public (but not private) funding was interpreted as a threat to the self-determination of scientists.[18]

Hyperbolic representations of scientific knowledge as an agent, if not as a mystical force, were common coin also in another sphere of public discussion: the coverage of science news by journalists. In one journalistic summary of 1936, for example, entitled *The March of Science*, H. Gordon Garbedian ran through one department of knowledge after another, noting the "awe-inspiring" feats of our "wizards" of research, which amounted to a series of episodes in a serial motion picture, "science to the rescue." Young men, pictured in white coats, bent over test tubes, were captioned as the Magellans and Columbuses of our time. A galaxy of scientific superstars were willing to let their names be listed at the front of this hilarious book as expert consultants. Garbedian's fawning adulation of scientists was consistent with his vision of knowledge as a vast, anthropomorphic entity, always "marching," and having "impacts" on each and every aspect of civilization.[19]

These images of a mobile, self-directing, dynamic science were ideally suited for organizing yet another sphere of discussion of the 1920s and 1930s: writings about the history of science. Although history of science was not yet established as a discipline, many scientists, philosophers, and journalists shared with a handful of historians the task of narrating science's great discoveries.[20] Perhaps the most widely quoted of these works was *Science and the Modern World*, by Alfred North Whitehead. He saw the scientific intellect as the prime mover in all history, of course. Whitehead closed his book with the happy judgment that the scientific men of history were "ultimately rulers of the world," while the influence of "the great conquerors, from Alexander to Caesar, and from Caesar to Napoleon," had shrunk to "insignificance."[21] Even George Sarton, one of the period's few specialists in the technical study of the history of science, never tired of informing his contemporaries that the progress of civilization had worked itself out through the lives of a small number of individual men of genius.[22] This message was conveyed by shelves of popular histories less sophisticated than the works of Whitehead or Sarton.[23]

Philosophers displayed more awareness of the communal aspects of the scientific endeavor than did historians, journalists, and science-entrepreneurs, but even in the discourse of philosophy, individualist conventions were dominant. The feature of science most addressed by American philosophers of the 1930s was its ideal logic of justification as designed to be mastered by individual inquirers. The terms of the discussion were set by adherents of logical positivism, a movement significant for our story chiefly on account of its de-emphasis of the social matrix of inquiry. The logical positivists insisted that knowledge could be adequately analyzed without reference to whatever social, economic, and political conditions may have facilitated its growth in this or that specific case. This belief was popularized in the form of Hans Reichenbach's famous distinction between the "context of justification" and the "context of discovery."[24] Discovery, in this view, was a mysterious process about which nonphilosophers might choose to speculate, but philosophers had plenty of important work to do in establishing standards for the justification of true belief. The logical positivists did not convince everyone, but they certainly had the initiative in philosophical circles where the nature of science was discussed. They reinforced the traditional individualist orientation of the epistemological mainstream since Descartes,[25] and thereby helped to promote a vision of knowledge as more strictly defined, and as more distant from any social context, than knowledge had been envisioned to be by their immediate predecessors in defining the terms of philosophical discourse in America, the pragmatists.

It was indeed the aging pragmatist John Dewey—eighty years old in 1939, when the logical positivists were sweeping much of their opposition away, and when the war that would transform the political economy of research began—who came the closest during the 1920s and 1930s to becoming a genuine and effective critic of the laissez-faire, individualist, socially detached conceptions of science inherited by Bush and his contemporaries. By looking briefly at Dewey, we can turn now from this quick overview of discourse conducive to the development of Bush's perspective to consider instead items in the prewar cultural inventory that might foster a critical alternative to Bush's perspective.

Dewey was uncomfortable with the claim that social influences were bound to inhibit science. The instrumentalist Dewey preferred to regard knowledge as a response to social needs, and was generally suspicious of the very concept of "pure science." But Dewey and his followers distinguished sharply between social needs that were perceived and acted upon by "free intelligence," and those prejudices and vested interests, on the other hand, that merely masqueraded as "social needs." There were, moreover, persistent ambiguities in Dewey's account of "free intelligence" that rendered his work less helpful than one might expect to followers like Kaempffert—who admired Dewey, and quoted him frequently—when they tried to take on Vannevar Bush and the scientific establishment. Dewey sometimes wrote rigorously enough about knowledge to distinguish between science as an "attitude," as a body of "warranted belief," and as a set of "technical applications," but when he came to talk about "science and society" the meaning of "science" was extremely vague. For example, in a widely anthologized piece of 1931 entitled "Science and Society," Dewey depicted science as both an autonomous force and as a neutral instrument of prior purposes. Dewey condemned laissez-faire in the technological application of scientific knowledge, but he did not confront the question of the appropriateness of planning in what others would call "basic science."[26] Since Dewey wanted society as a whole to become more "scientific," and since he regarded "scientific method" as something anyone could adopt and practice, he was reluctant to distinguish "scientists" from the proto-scientific individuals and groups that made up the rest of society.[27] Hence Dewey's works could be of only limited use in the task of criticizing Bush, who had brought the received wisdom about "knowledge and society" to bear specifically on the relationship between "scientists" in the most narrow sense of the term and the larger society to which these distinctive people now looked for greater support. As a liberal, Dewey was a strong advocate of planning, and as an instrumentalist he had a vision of knowledge very much at odds with that of Bush. Yet Dewey's voluminous and widely quoted writings of the 1930s did not equip opponents of Bush with the weapons they needed.

Nor was the required help available in the sociological work done in the 1930s by Robert K. Merton. Merton did argue that some social settings were more conducive than others to the vitality of the scientific enterprise in general, but he stopped well short of suggesting that the specific content of knowledge could be affected by planning. Merton's work, far from challenging the conventional notions of scientific autonomy, reaffirmed them, and sought to chart the ups and downs of science in terms of the extent to which the autonomy was politically protected. Merton's writings of this era would have actually served the interests of Bush, had he been attentive to them. Merton even developed the notion of a "scientific community," and emphasized the discipline that scientists exercised over one another. Yet it is not surprising that the conservative Republican Bush and his free-enterprise allies overlooked, or shunned, whatever help they might have derived from Merton: in his account of science's communitarian aspect, Merton casually listed "communism" as a salient ideal of scientific communities.[28]

In the writings of a group of British Communists, indeed, there did surface in the 1930s a theoretical perspective according to which the planning of science was both possible and desirable. Yet much of what J. D. Bernal and his associates said about science as an agent of social progress was consistent with the views of Merton and Dewey, and even with science-hype popularizers like Garbedian. Willing as were these socialist men of science to assign real influence in history to organized social classes—something that would not have occurred to Whitehead, for example—the Bernalists tended to depict science very idealistically, as an independent, almost mystical force.[29] What most distinguished the Bernalists was, first, their frank advocacy of the planning of research by an enlightened state, of which they took the Soviet Union to be an appropriate model, and second, the misgivings they sometimes expressed about the bourgeois concept of "freedom." Freedom exists chiefly in the "interest of some powerful social class," observed J. G. Crowther, who insisted that the decision to control or to free science ought to depend on an assessment of which socioeconomic class would benefit.[30] The Bernalists would loom large in any study of British discourse about the autonomy of knowledge, but on the American side of the Atlantic their work generated relatively little interest until it was virtually rediscovered after the early 1960s.[31]

Bush might not have won so easy a victory in the science policy debates with Kilgore and Kaempffert had the latter been equipped with an alternative set of ideas about knowledge and society that were reasonably well developed, and that had been sanctioned by extensive public use. In the absence of such a resource, Bush's opponents had to make do with arguments that did not speak effectively to the apparently special nature of "basic science." Bush's opponents complained that "old man Profit" was allowed to have his way too often, and they protested that democracy was being undermined by a scientific elite eager to avoid accountability. They countered Bush's abstractions about "basic science" with abstractions of their own about politics and economics: Kaempffert's review of Bush attacked "free enterprise in the laboratory" as an inefficient basis for research funded by the public.[32] In response, Bush and Bush's allies in the foundations and the universities invoked the received wisdom about knowledge and society,[33] and they added the very pointed, Red-baiting charge that Kaempffert was trying to impose totalitarianism on American science.

In a lengthy and widely discussed letter to the *Times*, the science officer of the Rockefeller Foundation, Warren Weaver, explained to Kaempffert that sciences had not been advanced by government coordination at all. The recently exploded atomic bomb was not a product of government science. Contrary to popular belief, the Organization for Scientific Research and Development was not a model for the doing of research; what this office had done during the war was merely to coordinate the "practical application of basic scientific knowledge." That knowledge, Weaver insisted, had been produced earlier "by free scientists, following the free play of their imaginations, their curiosities, their hunches, their special prejudices, their unfounded likes and dislikes." Skillfully ignoring Kaempffert's repeated commitment to basic science, Weaver treated any proposal for planning as, by definition, a call for applied rather than basic science. Weaver compared Kaempffert's vision of a planned science to a business corporation that would spend all its capital without providing for any new income. Another comparison occurred to Weaver: Kaempffert was advocating, in effect, the holding of a gun to the head of scientists and telling them what to think.[34]

Although the National Science Foundation, as actually constructed in 1950, entailed more government involvement in the administration of science than Bush had desired, there is no doubt that Bush and his allies prevailed over Kilgore, Kaempffert, and other critics of *Science— The Endless Frontier*.[35] Bush's triumph, it must be emphasized, was not to have vindicated one theoretical perspective on knowledge and society against the claims of another, but rather to have persuaded enough people that knowledge and society, not politics, was the topic of conversation. Once it was implicitly conceded that the issue was not liberalism versus conservatism, but simply the freedom to do basic science, it followed that one could decide the nature of federal support for science by merely invoking a set of apparent truisms about knowledge and society. Knowledge cannot be planned, and it advances best if individual scientists are freed from social influences of any kind. In the absence of a coherent, alternative view of how "pure science" operated, Bush's position was a strong one.

The "scientists" of Weaver's letter and of Bush's report were individuals whose contributions to knowledge might be thwarted if the government tried to manage their work. Did this mean that the scientists required no management? Spokesmen for scientific institutions had often been content to leave this impression. Weaver's letter to the *Times* had said nothing about the careful planning that had gone into the Rockefeller Foundation's support of science, and that is now the subject of many history-of-science monographs.[36] Weaver called forth instead the administratively indefinite image of individual scientists following their hunches, freely, of course. But massive federal funding and the creation of an attendant bureaucracy eventually forced the recognition that someone was going to have to decide exactly who would get the money and why. *Science—The Endless Frontier* implied that scientists themselves had adequate devices for making such decisions. The closest Bush came to specifying these devices was his repeated reference to the universities and research institutes which he regarded as the proper recipients of federal funds. What Bush consistently implied, but did not spell out, was the existence of a scientific community: a complex of institutions through which scientists could administer the process of inquiry. Since this notion of a "scientific community" has subsequently become so prominent in discussions of the political and economic relations of science, its absence from Bush's text as an explicit organizing concept is now one of that text's most striking features. Bush came right to the brink of articulating the concept, but remained too embedded in an individualist rhetoric to take the step.

If the notion remained only implicit in Bush's report, it was vividly explicit in something else published in America in that pivotal year of 1945. In an obscure article entitled, appropriately enough, "The Autonomy of Science," the British physical chemist Michael Polanyi discussed in frankly political language the influence routinely exercised over the course of research by "a small number of senior scientists," the "unofficial governors of the scientific community" who advise on appointments, publications, awards, and special subsidies. "By their advice they can delay or accelerate the growth of a line of research." Governance functions were carried out within the professional communities of given disciplines, but also within the "body" of science as a whole.[37] Polanyi identified the missing link, institutionally, between the individual scientist and the public: that link was the scientific community.

The sharpness of Polanyi's account derived from the structure of British discourse. His essay had first been printed in Great Britain two years before, and responded directly to the apparent influence of the Bernalists in that nation.[38] Especially was Polanyi distressed at the willingness of the Bernalists to uphold the science policy of the Soviet Union as an appropriate model for the West. Much of Polanyi's "The Autonomy of Science" was an account of the damage done to genetics by T. D. Lysenko's effort to, in Polanyi's loaded words, "run science for the public good."[39] Polanyi was slow to acknowledge that state planning of science might produce different results according to the nature of the state. Could a Lysenko emerge in Great Britain or in the United States? But his own preoccupation with the Soviet case gave impetus to his writings, and eventually to an important international conference of 1953 on "Science and Freedom."

This conference was held in Hamburg under the auspices of the Congress for Cultural Freedom. Whatever services this conference may have performed in the Cold War, it served also to popularize Polanyi's ideas in the United States. The sociologist Edward Shils soon reported in *Bulletin of the Atomic Scientists* that the diverse papers and debates at the conference had again and again contributed to the development of the coherent idea of an "autonomous scientific community." In announcing the discovery of this idea, Shils criticized traditional analyses of science for failing to see that scientific activities form "a kind of social and cultural system with its own powers of self-maintenance and self-regulation." Shils's point was not that science had changed, but that *ideas* about science had changed, and for the better. Especially did Shils praise Polanyi's own paper, which explicitly assimilated "the structure of the scientific world" into the "free market in the economic sphere." Polanyi held close to the "free enterprise" tradition, yet was prepared to defend within its terms the powers of a community of scientists. Even amid all the disciplines of the scientific community, the prerogatives of individuals remained intact, Shils explained: for Polanyi, determinations about "what is to be investigated and which lines of inquiry followed up by further research are arrived at through a system of institutions operating through multitudes of individual decisions freely made."[40]

The notion of an autonomous scientific community, as popularized by Polanyi and Shils, gave helpful specificity to the abstract entity called "research" or "science," the support of which the federal government in the 1950s was being regularly asked to renew and expand.[41] The more socially concrete and administratively coherent "science" could be made to appear, the less suspicious became the demand that the government support an enterprise the necessary essence of which was ostensibly its freedom from the kind of accountability the state generally required of recipients of tax dollars. During the 1950s, Bush's arguments of 1945 were explicitly supplemented along exactly this line. Science, explained one academic consultant to government in 1956, is a "social system" complete unto itself. "Pure science is self-sustaining as a system of social control"; once the public and their elected representatives are made to understand this point—that the scientific community is indeed a system of social control—support for "basic research" becomes "an intelligible and attainable goal."[42]

It was through the idea of scientific community, then, that the conflicting claims for "planning" and "laissez-faire" were reconciled. Of course there had to be planning, but it was to be carried out within a genuine body politic, with its own rational system for evaluating priorities and personnel. Of course there would be freedom of inquiry, because the investigators who were accountable to the scientific community were in no way subject to pressures from outside that community. The vaunted "autonomy" of knowledge was thus particularized: it resided in a concrete social constituency that could be marked off from the rest of society. Laissez-faire would continue, but it was no longer laissez-faire individualism. It amounted to what we might call "laissez-faire communitarianism." Let the community of science alone.

The community addressed in this particular species of communitarianism was no ordinary community. It was often said to be organized around a set of values which, as it happened, were ideally suited to neutralize the negative connotations some people associated with laissez-faire, and to keep "free inquiry" at a safe distance from its more controversial ideological sibling, "free enterprise." Although Polanyi was quite happy to have science vindicated in terms of classical capitalist ideology, only slightly revised, some others preferred to depict scientists in more altruistic terms, and to stress the tension between the putative values of science and those of capital accumulation. This was true of Merton, for example, who in 1942 had sought to outline "the scientific ethos" in antifascist terms.[43] Merton formulated this ethos in terms of four basic "norms"—universalism, disinterestedness, communism, and organized skepticism—that were supposedly enforced by scientists themselves, as they policed one another. No one paid much attention to this formulation in 1942. Indeed, it was not until well into the 1960s, after Kuhn had consolidated the idea of the scientific community in the common academic consciousness, that this formulation of Merton's became the basis for a scholarly industry on the part of sociologists. Yet this early analysis of Merton's was kept ready for quick access through the 1949 and 1957 editions of Merton's *Social Theory and Social Structure*, in which the 1942 formulation had been reprinted as a chapter entitled "Science and Democratic Social Structure."[44] Merton's construction of the value-system of the community of science was carried along on the shoulders, one might say, of other contributions of Merton then more influential, including those flagged by the buzzwords "latent and manifest functions," and "middle range theory." Social scientists of the 1950s sometimes mentioned Merton's analysis of the "scientific ethos,"[45] which attributed to scientists as a collectivity a set of moral virtues commonly attributed to them as individuals by centuries of sympathetic commentators.

The significance of Merton's "norms" in the context of growth in popularity of the notion of a scientific community is twofold. First, Merton's scientists constituted a virtually ideal democratic society in themselves; it was all the more legitimate, then, to allow such a community to have autonomy within a democratic society like the United States. Second, Merton emphasized the least selfish of the traits of scientists: their inquiries were not only "disinterested," he insisted, but the "property" that resulted from their labor was treated "communistically," in the sense that the property belonged to all. Scientists may compete for the honor of solving a given problem, and thereby making contributions to knowledge, but the knowledge itself was not an item of commerce. Although the enterprise of individual inquirers was free within the perimeter of the norms of a community wisely supported yet left alone by the public, the outcome was intellectual capital at the disposal of all. As Bernard Barber put it in 1952, men in "the larger society" are expected to be "'self-interested' in their occupational activities . . . in the sense that they serve their own immediate interests first." But in science, Barber explained, "a different moral pattern prevails": people are "expected by their peers" to serve themselves by "serving the community."[46] No robber barons here, just *Gemeinschaft*.

The idea that scientists constituted a peculiarly virtuous community possessed of distinctive interests in the context of the American political order was advanced with increasing frequency during the Eisenhower era, especially by the community's "political arm," the American Association for the Advancement of Science.[47] By the time of the "science studies renaissance" of the early 1960s, the concept of the "scientific community" was taken for granted and ready to be developed systematically, even by scholars who had been oblivious to the political dynamics of the process by which the concept came to prominence. Kuhn, for example, was a physicist-turned-historian who worked in an intensely academic setting. Yet Price had been an official of the Truman administration during the debates over Bush's plan, and hence came to his scholarly work in exactly the context reviewed above. Price and Kuhn were perhaps the most creative of the scholars who made the years 1962–1965 the watershed they now appear to be. Their work constitutes the climax of the story this article tries to tell.

"The scientific community of the United States," Price argued, is an "establishment" of a certain character, "a loosely defined estate with a special function in our constitutional system."[48] Price invoked the image of an "estate" in order to compare the status and standing of the modern scientific community to that of the clergy, nobility, and burgesses of early modern England.[49] Scientists were thus an establishment whose authority and relations with other estates demanded clarification. He posited a spectrum of functions "from truth to power," with pure science at one end and pure politics at the other. Price granted that neither existed in a truly pure state, but he proposed that the closer any given estate is to the "truth" the more "is it entitled to freedom and self-government." Although administrators and professionals were certainly farther than scientists were from "truth," and closer to "power," even scientists couldn't help getting entangled with power, given society's need to use scientists in its public affairs. Much of Price's book was a detailed account of how a system of checks and balances enabled a knowledge-dependent society to remain democratic and a funding-dependent science to remain autonomous.[50] Price's basic views about science and power were not strikingly different from those of Bush, although Price was much more sanguine than Bush about science's ability to flourish under a measure of public control.[51] Price understood the logic of the new political economy of science much better than Bush did, and Price proved to be the commanding theorist Bush vainly tried to be. In an ideal science, there is no power; in an ideal polity, there is no truth. Price did not put it as starkly as that, but on the basis of these ideal types Price predicated the rights of the scientific community to the degree of political independence it could demand in a society with democratic aspirations.[52]

If *The Scientific Estate* arose from the most vividly contemporary of contexts—the political relations of science in the United States since 1945—*The Structure of Scientific Revolutions* emerged from one of the most cloistered of settings: the increasingly academic study of increasingly outdated ideas. As scholars developed the will to take science seriously as a historical subject, they found it hard to confirm the popular belief that science's history was the "accumulation of individual discoveries and inventions" through which "myths" were replaced by genuine "knowledge."[53] Yet Kuhn was not altogether isolated from the larger environment in which the notion of the "scientific community" gained currency in response to the new political economy of science. Kuhn was the protégé, after all, of Bush's chief coworker in government service, Harvard president James B. Conant, himself a prominent figure in the public discussion of science and society during the late 1940s and 1950s.[54] Kuhn is important in relation to many themes in recent intellectual history, but his significance for our story is in the role he ascribed to the scientific community.[55]

This role was, of course, enormous, by contrast to its size within most earlier histories and philosophies of science. Not only did Kuhn "set in the sociology of the scientific community" his ideas about scientific change, arguing that innovation is peculiarly facilitated by the community's determination to extend the range of phenomena explicable in terms of the theories to which it is committed; Kuhn went on to propose that we have no better standard for scientific truth than what the scientific community decides. It is not always obvious, Kuhn insisted, which explanation of a given range of phenomena ought to count as an advancement of knowledge and as a basis for further inquiry; it will not do to say that the "facts" always compel us to accept one explanation over another. When alternative, plausible paradigms compete for the loyalty of a scientific community, and hence for standing as "scientific knowledge," what actually happens, Kuhn held, "is the selection by conflict within the scientific community of the fittest way to practice future science." Kuhn acknowledged that the world studied by science must "possess quite special characteristics" in order for science to work, but he was content to leave the nature of these characteristics a mystery.[56]

This conclusion implied a sweeping reversal of conventions in the representation of science. Scientific discovery had been a mysterious process, and the learned world had been willing to tolerate a language of candid mystification for the purposes of describing this process. This language had been acceptable even to those people—above all, scientists—who demanded an austere, technical language for talking about the objects of knowledge. Kuhn had integrated "justification" and "discovery," and tried to begin an austere, technical analysis of science as a process carried out by people interacting in highly specific and contingent social circumstances. Kuhn's work demystified discovery, but at the same time left the world itself more mysterious than ever.

If ideas about what was mysterious and what was not were reversed in the pages of The Structure of Scientific Revolutions, these same pages confirmed the received faith in the autonomy of knowledge, thereby rendering this book vital grist for the mill of the new laissez-faire communitarianism of which Price's The Scientific Estate was the most complete statement. Indeed, for all its aloofness from the surrounding "science policy" debates of its day, this book was perhaps the most formidable brief for "peer review" ever written. Kuhn's successful scientific communities were tightly knit bodies decisively set apart from the larger society, yet exercising undisputed authority over what shall count as "knowledge" in their field. The "insulation" of such communities from society was "unparalleled," said Kuhn, by any other professional group, including those practicing social science. Indeed, when deciding what was and was not a "real" science, one could scarcely do better than to ask whether a candidate-community functioned in relation to society in the ways that physics did: commandingly authoritative, dogma-defined, highly specialized, distinctively isolated, autonomous. The autonomy of knowledge had long been assumed to follow from characteristics of the object of knowledge itself, that "nature" the "truth" about which was gradually being uncovered. Sometimes a second, cultural basis had been invoked: the distinctive attitude of disinterestedness that scientists allegedly brought to their inquiries. Kuhn predicated the autonomy of knowledge on neither of these grounds, but on the special characteristics of certain human communities, a call for the further study of which he chose to conclude the second edition of his famous book.[57]

It is an irony of Kuhn's influence that much of the sociological and philosophical work he helped to inspire has entailed a challenge to the very idea of the autonomy of scientific knowledge. Students of scientific communities during the 1970s and early 1980s spoke less and less of the impact of science on society, and more and more of the impact of society on science.[58] In the late 1980s, studies of the dynamics of scientific communities attained unprecedented ethnographic detail and theoretical rigor.[59] The autonomy of knowledge, an idea that once ruled unquestioned and virtually unexamined, has found in the scientific community a vehicle of uncertain strength, made up of human parts whose now demystified properties are the most popular items on the agenda of historians, sociologists, and philosophers of science.

NOTES

1. Abraham Flexner to Franklin D. Roosevelt, November 3, 1933, in *Science in America: A Documentary History 1900–1939*, ed. Nathan Reingold and Ida D. Reingold (Chicago, 1981), 451.

2. Abraham Flexner to Simon Flexner, October 18, 1933, in *Science in America*, 450. See also other letters involving this episode, and the Reingolds' comments, 435–436, 451–454.

3. Sinclair Lewis, *Arrowsmith* (New York, 1925), 425–430.

4. For a pungent, early critique, see the attack on this "Robinson Crusoe" theory of scientific progress in Karl Popper, *The Open Society and Its Enemies* (London, 1945), 2:219–220.

5. E.g., Charles Peirce, "Some Consequences of Four Incapacities," an essay of 1868 reprinted in *Writings of Charles S. Peirce: A Chronological Edition* (Bloomington, Ind., 1984), 211–242.

6. Fritz Machlup, *The Production and Distribution of Knowledge in the United States*

(Princeton, 1962); Derek Price, *Little Science, Big Science* (New York, 1963); Don K. Price, *The Scientific Estate* (New York, 1965); Karl Hill, *The Management of Scientists* (Boston, 1964); Warren Hagestrom, *The Scientific Community* (New York, 1965); Thomas S. Kuhn, *The Structure of Scientific Revolutions* (Chicago, 1962). See also Joseph Agassi, "Toward a New Historiography of Science," Beiheft 2 of *History and Theory*; Clark Kerr, *The Uses of the University* (Cambridge, Mass., 1964); Michael Polanyi, "The Republic of Science: Its Political and Economic Significance," *Minerva* 1 (1962): 54–73; and Joseph Ben-David, "Scientific Growth: A Sociological View," *Minerva* 3 (1964): 455–476. It was during these same years that American scholars began to devote more attention to the ideas of Karl Popper, whose 1935 work, *Logic of Scientific Discovery*, appeared in English in 1959.

7. Vannevar Bush, *Science—The Endless Frontier* (Washington, D.C., 1945).

8. Even when comparing the growth of science to the building of a cathedral, Bush spoke in an individualistic idiom. In his essay "The Builders," written in 1945 and published the following year in his collection *Endless Horizons* (Washington, D.C., 1946), 179–191, Bush celebrated not discipline and organization, not planning and coordinating, but the harmonious labor of differently skilled and equipped individuals. See also the analysis of Bush's essay in Nathan Reingold, "Vannevar Bush's New Deal for Research: or, The Triumph of the Old Order," *Historical Studies in the Physical Sciences* 17 (1987): 304.

9. This revolution in the political economy of science has finally begun to draw the attention it deserves from historians. An exemplary study is Stuart W. Leslie, "Playing the Education Game to Win: The Military and Interdisciplinary Research at Stanford," *Historical Studies in the Physical Sciences* 18 (1987): 55–88.

10. Daniel J. Kevles, "The National Science Foundation and the Debate over Postwar Research Policy, 1942–1945: A Political Interpretation of *Science—The Endless Frontier*," *Isis* 68 (1977): 5–26.

11. See the documents reprinted in *The Politics of American Science, 1939 to the Present*, ed. James L. Penick, Jr., et al., rev. ed. (Cambridge, Mass., 1972), 82–95. Cf. Waldemar Kaempffert, "The Case for Planned Research," *American Mercury* 57 (1943): 441–447.

12. Bush, *Science—The Endless Frontier*, 1–2, 13–14.

13. For a typical, popular formulation of these two rudimentary theories, see the book designed as the ideological statement of the New York World's Fair of 1939, Gerald Wendt, *Science for the World of Tomorrow* (New York, 1939), 14.

14. In a book widely circulated among scientific intellectuals in the United States during the period, a leading British scientific statesman depicted each investigator as a sea captain, going his own way, oblivious to the needs and interests of others, yet contributing harmoniously to knowledge on account of having "hope at the helm and truth at the prow"; see Sir Richard Gregory, *Discovery, or The Spirit and Service of Science* (New York, 1926), 11.

15. On this episode, see Ronald C. Tobey, *The American Ideology of National Science, 1919–1930* (Pittsburgh, Pa., 1971), esp. 133–232; and Lance E. Davis and Daniel J. Kevles, "The National Research Fund: A Case Study in the Industrial Support of Academic Science," *Minerva* 12 (1974): 207–220.

16. George Ellery Hale, "Science and the Wealth of Nations," *Harper's* 156 (1928): 243–251.

17. Robert A. Millikan, *Science and the New Civilization* (New York, 1930), 67; on Millikan's remarkable career as an "operator" and propagandist, see Robert H. Kargon, *The Rise of Robert Millikan: Portrait of a Life in American Science* (Ithaca, N.Y., 1982).

18. The constraints placed by this tradition on scientists involved in the New Deal's Science Advisory Board have been addressed by Lewis E. Auerbach, "Scientists in the New Deal: A Pre-War Episode in the Relations between Science and Government in the United States," *Minerva* 3 (1965): 457–482, esp. 458: "the bearers of a tradition of pure and disinterested science" failed "to adapt themselves to a new situation in which government sought their assistance and offered its support"; they distrusted government, and "feared that the autonomy of their intellectual activities would be damaged in ways which they could not foresee if they allowed themselves to become financially dependent on it." The halting steps made toward "planning" by some members of the Science Advisory Board have been emphasized by Robert Kargon and Elizabeth Hodes, "Karl Compton, Isaiah Bowman, and the Politics of Science in the Great Depression," *Isis* 76 (1985): 301–318.

19. H. Gordon Garbedian, *The March of Science: A Popular Introduction to the Story of the Universe and Man's Place on Earth* (New York, 1936), 61, 130, 266, 268, 297. For another example of this genre, see *Science Remaking the World*, ed. Otis W. Caldwell and Edwin E. Slosson (New York, 1923). Slosson's endeavors as a propagandist for science are analyzed in Tobey, *The American Ideology of National Science*, 71–89. Yet journalistic writings about the "impact" of science remain largely unstudied by historians of the United States. The most revealing and detailed study for the 1930s is Robert W. Rydell, "The Fan Dance of Science: America's World's Fairs in the Great Depression," *Isis* 76 (1985): 525–542.

20. For an informative account of the protodiscipline of history of science, see Arnold Thackray, "The Pre-History of an Academic Discipline: The Study of the History of Science in the United States, 1891–1941," *Minerva* 18 (1980): 448–473. Although Thackray gives some attention to the messages contained in writings on the history of science during the 1920s and 1930s (esp. 460, 465–470), his chief contribution is to clarify the relationship between these writings and their patrons. The intellectual content of the many relevant books and articles remains to be analyzed in appropriate detail.

21. Alfred North Whitehead, *Science and the Modern World* (New York, 1925), 299–300.

22. These views were expressed, for example, in George Sarton, *The History of Science and the New Humanism* (Cambridge, Mass., 1937), 46. See also Arnold Thackray and Robert K. Merton, "On Discipline Building: The Paradoxes of George Sarton," *Isis* 63 (1972): 473–495.

23. See, for example, Joseph Mayer, *The Seven Seals of Science*, rev. student's ed. (New York, 1937). This work begins with a frontispiece depicting a single, Hercules-like male pushing a globe upward amid a shower of meteors, with the caption "Science Moves the World Upward toward the Light."

24. Hans Reichenbach, *Experience and Prediction: An Analysis of the Foundations and Structures of Knowledge* (Chicago, 1938), 6–7, 382–383.

25. See Anthony Quinton's discussion of epistemological individualism in his "Authority and Autonomy in Knowledge," in *Thoughts and Thinkers*, ed. Anthony Quinton (London, 1982), 65–74.

26. John Dewey, "Science and Society," in *Philosophy and Civilization*, ed. John Dewey (New York, 1931), 318–330. See also one of Dewey's most extensive and direct discussions of "freedom" and "science," "Science and Free Culture," in his *Freedom and Culture* (New York, 1939), 131–154, esp. 132, 141–142, 145.

27. On this theme in Dewey and in Dewey's followers, see my "The Problem of Pragmatism in American History," in *In the American Province: Studies in the History and Historiography of Ideas* (Bloomington, Ind., 1985), 35–36, 41.

28. Robert K. Merton, "Science, Technology and Society in Seventeenth Century England," *Osiris* 4 (1938), pt. 2, 360–632; "Science and the Social Order," *Philosophy of Science* 5 (1938): 321–327; and "A Note on Science and Democracy," *Journal of Legal and Political Sociology* 1 (1942): 115–126.

29. This has been noted ruefully even by Gary Wersky, author of a sympathetic and very able study of Bernalism: *The Visible College: The Collective Biography of British Scientific Socialists in the 1930s* (New York, 1978), esp. 187–188.

30. J. G. Crowther, *The Social Relations of Science* (1941; 2d ed., London, 1967), 247.

31. The Marxist journal *Science and Society* included extremely few contributions from Americans, as has been noted in a recent study of left-wing scientists in the United States: Peter J. Kuznick, *Beyond the Laboratory: Scientists as Political Activists in 1930s America* (Chicago, 1987), 69. One of the most serious and extensive American responses to the Bernalists was a skeptical assessment by a physicist-philosopher, V. F. Lenzen, "Science and Social Context," *University of California Publications in Philosophy* 33 (1942): 3–26.

32. Kaempffert, "Planned Research," 445–446; Kaempffert, review of Bush's *Science—The Endless Frontier*, in *New York Times*, July 22, 1945, E13; Kevles, "Political Interpretation," 7.

33. James Bryant Conant, "National Research Argued: Dr. Conant Favors Federal Subsidies but Wants Freedom for Science," *New York Times*, August 13, 1945, 18. See also the long interview with Bush, "Dr. Bush Sees a Boundless Future for Science," *New York Times Magazine*, September 2, 1945, 14, 46.

34. Warren Weaver, "Free Science Sought: Control, It Is Argued, Would Hamper Advances," *New York Times*, September 2, 1945, sec. 4, 8.

35. For a cogent account of Bush's qualified victory, see Daniel J. Kevles, "Victory for Elitism," in his *The Physicists: The History of a Scientific Community in Modern America* (New York, 1978), 349–366.

36. See, e.g., Robert E. Kohler, "A Policy for the Advancement of Science: The Rockefeller Foundation, 1924–1929," *Minerva* 16 (1978): 480–515; and Pnina Abir-Am, "The Discourse of Physical Power and Biological Knowledge in the 1930's: A Reappraisal of the Rockefeller Foundation's 'Policy' in Molecular-Biology," *Social Studies of Science* 12 (1982): 341–382.

37. Michael Polanyi, "The Autonomy of Science," *Scientific Monthly* 61 (1945): 143.

38. Polanyi described the intensity of his reaction to the Bernalists in a 1964 preface to his *Science, Faith and Society* (Chicago, 1964), 8–9. See also William

McGucken, "On Freedom and Planning in Science: The Society for Freedom in Science, 1940–1946," *Minerva* 16 (1978): 52–72.

39. Polanyi, "The Autonomy of Science," 147–150. Cf. Leo Kartman, "Soviet Genetics and the 'Autonomy of Science,'" *Scientific Monthly* 61 (1945): 67–70. The difficulties felt by the Bernalists in dealing with Lysenkoism are explored by Wersky, *The Visible College*, 209–210, 292–301, who also provides a brief account of the conflict between the Bernalists and Polanyi (282–284).

40. Edward Shils, "The Scientific Community: Thoughts after Hamburg," *Bulletin of the Atomic Scientists* 10 (1954): 151–155. The increased attention by professional sociologists to science considered as a "community" during the 1950s and 1960s has been noted by Joseph Ben-David, *The Scientist's Role in Society: A Comparative Study* (Englewood Cliffs, N.J., 1971), 3, who cites Shils's article as an early example.

41. That government officials in the early 1950s looked at science policy in terms of an enduring conflict between "laissez-faire" and "planning or control" is established by Morgan Sherwood, "Federal Policy for Basic Research: Presidential Staff and the National Science Foundation, 1950–1956," *Journal of American History* 55 (1968): 599–615, esp. 602.

42. Herbert A. Shepard, "Basic Research and the Social System of Pure Science," *Philosophy of Science* 23 (1956): 48, 51, 56.

43. Merton, "A Note on Science and Democracy." For a study of this work in its immediate political context, see David A. Hollinger, "The Defense of Democracy and Robert K. Merton's Formulation of the Scientific Ethos," *Knowledge and Society* 4 (1983), 1–15, reprinted as chapter 5 of the present volume. The ideological superiority—from a democratic viewpoint—of Merton's "scientific ethos" over "the free market mechanism in classical economic thought" has been noted explicitly in a perspicacious but all-too-neglected essay by Yaron Ezrahi, "Science and the Problem of Authority in Democracy," in *Science and Social Structure: A Festschrift for Robert K. Merton*, ed. Thomas Gieryn (New York, 1980), 50.

44. Robert K. Merton, *Social Theory and Social Structure* (Glencoe, Ill., 1949), 307–316; 2d ed. (1957), 550–561.

45. See, e.g., Bernard Barber, *Science and the Social Order* (New York, 1952); and Talcott Parsons, *The Social System* (New York, 1951), 335–345. An especially interesting example is Shepard, "Basic Research," 48, because there Merton's account of science as a value-system is fully integrated with the concern for the political relations of science to which Shepard's article is directed.

46. Barber, *Science and the Social Order*, 131–132.

47. See for example, the statement of the association's Committee for the Promotion of Science and Human Welfare, as reported in *Science* 132 (July 8, 1960): 71.

48. Price, *The Scientific Estate*, 19–20.

49. The notion of scientists as an "estate" had been advanced in the 1920s by the biologist A. D. Little, "The Fifth Estate," *Science* 60 (1924): 299–306. Yet Little, unlike Price, had no sense of scientists as a community, and had little use for democracy. Specifically, Little wanted scientists to have more power in order

that they might put the principles of eugenics into practice without delay. The laws of eugenics, like other laws of "knowledge," Little believed to be autonomous entities which humans were simply to find and obey: "the laws of nature are the will of God," and "their discovery is a revelation as valid as that of Sinai" (see 304).

50. Price, *The Scientific Estate*, 135, 137–138, 148.

51. Price had been an official of the Bureau of the Budget during the controversy over *Science—The Endless Frontier*, and had been an influential critic of Bush's effort to isolate the National Science Foundation from what Price thought was appropriate political accountability. Price's role in the Truman administration's consideration of the issues is well set forth by Kevles, *The Physicists*, 350–362.

52. The reluctance of more recent theorists of "science and power" to work within these terms is a mark of how far the discussion has traveled since the watershed of a quarter-century ago. Now, most theorists emphasize the power-laden character of scientific practice, and interpret much of the behavior of scientists as exercises of power. Perhaps the most influential single work in this recent discussion has been Michel Foucault, *Power/Knowledge: Selected Interviews and Other Writings, 1972–1977*, ed. Colin Gordon, trans. Colin Gordon et al. (New York, 1980), esp. 109–133. The most comprehensive and systematic work in this vein is Joseph Rouse, *Knowledge and Power: Toward a Political Philosophy of Science* (Ithaca, N.Y., 1987). I have addressed the intellectual gap between Price and Rouse in my "Giving at the Office in the Age of Power/Knowledge," *Michigan Quarterly Review* 29 (1990): 123–132, esp. 130–132.

53. Kuhn, *The Structure of Scientific Revolutions*, 2–3.

54. Kuhn's *The Structure of Scientific Revolutions* is dedicated "to James B. Conant, who started it." Conant's important book of 1947, *On Understanding Science*, Mentor ed. (New York, 1951), does not explicitly invoke the concept of the "scientific community," but it does criticize in a proto-Kuhnian manner the heroic-individualist conventions for representing scientists; Conant emphasizes instead the discipline institutionalized by the "crowd of witnesses that surrounds" any working scientist (23).

55. Kuhn attributes (in *The Structure of Scientific Revolutions*, viii–ix) his sensitivity to "the sociology of the scientific community" to the then "almost unknown monograph" by Ludwik Fleck which has since been translated into English and become, despite its mid-1930s origins, another "post-60s" work in science studies: Ludwik Fleck, *The Genesis and Development of a Scientific Fact*, trans. Frederick Bradley and Thaddeus J. Trenn (Chicago, 1979). See also Jonathan Harwood, "Ludwik Fleck and the Sociology of Knowledge," *Social Studies of Science* 16 (1986): 173–187.

56. Kuhn, *The Structure of Scientific Revolutions*, 170–173.

57. Ibid., 164, 168; and 2d ed., 210.

58. These scholars were divided, to be sure, about the extent to which the knowledge produced by scientific communities has been generated, or even warranted, by a variety of cultural, economic, sexual, and political considerations "external" to science's intellectual development, but they have debated such is-

sues openly. For a convenient selection of this body of scholarship, see *Science in Context: Readings in the Sociology of Science*, ed. Barry Barnes and David Edge (Cambridge, Mass., 1982).

59. Four of the most widely discussed of these studies were Andrew Pickering, *Constructing Quarks: A Sociological History of Particle Physics* (Chicago, 1984); Bruno Latour, *Science in Action: How to Follow Scientists and Engineers through Society* (Cambridge, Mass., 1987); Ronald N. Giere, *Explaining Science: A Cognitive Approach* (Chicago, 1988); and David L. Hull, *Science as a Process: An Evolutionary Account of the Social and Conceptual Development of Science* (Chicago, 1989).

CHAPTER SEVEN

Academic Culture at the University of Michigan, 1938–1988

This case study in the intellectual and political history of the American research university is organized around the relationship between campus-specific and national dynamics. The University of Michigan is an especially challenging case for such a study because Michigan is, as I emphasize here, one of the most persistently generic of the institutions in its class. Hence at Michigan the prevailing culture of American elite academia has been visible in virtually all of its aspects, developing in certain directions selected not so much by deeply structural constraints— although a sponsoring midwestern public provided a matrix more conducive to some initiatives than to others—as by a complex of contingent circumstances and individual acts of enterprise.

To bring into bold relief the character of Michigan's academic culture and the "mainstream academic professionalism" that I claim largely defined it, I contrast Michigan to two of its peer institutions, Columbia and Stanford. These universities displayed campus cultures that were strikingly different from Michigan's yet in many specific respects antithetical to each other. To account, at least in part, for the vigor of Michigan's mainstream professionalism, I analyze the playing out on the Ann Arbor campus of two pivotal events national in scale during the decade following World War II: the struggle over McCarthyism, and the cultivation of entrepreneurship on the part of social scientists.

This inquiry was carried out at the invitation of John D'Arms, then dean of the Rackham Graduate School of the University of Michigan, for presentation on the occasion of the Rackham Building's fiftieth anniversary in 1988. This accounts for my chronological frame. In keeping with the occasion, the piece is celebratory as well as critical in tone. A longer and more extensively documented version of this article is available in the original publication, Intellectual History and Academic Culture at the University of Michigan: Fresh Explorations, *ed. Margaret A. Lourie (Ann Arbor, Mich., 1989).*

MAJOR research universities of the United States in the middle and late decades of the twentieth century have much in common, but they also display distinctive variations. This inquiry into the intellectual and political history of one such institution—the University of Michigan— over the course of a half-century tries to discern that university's particularity against the backdrop of the larger history of the entire class of

American universities to which Michigan obviously belonged. In what varieties of science and scholarship did the faculty at Ann Arbor make the most visible of marks? Did some fields or styles of academic work flourishing elsewhere languish at Michigan? Insofar as Michigan displayed a distinctive campus culture, what were its features? What do we learn when we look at this one campus's experience in relation to that of some of its institutional peers? Although these questions could be asked of any university for any era, this inquiry confronts Michigan during the years 1938–1988, the first fifty years of the Horace Rackham Graduate School. It is indeed the golden anniversary of Rackham that prompts the study.

When the Rackham Building was dedicated in 1938, Michigan was highly conscious of its reputation as a national university. Senior in years to Wisconsin and Berkeley, its only two intellectual peers among public universities, Michigan was decidedly more "eastern" in style and in composition.[1] Michigan boasted an out-of-state enrollment of about 43 percent.[2] It was said to possess the largest living alumni of any university in the English-speaking world.[3] And the Michigan alumni were formidable qualitatively as well as quantitively: Michigan was the fourth largest baccalaureate producer of the American scientists then designated as distinguished in *American Men of Science*, outproducing both Wisconsin and Princeton in that category at a rate of almost two to one.[4]

But Michigan was more egalitarian than its eastern, private counterparts. Unlike them, Michigan had long been committed to the education of women,[5] and it was quicker than many of the Ivy League universities to detach humanities instruction from Christian apologetics. A decade before Columbia made room for its first Jewish professor of English, Lionel Trilling, Jewish faculty at Michigan chaired the Departments of English and Romance Languages, as well as Economics.[6] It is true that as late as 1930, the Michigan Law School had accepted fifteen million dollars from the avowed Anglo-Saxon supremacist and confirmed anti-Semite William W. Cook, and the university was willing to publish in its alumni magazine Cook's detailed instructions for the conservative doctrinal slant he expected in the scholarship he was funding. Cook, a few years earlier, had written a book urging his countrymen to "make life so uncomfortable" for Jews that they would cease to exist as Jews. Cook also suggested that American blacks emigrate to New Guinea or Central America.[7] But this extremism was at the margin; the campus atmosphere in the 1930s has been recalled by the economist William Haber as remarkably free of the open prejudice against Jews that was so prominent a feature of academic life between the world wars in the urban northeast.[8] Michigan in 1938 stood culturally midway between the Ivy League and what we now call the Big Ten, displaying some of the stereotypical features of each. While Wisconsin prided itself on its special services to its state and region, Michigan looked eastward, and with the extensive support of the legislature in Lansing, fashioned for itself an image more national and more conservative than Wisconsin's.[9]

This image of a national, cosmopolitan university was largely sustained in the character, scope, and stature of its academic programs.[10] Ann Arbor had always been a distinguished humanities university, especially in philosophy, classics, and the Romance and Germanic languages; in 1938 this aspect of the tradition was intact. The social science departments were as a general rule smaller and less eminent, especially by contrast to the University of Chicago, but many of the professional schools at Ann Arbor were distinguished, particularly the Medical School.[11] Michigan's physics department was then one of the most important in the world, presided over by Harrison M. Randall. Chairman Randall, by being among the first to hire theoretical physicists from Europe and by orchestrating a unique summer seminar for the international community of theoretical physics, had made Michigan's department strikingly European in orientation.[12] The Departments of Mathematics, Biology, and Astronomy were also strong. Only Harvard and Princeton had a greater number of distinguished mathematicians in 1938 than did Michigan.[13] So Michigan entered the Rackham era as an extremely well-established research university. In the Midwest but not altogether of it, Michigan was a home for the national mainstream of academic professionalism and was known for the solidity and breadth of its programs, especially in the natural sciences, the humanities, and the professional schools.

In tracing what happened to this university during the following fifty years it is important to remember a truth that each individual university is tempted to deny. The major research universities of the United States are, in many respects, all alike, and they seem to have become more alike during this past half-century.[14] For all their celebration of their own unique achievements and ethos, these universities—public or private, eastern or western, urban or suburban—are all subject by degree to the same political and economic forces. Chicago, Wisconsin, Yale, Berkeley, Harvard, Michigan, Princeton, Stanford, Columbia—all respond to the same complex of interests and imperatives manifest in the National Science Foundation, the Department of Defense, the great private foundations, and the rather homogeneous body of trustees, regents, alumni, and in some cases legislators variously involved in the setting of policies and priorities for these institutions.[15]

Culturally, these universities all share a professoriat found by our sociologists of higher education to be much more secular, much more Jewish, and much more liberal than other, comparable occupational cohorts, including the faculties at less prestigious colleges and universities. Intellectually, moreover, all of these elite universities share the same disciplinary discourses: they develop their curriculum and their research programs in terms set by national and international professional communities of physicists, historians, economists, and so forth. In keeping with the popular bumper sticker "Think Globally, Act Locally," all of these universities are essentially physical sites for intellectual projects the basic character of which is determined elsewhere, in arenas of larger scale. Hence, when we inquire into the particular history of any one of these institutions, we necessarily encounter the generic research university as well as the specific institutional culture of one campus. It is not always easy to sort out the one from the other.

This sorting out is all the more difficult at the largest public universities, which are even more likely than their private peers to try to cover the waterfront, and to reproduce within each of their departments the contours and emphases of each discipline's national discourse at any given time. Throughout the past fifty years, Michigan has been known for one achievement above all others: for managing to perform reasonably well virtually every function major universities are expected to perform. This distinction for a single campus is more worthy of notice than it might first appear. Princeton has no schools of medicine, music, art, public health, education, natural resources, social work, nursing, or law. The Johns Hopkins University has conspicuously downplayed its undergraduate teaching mission. When Clark Kerr celebrated "the multiversity" in 1963, exactly at the midpoint of our half-century, he described Michigan just as accurately as he did his own Berkeley.[16]

Michigan, moreover, has been famous for the intellectual pluralism *within* its many academic units. This is not to claim that all varieties of science and scholarship flourished equally at Michigan at all times during the last half-century. Subspecialty strengths have affected the character of several departments and schools: in public health, epidemiology; in physics, spectroscopy; in psychology, social psychology; in music, composition; in classics, papyrology; and in mathematics, topology. The list of prominent examples could easily be extended. But even the units that attained great distinction in these specialties were often quite diverse. In philosophy, for example, William Frankena, C. L. Stevenson, and Richard Brandt made Ann Arbor unique in the United States as a center for the study of ethical theory, but the department, even while led by these men, became known for its breadth within the analytical tradition.[17] One can find exceptions to Michigan's reputation for pluralistic, comprehensive departments, but exceptions they truly are. There is a "Chicago School" of this and a "Chicago School" of that, but rarely a "Michigan School."[18]

Michigan, then, is surely *one of the most persistently generic* of the major universities in the United States. Hence Michigan, even more than most of the universities in its class, resists inquiries into campus-specific variations in academic culture. But recognition of this fact seems to me to be the first step toward understanding the Michigan tradition.

Michigan helped to invent the modern American university, after all, when the Ivies were still denominational colleges. Michigan has been historically content to exemplify the university "whole" rather than to particularize it.[19] While Princeton, Harvard, and Yale have manufactured and sustained campus lore, constantly reinforcing their own particularity, building upon traditions of undergraduate exclusivity,[20] Michigan has instead identified itself with ideals *common* to institutions of higher learning. If there is a Michigan mystique, it is more democratic than exclusive, more egalitarian than hierarchical; it is a mystique more of pluralism than of uniqueness of any sort. Within the Big Ten and within the state of Michigan, Ann Arbor is sometimes perceived as arrogant and precious, even snobbish, but its image among peer universities, especially in the East, is very different.

I dwell so long on the relatively generic character of Michigan because I have come to believe that Michigan's tradition is preeminently national rather than local. To dwell on local idiosyncrasies is to risk losing track of the chief historical significance of the University of Michigan as an embodiment of the national academic culture, as an institution successfully devoted to both excellence and comprehensiveness. Yet I want to take that risk. I want to try to address local variations on national tendencies and norms.

In this comparative perspective, when we turn to the chronological development of Michigan during the Rackham era, it makes sense to concentrate on the two decades following World War II. It is a commonplace that during these years, American universities experienced unprecedented growth and a prodigious increase in perceived social significance. By the 1960s public discourse was flooded with studies and symposiums and screeds about the transformation of American higher education and the growth, in particular, of research universities. These were the pivotal years of change, and it is on the Michigan events of these postwar decades that I want especially to focus. Michigan was then a major site of the entrepreneurial transformation of American academia; it was simultaneously an important site of the intellectual revolutions in American social science associated with behavioral perspectives and quantitative methods. In both cases, the Institute for Social Research (ISR) was a central factor. In 1945 the social sciences at Michigan did not amount to much, but by the 1960s, Michigan could claim one of the finest social science establishments in the world. In this same period, Michigan was a primary locus of the national struggle over McCarthyism.

These two sets of events—the story of ISR-related social science, and the story of how Michigan dealt with its accused Communists and ex-Communists—can help us understand the terms on which Michigan's mainstream academic professionalism was consolidated. The ISR story unfolds in the context of the period's unprecedented achievements of academic entrepreneurialism. Michigan psychologist James Grier Miller, flying back to Detroit after a conference in California in the early 1950s, found himself seated next to Governor G. Mennen Williams. Miller was an enterprising fellow and took advantage of the opportunity to educate the governor about the university's great potential for service to the people of Michigan and to the nation. He pointed out that a mental health research institute under his own direction would be a wonderful way for such service to be rendered. By the time the plane touched down at the Willow Run Airport, the governor had virtually promised several million dollars to support a mental health research institute to be directed by Miller. The unit was established in 1955 and staffed in part by a cadre of scholars from the University of Chicago, upon which Miller, equipped with the necessary capital, made a spectacular raid.[21]

The local gossip of every research university includes such tales of successful entrepreneurship, more often involving private or federal patrons. The neoconservative savant Robert Nisbet has argued that the sudden importance in the late 1940s and 1950s of grants to individual scholars and to "small company-like groups of faculty . . . for the purposes of creating institutes, centers, bureaus, and other essentially capitalistic enterprises within the academic community" was "the single most powerful agent of change" in the entire modern history of universities.[22] Nisbet exaggerates this transformation, as universities did not await the year 1947 to partake of capitalist social relations; but he is onto something. Direct grants from private foundations and industry as well as from agencies of the federal government played a large role in the history of many universities.[23] A prominent set of examples at Michigan is the creating of the foreign area studies centers in the early 1960s. Indeed, the openness of Michigan's administrative structure to the development of centers and institutions funded by outside sources is both an emblem for, and a source of, Michigan's pluralism. Nowhere in Ann Arbor was this entrepreneurial transformation carried out with more panache than at that supreme exemplar of academic enterprise, the Institute for Social Research.[24]

Although the name ISR was adopted in 1948, when the Research Center for Group Dynamics moved from MIT to Michigan to join forces with the Survey Research Center, the enterprise truly dates from 1946, when the Survey Research Center was established by a group of scholars who had spent World War II doing survey work for the federal government. Rensis Likert, Angus Campbell, George Katona, and others moved to Ann Arbor to try to find an institutional home for themselves at Likert's alma mater. If Michigan soon became the most entrepreneurial of America's universities in the social sciences, the credit belongs to these men and their closest colleagues, including psychology chair Donald Marquis, the chief agent in this group's move to Michigan.[25] Large database survey research is, of course, a capital-intensive endeavor, and ISR was chiefly responsible for raising its own money. ISR did business with industry and government to the tune of more than $200,000 in its first year of full operation and by 1951–1952 grossed $850,000.[26] By the 1980s its annual budget surpassed $15 million, and ISR was regarded as the largest university-based social science research institute in the world.

A distinctive administrative arrangement helpful to ISR was the university's willingness to allow ISR to keep the "overhead" component of its gross revenue. In the name of "indirect costs," the university took a substantial cut off the top of grants and contract payments made to other affiliated institutes and individuals but suspended this standard practice in the case of ISR. The decisive factors in maintaining the arrangement seem to have been the political skills of ISR leaders, especially Likert and Campbell, in integrating themselves and their staffs into the university's social science departments, and the formidable influence of Marquis on the central administration.[27]

Through the late 1940s and 1950s a number of ISR researchers were appointed to faculty positions, and others were hired by various departments to teach particular courses. Especially did the psychology department take advantage of the opportunities presented by ISR to make fractional and joint appointments; in a span of five years the ingenious operator Marquis enlarged the psychology faculty from eight to forty.[28] The departments most affected intellectually by ISR's presence appear to have been Psychology and Political Science, but the results were rather different in the two cases. The effect on the Department of Psychology was to facilitate pell-mell expansion and eclectic diversification, enabling Psychology, since it simultaneously pursued non-ISR opportunities, to become a classic case of the comprehensive, pluralistic Michigan department, embodying the diversity—however chaotic it seemed to some—of the national discipline.[29] Political science is also a diverse discipline, but not nearly so diverse as psychology. And the national trend among political scientists was decidedly in a behaviorist, quantificationist direction precisely when the political science department began to take advantage of ISR around 1960.[30] Although Political Science grew in size through the use of joint appointments with ISR, its growth was more focused, methodologically and doctrinally, than the psychology department's. By aggressively identifying itself with the best work being done in the "behaviorist revolution in political science," Michigan's political scientists raised their national ranking decisively.[31]

Sociology also made important appointments in connection with ISR, as eventually did Psychiatry, History, Statistics, Economics, Architecture, Internal Medicine, and Public Health. A great deal of distinguished social scientific work was done at Michigan in the 1950s and 1960s with no ISR connection whatsoever, to be sure;[32] and there did take place at ISR some work that the departments found "too applied" to be appropriate for a university. But ISR did much to make Michigan the social scientific powerhouse it had become by the early 1960s. It was through an ISR connection that the Department of Economics recruited its only member to be elected to the National Academy of Sciences, James Morgan, and it was through the same ISR connection that Economics would have recruited the eventual Nobel laureate Lawrence Klein had the regents not stopped the tenured appointment on political grounds.

Before turning to the story of Michigan's struggles over accused Communists and ex-Communists like Klein, I want to acknowledge that while the ISR-driven social sciences were attaining national leadership, Michigan's programs in natural science and mathematics underwent a very different experience. Although these programs grew and generally prospered amid the enormous increases in federal dollars then available, a number of other universities were more successful in expanding their research capabilities and stature, especially in the physical sciences. By standard indicators, Michigan was not as formidable a science university in 1963, relative to its peers, as it had been in 1938. Michigan membership in the National Academy of Sciences, for example, had only doubled, while several of Michigan's peer institutions had tripled and quadrupled their representation in the academy during the same period.[33] Institutions as different as Wisconsin and Princeton, Berkeley and Stanford, advanced aggressively and visibly into "big science," while the attainments of Michigan's science departments came to seem modest by comparison.[34]

But Michigan's scientists as well as its social scientists were prominent actors in the second story of the postwar decades I want to tell, the story of Michigan as a setting of the academic struggle over McCarthyism.[35] Indeed, one reason this episode looms so large in Michigan's history is its campuswide character. In this episode, the Michigan faculty experienced a rare moment of high institutional consciousness, acting not on the basis of disciplinary and departmental identities, but on the basis of their identities as members of the academy in general, and as members of a particular faculty confronted with a particular adminis-tration. In the course of these events, faculty and administrators helped to define the political dimension of Michigan's academic culture. In the process, the faculty actually cast out one of its members—the math-ematician Chandler Davis[36]—a step it would not take again until 1983, when it cast out a member of the psychology department for sexual misconduct.

Everyone at Michigan was in favor of academic freedom, of course, but another ideal, potentially at odds with academic freedom, was sud-denly on the agenda: "intellectual integrity." It was the possession of "in-tellectual integrity" that now entitled individual faculty to academic free-dom. If it could be shown that a given colleague lacked this quality, the obligation to defend that colleague's academic freedom disappeared. Hence there was a great deal at stake when discussion turned to whether it was possible for a Communist to have this supreme academic virtue, "intellectual integrity." By early 1953, when congressional committees began the most active phase of their inquiries into American universi-ties, a number of powerful voices had gone on record in the negative: to be a Communist was to betray intellectual integrity, and to show oneself unfit to serve on a faculty.

This argument was made most portentously in a statement signed by the presidents of all thirty-seven of the leading universities constituting the Association of American Universities (not to be confused with the faculty organization, the American Association of University Profes-sors).[37] Michigan president Harlan Hatcher was, of course, a signer of this statement, and in May of 1953 he tried to get the faculty senate to endorse it. In the course of a lively debate Kenneth Boulding attacked the presidential statement for weakening academic freedom, and histo-rian Preston Slosson argued that mere membership in the Communist Party should not be taken as evidence that a colleague was simply a prop-agandist and was therefore subject to dismissal. Law dean E. Blythe Stason addressed the senate in an effort to clarify the meaning of the statement Hatcher had placed before it. According to this statement, a faculty person who invoked the Fifth Amendment, Stason explained, be-came guilty, in effect, until proven innocent: invoking the Fifth Amend-ment "places upon a professor a heavy burden of proof of his fitness to hold a teaching position and lays upon his university an obligation to reexamine his qualifications for membership in its society."[38] Although the senate tabled the AAU statement and endorsed instead an AAUP document affirming academic freedom in more conventional terms, it was the Hatcher-AAU position—precisely as interpreted by Stason—that controlled events on campus a year later when pharmacologist Mark

Nickerson and biologist Clement Markert pleaded the Fifth, and mathematician Chandler Davis pleaded the First Amendment, in refusing to answer the questions of a congressional subcommittee at a session held in Lansing.[39]

Hatcher suspended all three the day after they refused to answer the subcommittee's questions,[40] and the university went forward with its own investigation. The faculty senate's Committee on Intellectual Freedom and Intellectual Integrity, chaired by the distinguished psychologist Angus Campbell of ISR, was ready to act as an appeal board, but the original jurisdiction fell to a Special Advisory Committee appointed by Hatcher and chaired by law professor Russell A. Smith. The Smith committee made clear at the outset that the issue was one of "integrity," not of research or teaching competence, and that the test of integrity was a willingness to answer specific and pointed questions about one's politics, especially about membership in the Communist Party. By this standard, Markert was found to have integrity. Before his colleagues he was willing to answer questions he would not answer before the House Un-American Activities Committee (HUAC). Yes, he had been a Communist, Markert acknowledged, but he had become disillusioned with the party's dogmatism and its subservience to Moscow. The Smith committee recommended that Markert be retained on the faculty, and Hatcher accepted this recommendation.[41]

In the matter of Nickerson's integrity, the Smith committee split, voting three to two for his integrity and his retention. Nickerson, like Markert, had answered the questions put to him by the Smith committee, but Nickerson reported merely drifting away from the party as he became more involved in his scientific work, not having experienced direct disillusion with the party. This was insufficiently decisive, and it was suggested that Nickerson had gone underground in 1948 and remained an agent of the Communist conspiracy. As the chair of Pharmacology, Maurice Seevers, put the point when meeting with the Smith committee, Nickerson's table talk at lunch "is a leftish type of conversation . . . basically following the communist line without saying so." When Hatcher eventually dismissed Nickerson, he characterized him as still "a communist in spirit" regardless of whether he happened to be a member of the party.[42]

The Smith committee had a more difficult time with Davis, who, unlike both Markert and Nickerson, refused to answer questions about his politics even when faculty colleagues were the interrogators, and who denied that his integrity depended on whether or not he was a Communist. Davis, like Markert, had strong faculty support within the College of Letters, Science, and Art. When the Smith committee met with the Executive Committee of that college, philosopher William Frankena took direct and repeated issue with the widespread presumption that Communist Party membership in itself compromised integrity and therefore justified dismissal. The opposite, more conservative side of this crucial theoretical dispute was argued, however, by economist William Haber.[43] The Smith committee not only agreed with Haber but was unanimous in its own recommendation that Davis be dismissed. Yet before either Davis or Nickerson could actually be severed from the faculty, the two cases had to be heard by the senate's own Campbell committee, to which both Davis and Nickerson appealed.

The deliberations of the Campbell committee are by far the most important phase of this entire episode. Here was a group appointed by the faculty's own governance system, charged not with the general task of advising the president on how to handle a complex crisis but with the explicit responsibility of defending "Intellectual Freedom and Intellectual Integrity" in the face of HUAC-instigated inquiries into the politics of Michigan faculty. The Campbell committee was literally the interpreter and guardian on the Ann Arbor campus of the classical intellectual values at a historic moment when these values were put under severe public strain. What limits would the Campbell committee place on the "freedom" of Davis and Nickerson? What did "integrity" mean to the Campbell committee?

Integrity meant, above all, a willingness to tell one's colleagues exactly what one's politics were, and academic freedom did not extend to a right to refuse to do so. The Campbell committee wanted Davis to say whether he was a Communist at that moment, whether he had been a Communist in the past, and specifically whether he had been a Communist at the time he joined the faculty and signed a routine oath. These are precisely the questions Campbell personally put to Davis in the opening moments of the Campbell committee's hearing of August 11, 1954. "Are you being honest in your associations with the University?" Campbell summarized his concern.[44] Davis's response to the effect that honesty about whether or not he was a Communist was irrelevant did not cut Campbell's ice, nor that of others on the committee. Hence Nickerson, who answered all the questions put to him by the Campbell committee, passed the integrity test, and the committee unanimously recommended his retention. Davis did not pass the integrity test; the Campbell committee unanimously recommended his dismissal.

The fact that Hatcher ignored the Campbell committee and fired Nickerson[45] as well as Davis[46] conveys familiar, unremarkable lessons about the limits of faculty authority. Hatcher, too, claimed to be applying the integrity test; he simply evaluated Nickerson's performance differently, agreeing with the negative conclusion offered by the Executive Committee of the Medical School.

One can still argue about whether the Campbell committee was correct to judge Chandler Davis a moral failure, but a striking implication of that judgment was its affirmation of the supremacy of professional solidarity. Faculty who wanted to support Davis balked when he insisted on placing other principles or interests above this solidarity with his professional colleagues. Even had he told the Campbell committee that he retained Communist sympathies, there is good reason to believe that all or some members of that committee would have defended Davis, arguing that no matter how "Red" his politics might be, his teaching and scholarship had integrity. The Campbell committee and many other of Davis's colleagues desperately wanted him to join Markert and Nickerson in treating the professoriat as the salient community, distinct from the alien political world of HUAC and its critics. One can argue that Davis was wrong to hold out as he did for a higher loyalty, to his own conception of what he owed and did not owe to the academy, but his holding out was truly the gravamen of his dispute with those faculty most responsible for casting him out. Michigan's pluralism was thus narrowed by its professionalism: Michigan, at least in 1954, was not plural enough to accommodate the likes of Chandler Davis.[47]

The long-term and even the short-term effects of the Davis and Nickerson firings are not easy to assess. In the long run, the faculty cannot have been terribly intimidated; otherwise there would not have been by 1965 so many faculty in Ann Arbor ready to take a lead in organizing the earliest opposition to the Vietnam War. But in the short run, there were some obvious indications at Michigan of the kinds of caution said to be characteristic of the academy nationally in the wake of the HUAC investigations.[48] The economics department put on hold the plans it was then making to add to its tenured ranks the ISR economist Lawrence Klein, even though Klein had repudiated Communism in a private HUAC hearing. Even the following year when the economists, under the new and vigorous chairmanship of Gardner Ackley, tried to appoint Klein,[49] the appointment was stopped.[50] The chief agent in Klein's destiny was accounting specialist William Paton, for whom the regents later named a building. Paton lobbied personally with five regents against the appointment, pointing out that Klein sympathized with Norwegian socialism.[51]

Klein was an ISR man, and the work that had won the attention of his colleagues across campus and indeed throughout his discipline was econometric model-building, soon to become the most visible white water in the mainstream of professional economics. Hence reference to Klein, and to the genuine excitement that Michigan's economists felt about his work, provides a convenient opportunity to turn to the matter of what styles of scholarship flourished there in the wake of the two sets of events I have just described.

Since I am suggesting that both of these very different sets of events were conducive to the consolidation at Michigan of mainstream academic professionalism, Klein's having been both an ISR stalwart and Michigan's most obvious and well-known victim of McCarthyism can serve to prevent the misunderstanding that ISR and McCarthyism were somehow allied with each other.

The concept of "mainstream academic professionalism" is fairly straightforward. It involves a suspicion of grand theory and of epistemological quibbling, a preference for concrete and clearly manageable projects, a penchant for technical methodological refinements, and, above all, attention to aspects of the social sciences and humanities least likely to be mistaken for political advocacy, cultural criticism, or journalism. The Michigan that had come into being by the late 1950s and early 1960s was a mighty engine of scholarship and science of just this type. Michigan's mainstream academic professionalism may be more readily recognized for what it was if we recall what was going on at the same historical moment at Columbia.

Columbia had plenty of mainstream academic professionalism of its own, of course, but it also had something else. Robert K. Merton, Paul F. Lazarsfeld, David Truman, and Ernest Nagel of Columbia helped to endow their generation of American intellectuals with a language in which to talk about empirical social research, and their colleague C. Wright Mills provided the era's most enduring, most widely quoted critique of quantitative social science. Yet there issued from Michigan no theoretical works of the stature of Merton's *Social Theory and Social Structure* and Nagel's *The Structure of Science*, no manifestos for social research as widely quoted as Lazarsfeld's papers, no theoretical synthesis of behaviorist political science as influential as David Truman's *The Governmental Process*, nor any critiques of the whole enterprise comparable in bite and in influence to Mills's *The Sociological Imagination*.[52] This is not to deny that Michigan faculty wrote creatively about these issues; but it is to insist that the marks on the world of social science they made as theorists and critics were not nearly so deep as those they made as practitioners. Even behaviorist social science, Michigan's greatest glory during most of our period, was more commandingly practiced and exemplified at Michigan than it was vindicated theoretically or subjected to sustained criticism.[53]

Then in residence on Morningside Heights were not only Merton, Lazarsfeld, Nagel, Truman, and Mills, but also the historian Richard Hofstadter, the literary critic Lionel Trilling, and the all-purpose savant,

Jacques Barzun. There, too, were Daniel Bell, Charles Frankel, Henry Steele Commager, John Herman Randall, Jr., Robert S. Lynd, Gilbert Highet, I. I. Rabi, Moses Hadas, and Meyer Schapiro.[54] Whatever else these men[55] accomplished or failed to accomplish, they articulated some of the central concerns of their respective callings in theoretical terms general enough to engage the attention of men and women of other academic fields.

Some of these Columbia scholars sought to address the implications for American politics and public doctrine of work within their disciplines.[56] Trilling and Bell, for example, functioned openly as moralists, as public intellectuals. One can speculate on the role played by New York City in attracting these intellectuals to Columbia, in giving a special intensity to their collegial discourse, in providing them with inspiration to serve a public wider than their own disciplinary communities, and—through that city's unique media and publishing apparatus—in giving them the visibility that helped make them figures of national repute.[57]

Michigan at the same moment did have the popular naturalist Marston Bates[58] and Kenneth Boulding, who, even while surrounded by Michigan's increasingly econometric economists,[59] had the brass to write a book entitled *The Meaning of the Twentieth Century*.[60] But the work then being done at Michigan making the most waves, at least in the social sciences and humanities, where campus-to-campus variation among elite universities is the most evident, was rather different. In 1960 there issued from ISR the book remembered by one study of the era as "the great monument of postwar political science," *The American Voter*, by Angus Campbell, Philip Converse, Donald Stokes, and Warren Miller.[61]

This book's unflinching picture of an overwhelmingly apathetic, ignorant, irrational electorate was replete with implications for the state and fate of democracy, but the authors did no hand-wringing, foot-stamping, or arm-waving. Other political scientists disturbed by the book were quick to address its policy implications, but the Michigan group had produced an austere, methodologically painstaking volume now remembered as a landmark in the effort of political scientists to distinguish sharply between their scientific contributions and the discourse about policy in which any citizen could, of course, participate at will.[62] *The American Voter* was a scientifically self-conscious, rigorously professional work of data and methods that made no compromises with the world of the *New Republic*. Studied in its aloofness from political advocacy, this book was mainstream academic professionalism at its confident best. Shortly after *The American Voter* appeared, Rensis Likert produced *New Patterns of Management*, and yet another ISR mainstay, George Katona, published *The Powerful Consumer*.[63] All three emanated from projects in large-database survey research, connected to middle-range theories.[64]

By far the most distinguished of Michigan's humanities departments in the late 1950s and early 1960s was the Department of Philosophy, then ranked second only to Harvard's. Here, too, mainstream academic professionalism was practiced at its best. I have already alluded to the department's distinction in ethics, and it should be pointed out that the work of Frankena, Stevenson, and Brandt was not applied ethics; these men did technical ethical theory in a rigorous, disciplinary tradition.[65] Classical Studies, too, was very distinguished, and my emphasis on strict professionalism is borne out by the fact that the emblem for classics at Michigan was the great papyrologist H. C. Youtie, not someone like the highly interpretive, even prophetic Norman O. Brown.[66] The Law School was filled with prolific scholars, known primarily for their codifications of private law.[67] Harold Wethey, the art historian, enjoyed a spectacular career as a cataloger and classifier of the paintings of Titian. H. W. Nordmeyer, for twenty-five years chair of German, was famous chiefly as a bibliographer.

Wethey and Nordmeyer were both "scholars" rather than "critics," in fields for which this distinction has traditionally marked off mainstream academic professionalism from a variety of alternatives. Michigan's English department was then more oriented to teaching than to either scholarship or criticism, but its publishing members were certainly more scholars than critics. A major success of that department was *The Middle English Dictionary*, a monument of specific information.[68] Robert H. Super's enduring editorial work on Matthew Arnold is also a great legacy of those years, but Super himself accounted for two of his department's four Guggenheim Fellowships during one span of a dozen years in which some other, smaller Michigan departments won six, eight, or ten Guggenheims.[69] The illustrious critic Austin Warren was in isolated residence there at the midpoint of the Rackham era;[70] he is the only Michigan person cited with any frequency in histories of literary criticism.[71]

In 1963 the *New York Review of Books* was established, but neither then nor in the subsequent quarter-century have Michigan faculty been prominent in the pages of this periodical, probably read by more American academic intellectuals than any other. The distance between Michigan and this important, transdisciplinary journal of critical opinion is at least consistent with the dominance at Michigan of the style of professionalism to which I have referred.[72]

Reference to the *New York Review of Books* can bring us back again to the matter of New York City versus a small midwestern city as contrasting settings in which Columbia and Michigan had achieved their rather different character by about 1960. A striking fact about many of the great urban universities, including Columbia, is the number of central European refugee intellectuals they added to their faculties during the era of World War II. Given its great size and prestige, and its relatively cosmopolitan prewar tradition, Michigan appears to have recruited disproportionately few of these scholars. Of the forty-eight leading humanists and social scientists whose careers are summarized in Lewis Coser's recent book, *Refugee Scholars in America*, only one, George Katona, ended up at Michigan.[73] Hence the legendary enlivening and deprovincializing effect these intellectual immigrants had on American academia was less pronounced at Michigan.[74] More of these men and women might have made Michigan's pluralism yet more pluralistic and its professionalism a bit more diversified intellectually than it was.

Is it possible that Michigan through the mid-1960s was the most persistently Protestant and native-born—with the exception, perhaps, of Wisconsin—of all the leading faculties in the United States? I have not been able to obtain reliable campus-to-campus data to support this impression, but it is an intriguing hypothesis. The situation at Michigan seems to have varied considerably from unit to unit. The Law School was long a midwestern-Protestant monolith; it appointed no one of Jewish origin until 1952, no Jew who had failed to convert to Christianity until 1955, and no Jew of East European descent until about 1960.[75] In any event, of the sixteen names I invoked earlier to remind us of Columbia's reputation for theorists and public intellectuals, more than half were Jewish. The irony is that easygoing Michigan, traditionally not much concerned with the question of who was Jewish and who was not,[76] turned out to be less dramatically affected in the 1940s and 1950s by the great opening of academia's gates to Jews than was Columbia, so long resistant to the Jewish population of the city around it and then suddenly so responsive to many of the nation's most prominent Jewish scholars.

If Columbia in the late 1950s and early 1960s was distinguished by the number and brilliance of its theorists and its critically engaged, public intellectuals, and obviously enriched by the sudden ethnic diversification of American academic life, Stanford affords a contrast to Michigan of an altogether different sort. Theorists and public intellectuals of any ethnicity were harder to find at Stanford than at Michigan. Stanford had almost no distinguished departments of any orientation in the humanities. In the social sciences, Stanford ranked well only in psychology and economics, the two social science disciplines closest to the mathematical, technological, and natural scientific fields in which Stanford had chosen to concentrate.[77]

And concentrate is the right word. Back in 1938 Stanford had been an institution of little distinction in any area of learning, but after World

War II it propelled itself upward in the rankings through intensive enterprise on behalf of selected programs. Frederick Terman, the engineering dean most influential in shaping Stanford's research policy, fought
against comprehensiveness and succeeded in directing Stanford's resources into what at Stanford were called "steeples." Terman sought to
build "superb programs in a few crucial fields" rather than "to try for
comprehensive coverage and end up doing lots of things well but none
with distinction." Terman said he would rather have one seven-foot high
jumper than lots of six-foot jumpers. Michigan, as a public university
with a pluralistic tradition, was trying to sustain its leadership and its
comprehensive scope amid economic pressures threatening to reduce it
to just another garden-variety state university; Stanford, meanwhile—a
relatively small, highly centralized, extremely wealthy private school—
roared past Michigan in the rankings in physics, math, chemistry, biochemistry, zoology, mechanical engineering, and electrical engineering.
These events at Stanford were predicated, in part, on a calculated decision to allocate resources without specific reference to the needs of undergraduate programs. When Terman retired, he explained privately to
his successor that indifference toward undergraduate programs was
among the secrets of Stanford's success.[78]

Stanford and Columbia afford more striking contrasts to each other
than either does to Michigan, but all the more do these two relatively
ungeneric universities serve to bring out Michigan's character at the
midpoint of the Rackham era. If Michigan by 1963 had lost some of its
eminence in the natural sciences, it had retained much of its leadership
in the humanities and had made social science its most distinguished
specialty. Its proliferating institutes and centers, growing apace with the
new entrepreneurialism, were making Michigan more pluralistic than
ever, and more responsive to those intellectual initiatives of its faculty
for which federal and private dollars could be the most easily found.
The most widely influential and respected work done at Michigan,
whether within departments or institutes, perpetuated the mainstream
academic professionalism that had always been preeminent in Ann
Arbor. Michigan's pluralism had flowered within, rather than beyond,
this professionalism.

The mainstream academic professionalism that flourished at this midpoint of the Rackham era was sustained by a certain epistemological confidence, a presumption of the autonomy of knowledge from its socio-
political matrix, and a faith in the social beneficence of knowledge
honestly produced.[79] These protections were soon weakened by the work
of Thomas Kuhn and Michel Foucault, by conflicts over the role of academic research in the Vietnam War, and by the development of its Marx-

ist and feminist perspectives in many disciplines. Knowledge and the processes of its production as well as its use came to be analyzed in political terms; the technical languages of the disciplines, once heralded for their autonomy, were said to be constituted by power relationships. Although these new winds of academic doctrine blew in a number of different directions in the 1970s and 1980s, all served to encourage an increase in theoretical and political self-consciousness. If Michigan did not become a conspicuous leader in defining and acting upon this self-consciousness, neither was Michigan a notorious holdout against it. Michigan's mainstream academic professionalism was supplemented by projects of a more theoretical and critical character than had been the norm in Ann Arbor. If American academia as a whole was moving in these directions, Michigan, true to its generic character, was part of the action.

Whatever may have changed at Michigan in the past twenty-five years, the university has continued to set the national standard for productivity in professional journals. If Michigan faculty have not been writing for the *New York Review* and *Daedalus*, they have been prolific in advancing the technical progress of their disciplines. In a national assessment of research and doctoral programs carried out in 1979, Michigan's leadership in social science was even more decisive in sheer bulk of publications than in perceived intellectual value.[80] But indicators of high intellectual value were also numerous. In many recent seasons, Michigan has produced more fellows of the Center for Advanced Study in the Behavioral Sciences than has any other institution.[81] Although Michigan's natural science membership in the National Academy of Sciences in 1988 has slipped yet lower than it was in 1963, relative to its peer universities, Michigan's extremely high social science membership in that body is consistent with other signs of the university's continued leadership in social science.[82]

We learn something about the University of Michigan from national rankings, from lists of academy memberships and prestigious fellowships, and from citation counts, but the feeling persists—in me, and in many others—that Michigan is a more impressive university as a whole than in those of its parts that are measured by these conventional indices of excellence. Hence I have emphasized the range and diversity of the place. If Michigan's pluralistic tradition has been a liability in some respects, inhibiting the concentration of resources in selected areas, that tradition has also sustained Michigan's overall greatness.

Pluralism is easy to fault. It offers few principles by which to set priorities, so it tends to respond uncritically to whatever initiatives and influences come upon it with the most force and capital. An institution devoted to pluralism is essentially passive, allowing itself to be pushed and pulled in various directions by agents who know what they want. Such pushes and pulls—by political forces, by the shifting methodological and doctrinal fashions of the national disciplines, by the enthusiasms and prejudices of private capital and the federal government—have, of course, been a large part of the Michigan story during the Rackham era. These pushes and pulls have been contained and to some extent directed by two considerations, one of principle, one of chance.

The principled constraint has been the university's effort to govern itself by the standard academic values of free and open inquiry, veracity, objectivity, reasoned argument, and reliance on evidence. These are amorphous values, and their meaning is often contested. But mainstream academic professionalism is certainly an expression of these values. Both critics and defenders of Davis, Nickerson, and Markert saw themselves as the true champions of these values. The disagreements about classified and other secret research that have taken place on campus periodically during the last twenty years have been largely couched in terms of these classical cognitive values.

If this loyalty to the standard academic ethic has helped Michigan to resist or welcome different initiatives, a more decisive influence in shaping the university appears to have been chance—the chance by which a given department or school has been in possession of the basic vision and the leadership skills to promote a given enterprise at a time when funds happen to be available and when the predilections of executive officers are propitious. Donald Marquis and Psychology and ISR together constitute a clear-cut positive example, but can we doubt that there were other chairs at other times in other units as talented as Marquis, other executive officers as responsive as Marvin Niehuss, other funds as available as those provided by the sponsors of early ISR research? It sounds like a simple combination of conditions, but I am not aware of any set of rules by which we can predict when this combination will come into being.

Multitudinous, sprawling, decentralized, contingent, imperfect, Michigan retains its capacity to inspire. That capacity derives in large part, I believe, not from any claims to uniqueness that might be made for Michigan, but from the enormous range of learned pursuits and doctrines available there. The University of Michigan has served the people of Michigan by its determination to remain a truly national rather than merely a state institution, making available locally a diversity of intellectual opportunities and a level of excellence unmatched in the public sphere except at Berkeley and Madison. The University of Michigan has served the Midwest by refusing to be as narrowly midwestern as many of its circumstances invite it to be.

NOTES

1. Although the university now treats 1817 as the year of its founding, its development as a university dates from the early 1850s. Wisconsin was founded in 1849, California in 1868. Neither attained distinction until the 1890s. The standard work on late-nineteenth-century American universities is Laurence R. Veysey, *The Emergence of the American University* (Chicago, 1965).

2. "Report on Student Residency Issues," Office of the Provost and Vice President for Academic Affairs (December 1987), 18.

3. The numbers of Michigan's alumni had long been a staple of conversation about American universities; see, for example, Edwin E. Slosson's popular *Leading American Universities* (New York, 1910), 477.

4. Steven Sargent Visher, *Scientists Starred, 1903–1943* (Baltimore, Md., 1947), 151. Visher's compilation is actually for 1943, not 1938; by 1943 the leading baccalaureate producers of scientists honored with a "star" in *Leading American Men of Science* were as follows: Harvard, 233; Yale, 109; Cornell, 89; Michigan, 82; Columbia, 65; Chicago, 64; MIT, 63; and Berkeley, 61.

5. See the informative book brought out by the university's Center for Continuing Education of Women, Dorothy Gies McGuigan, *A Dangerous Experiment: One Hundred Years of Women at the University of Michigan* (Ann Arbor, Mich., 1970). Part of the significance of Michigan's decision to admit women in 1870, McGuigan correctly notes, followed from the fact that Michigan was then "the largest university in the country and had by far the greatest prestige of any college west of New England" (30).

6. The chairmanships of Louis A. Strauss (English), Mordecai Levy (Romance Languages), and Leo Sharfman (Economics) were called to my attention by Otto Graf; interview, June 23, 1988.

7. See Cook, *American Institutions and Their Preservation* (New York, 1927), esp. 142, 146. See also *Michigan Alumnus* 35 (1929): 626ff., as cited by Elizabeth Gaspar Brown, *Legal Education at Michigan, 1859–1959* (Ann Arbor, Mich., 1959), 773–775, for the university's apparently unembarrassed public display of its tolerance for Cook's views even in the form of explicit expectations for the scholarship appropriate for the law faculty (e.g., "Better no legal research at all than research for socialistic purposes").

8. William Haber, interviews with Marjorie Brazer, May 2 and May 31, 1979, transcripts in Michigan Historical Collections (henceforth cited as MHC), Department of Economics, Box 5. Haber came to Michigan in 1936. Otto Graf, who was an undergraduate at Michigan from 1926 to 1930 and began teaching in the German department immediately upon his graduation, recalls that antiradicalism was more prominent at Michigan in the 1930s than was anti-Semitism. Graf has the impression that admissions recruiters, on trips to New York, would exclude as "too liberal" applicants who admitted to reading the *New York Times* rather than one of the many papers with a more conservative editorial outlook. Graf, interview, June 23, 1988.

9. The Madison campus's association with "The Wisconsin Idea" favored by turn-of-the-century reformers is properly emphasized in Merle Curti and Vernon Carstensen, *The University of Wisconsin, 1848–1925: A History* (Madison, Wis.,

1949), one of the best institutional histories ever written of an American university. The state of Michigan's traditionally Republican politics established for the university at Ann Arbor a political context very different from that provided by the state of Wisconsin for the Madison campus.

10. In 1934 a study of the American Council on Education listed fourteen of Michigan's departments in the "high excellence" category. On the basis of this study, a widely noted magazine article ranked Michigan sixth in overall quality of American universities, after Harvard, Chicago, Columbia, California (Berkeley), and Yale. See Edwin R. Embree, "In Order of Their Eminence," *Atlantic Monthly* 155 (1935): 655.

11. Bacteriologist Frederick Novy was the leading scientist in the Medical School; he was one of four Michigan faculty and emeriti to be members in 1938 of the National Academy of Sciences. The other three National Academy members with Michigan affiliations recorded on the 1938 membership list were astronomer Heber Doust Curtis, chemist Moses Gomberg, and psychologist Walter Bowers Pillsbury. See *Report of the National Academy of Sciences, 1937–39* (Washington, D.C., 1938), 108–115.

12. Spencer R. Weart, "The Physics Business in America, 1919–1940: A Statistical Reconnaissance," in *The Sciences in the American Context: New Perspectives*, ed. Nathan Reingold (Washington, D.C., 1979), 300; Samuel A. Goudsmidt, "The Michigan Symposium in Theoretical Physics," *Michigan Alumni Quarterly Review* 67 (1961): 178–182.

13. Visher, *Scientists Starred*, 485.

14. Perhaps this is why the large literature on the sociology of American higher education almost invariably treats the elite universities as a single entity and offers little institution-by-institution comparison and specificity. This is true even of the work of the best students of higher education, Martin Trow and Burton Clark. See, e.g., Burton Clark, ed., *The Academic Profession: National, Disciplinary, and Institutional Settings* (Berkeley, Calif., 1987). Howard H. Peckham, *The Making of the University of Michigan, 1817–1967* (Ann Arbor, Mich., 1967), is a useful source of basic information but offers little analysis. The intellectual development of the schools and departments of the university is dealt with more directly in *The Encyclopedic Survey of the University of Michigan*, 6 vols. (Ann Arbor, Mich., 1941–1981), but the departmental entries vary greatly in orientation, scope, and quality.

15. For a refreshingly realistic acknowledgment of these truths, see Robert M. Rosenzweig, "Public and Private Universities: Much Alike, Usefully Different," in *The Future of State Universities: Issues in Teaching, Research, and Public Service*, ed. Leslie W. Koepplin and David A. Wilson (New Brunswick, N.J., 1985), 295–303.

16. Clark Kerr, *The Uses of the University* (Cambridge, Mass., 1963). This remains one of the most candid books yet addressed to the problems and potentialities of the large university determined to pursue excellence and comprehensiveness at the same time. Kerr deals with some of the same issues in his perspicacious but too-often ignored essay, "Remembering Flexner," which served as an introduction to a 1968 reprint of Abraham Flexner's important work of 1930, *Universities: American, English, German* (New York, 1968), vii–xx.

17. My understanding of the history of Michigan's Department of Philosophy

has been greatly aided by interviews with Arthur Burks (May 19, 1988) and William Frankena (July 14, 1988). See also Arthur W. Burks, "Department of Philosophy," *Encyclopedic Survey*, 6:190–192.

18. One does see references to the "Michigan School of Political Science," associated above all with the work of Philip Converse and his collaborators, discussed below.

19. "Content to exemplify" might be contrasted to "vindicate theoretically." Michigan leaders have not made much effort to do the latter since the time of Henry Tappan, whose *University Education* (1851) is perhaps the most recent pronouncement of note on the nature and ideal course of American higher education to be written by a Michigan president (Tappan, moreover, wrote this book prior to his appointment at Michigan). Leadership in the national discourse about the aims and dilemmas of higher education has fallen to others— e.g., since the 1930s, Harvard's Conant, Pusey, and Bok; Chicago's Hutchins; and Berkeley's Kerr.

20. The extreme of this mystification is perhaps Princeton's annual P-rade, in which alumni march through campus in period-specific blazers.

21. I first learned of this incident from Donald Brown (interview, June 20, 1988). There are several versions of this tale. Some place the crucial Miller-Williams conversation chronologically after the institute's creation but before its full capitalization.

22. Robert Nisbet, *The Degradation of Academic Dogma: The University in America, 1945–1970* (New York, 1970), 72–73. At almost the same time Nisbet issued his jeremiad on behalf of traditional academic virtues, journalist Spencer Klaw identified "the academic entrepreneur" as "the most conspicuous symbol" of the "new order" of scientific life that had developed in World War II and its aftermath; see Klaw, *The New Brahmins: Scientific Life in America* (New York, 1969), 107.

23. There remains a good bit of disagreement and uncertainty about just what effect the interests of federal and private patrons have on the intellectual shape of the science and scholarship carried out in this entrepreneurial environment. An unusually careful, discerning discussion is Barry D. Karl and Stanley N. Katz, "Foundations and Ruling Class Elites," *Daedalus* 116 (1987): 1–40. In the large and often contentious literature on this question as it applies to the military and the natural sciences, one of the most challenging and technically detailed studies is Paul Forman, "Behind Quantum Electronics: National Security as [*sic*] Basis for Physical Research in the United States, 1940–1960," *Historical Studies in the Physical Sciences* 18 (1987): 149–229. See also Ian Hacking, "Weapons Research and the Form of Scientific Knowledge," *Canadian Journal of Philosophy*, suppl. vol. 12 (1986): 237–260.

24. The early history of the Institute for Social Research is one of the best-documented and most closely analyzed of any aspect of University of Michigan history, thanks to Charles F. Cannell and Robert L. Kahn, "Some Factors in the Origins and Development of the Institute for Social Research, The University of Michigan," *American Psychologist* 39 (1984): 1256–1266; and Jean Converse, *Survey Research in the United States: Roots and Emergence 1890–1960* (Berkeley, Calif., 1987); esp. chap. 11, "The Survey Research Center at Michigan: From the Margins of Government," 340–378.

25. Another activist in the cause was Robert Cooley Angell, chair of Sociology. The pivotal role of Marquis and Angell is plain from the Michigan administrative documents collected in the Marvin Lemmon Niehuss Papers, Box 1, "Institute for Social Research," MHC. I have also listened to Niehuss's recollections of these events; interview, July 19, 1988.

26. Converse, *Survey Research*, 344, 346. Just what to call these money-raising academics has been a delicate matter. Converse notes guardedly: "*Promoters, operators*, and certainly *hustlers* have all been used ironically among academics to lend a certain tarnish to these political skills of fund-raising and organizing" (264). Converse appears to prefer "research entrepreneur" and "managerial scholar."

27. ISR's high overruns did place the arrangement at risk more than once during the early years; sec, e.g., the testy memorandum of W. K. Pierpoint to Rensis Likert, September 21, 1951, Niehuss Papers, Box 1, "Institute for Social Research," MHC. Converse describes the salient relationships between ISR leaders and the central administration very well (344–349). Niehuss now remembers the early ISR social scientists as a very distinctive group; Niehuss and his colleagues in the central administration believed the group deserved special administrative attention; interview, July 19, 1988.

28. "Department of Psychology," *Encyclopedic Survey*, 6:207–208. In Marquis, Michigan was blessed with one of the nation's most sophisticated social science planners, possessed both of a coherent vision of what the social sciences should be intellectually, and of a program for organizing research communities in order to realize that vision. See his Presidential Address to the American Psychological Association, "Research Planning at the Frontiers of Science," *American Psychologist* 3 (1948): 430–438, and the then-confidential (May 1952) Ford Foundation document outlining the vision of the Center for Advanced Study in the Behavioral Sciences, coauthored by Marquis, and shared with Vice President Marvin L. Niehuss; Marquis to Niehuss, June 17, 1952, Niehuss Papers, Box 1, "Ford Foundation," MHC.

29. My understanding of the development of the psychology department depends heavily on Wilbert McKeachie (interview, May 6, 1988), and "Department of Psychology," *Encyclopedic Survey*, 6:207–212.

30. Of the many treatments of the behavioral revolution in political science, one of the most incisive and provocative is contained within the recent book by Raymond Seidelman with Edward J. Harpham, *Disenchanted Realists: Political Science and the American Crisis, 1884–1984* (Albany, N.Y., 1985), esp. 149–186.

31. For political science rankings, see Allan M. Carrter, *An Assessment of Quality in Graduate Education* (Washington, D.C., 1966); this study, known colloquially as "the Carrter Report," was based on 1964 evaluations. Compare, for 1969, Kenneth D. Roose and Charles J. Anderson, *A Rating of Graduate Programs* (Washington, D.C., 1970), and for 1978–1979, placing Michigan fourth in faculty quality, Lyle V. Jones et al., *An Assessment of Research-Doctorate Programs in the United States: Social and Behavioral Sciences* (Washington, D.C., 1982). According to the departmental history written by Joseph E. Kallenbach, "probably the most profound influence upon the department's curriculum and the approach to the subject matter of political science has come through its close relationship with the Insti-

tute for Social Research. . . . Employing the techniques and methodology of empirical research, rather than the normative, descriptive, and analytical approach characteristic of earlier stages in the development of political science as a field of study, the department's offerings now [ca. 1977] heavily emphasize political behavior studies." Kallenbach, "Department of Political Sciences," *Encyclopedic Survey*, 6:205–206.

32. The striking growth in size and stature of the Department of Anthropology is a prime example of non-ISR social scientific distinction at Michigan.

33. So far as can be gleaned from the academy's published membership list for 1963, Michigan had eight members in that year, compared with four in 1938. National Academy of Sciences, *Annual Report, 1963* (Washington, 1963), 141–164.

34. In California, the enterprising President Robert Gordon Sproul exploited the Atomic Energy Commission and other federal agencies for all he could get, which resulted in an unprecedented increase in buildings, equipment, and supporting funds for the natural sciences at Berkeley and UCLA. Verne Stadtman, *The University of California, 1868–1968* (New York, 1970), 369–370; Stadtman notes that Sproul's zeal for federal dollars was found to be excessive and incautious by some faculty leaders, including physicist Raymond Birge, chair of Berkeley's faculty Committee on Research. See also Robert Seidel, "A Home for Big Science: The Atomic Energy Commission's Laboratory System," *Historical Studies in the Physical Sciences* 16 (1986): 135–175. Any serious inquiry into the relative decline of Michigan's standing in the physical sciences in the postwar era would have to address the enterprise and initiative of several of Michigan's departmental chairs in the sciences. I have made no attempt to do this, but the story told above about Psychology chair Donald Marquis and the development of ISR leads me to believe that Michigan's central administration was responsive to innovative initiatives, even if not inclined, as was Berkeley's Sproul, to do the initiating. There is an oral tradition in some circles of lamentation that Michigan physical scientists were too proud of being able to build their equipment with "candle wax and baling wire" and insufficiently insistent about the needs of capital-intensive research. Some of Michigan's science old-timers complain bitterly, but not for specific attribution, about "social science hegemony," especially during the deanships of psychologist Roger Heyns and economist William Haber.

35. Michigan's importance is implied by the extensive attention devoted to the Michigan events in a recent, widely reviewed scholarly study by Ellen W. Schrecker, *No Ivory Tower: McCarthyism and the Universities* (New York, 1986). I have examined almost all of the documents in the Michigan Historical Collections Schrecker used, and some she did not; I find her account of the Michigan events to be accurate, and her judgments about the meaning of these events to be essentially sound. In the book as a whole, however, I believe Schrecker subsumes under "McCarthyism" too wide a range of conduct and belief. I am also persuaded by Lewis Perry that Schrecker, by concentrating on the stories of victims of McCarthyism, diminishes the real significance of academic efforts to fight McCarthyism; see Lewis Perry, review of Schrecker, *History of Education Quarterly* (Winter 1987): 563–568.

36. Michigan was subsequently censured by the American Association of University Professors. For the extensive justification of the AAUP's action, see the Academic Freedom and Tenure Committee's report, "The University of Michigan," *AAUP Bulletin* 44 (March 1958): 53–101.

37. The AAU statement, "The Rights and Responsibilities of Universities and Their Faculties," was adopted by the AAU at its meeting of March 24, 1953, at Princeton. For an account of the discussion among the AAU's leaders resulting in the adoption of the statement, see Schrecker, *No Ivory Tower*, 187–189. Copies of the statement itself are in many files in MHC, e.g., Niehuss Papers, Box 2, "Angell's Loyalty Committee."

38. Minutes of Senate Meeting, May 11, 1953, University Senate, Box 3, MHC. Stason was not, of course, declaring that persons who took the Fifth should be regarded as guilty of a criminal offense until proven innocent in court; the burden of proof he was addressing had to do not with crimes and courts, but with crimelike offenses and courtlike determinations of fitness for membership in a faculty. Yet he spoke formally in his capacity as dean of the Law School, after all; the conflation of two realms was obvious and presumably intentional. If it were not the case that a legal aura was desired, the text of the AAU statement could well have been interpreted for the senate by a professor of English, like Hatcher himself.

39. Why the HUAC subcommittee sent subpoenas to only four Michigan professors (Klein of ISR was also called; for a discussion of his case, see below) to appear at its session in Lansing has been a matter for speculation. Part of the answer may be that Niehuss had gone quietly to Washington beforehand to try to learn what HUAC had in its files on Michigan faculty. Upon being shown this information by HUAC staff, Niehuss cautioned that the evidence was very weak indeed. He warned that the committee would embarrass itself if it tried to depict certain individuals as Communists. Niehuss now refuses to reveal the names of other Michigan faculty on whom HUAC had designs in 1954. On other occasions, Niehuss also cautioned the FBI that its sense of who was subversive was open to question: an FBI agent once visited Niehuss's home and listed for him the Michigan faculty whom the FBI would "pick up tomorrow if war with the Russians broke out." On that list was Dean Hayward Keniston. When Niehuss pointed to the absurdity of this, the FBI agent explained that Keniston had once agreed to speak (but then did not) before a society devoted to American-Soviet friendship. Niehuss, interview, July 19, 1988.

40. Hatcher's action was widely protested. About two hundred faculty signed a statement published in the *Michigan Daily*, May 25, 1954, defending the constitutional rights of their colleagues and protesting the introduction of "extra-professional criteria" in the university's decision making about faculty. The signers of this statement were almost exclusively from the College of Letters, Science, and Art (LS&A). A list of the signers, with affiliations, is in Box 21 of the Niehuss Papers, MHC.

41. Markert soon left Michigan for Johns Hopkins and later went to Yale, where he became chair of his department and was elected to the National Academy of Sciences. Schrecker concludes on the basis of local FBI reports from the period found in Markert's FBI file that Hatcher accepted this recommendation

because he believed he would be able to get rid of Markert when his contract came up for renewal (*No Ivory Tower*, 227). Niehuss disputes this vehemently; interview, July 19, 1988.

42. "Proceedings at a Meeting of the Special Advisory Committee to the President on the Suspensions of Doctor Clement L. Markert, Doctor Mark Nickerson and Doctor H. Chandler Davis," Niehuss Papers, Box 21, MHC; see esp. 1, 49, 67. The transcript of the Smith committee's session on Nickerson with the Executive Committee of the Medical School reveals many dimensions of anti-Nickerson feeling within the Medical School, especially on the part of Seevers. "Nickerson is basically anti-authority," Seevers told the Smith committee, "and that is something that I personally am unable to put up with" (50). Hatcher's reference to Nickerson as a "communist in spirit" was an approving quotation from the minority report of the Smith committee; see his Report to the Senate, October 5, 1954, 16–17, in Niehuss Papers, Box 21, MHC.

43. "Proceedings," 2, esp. 76–81, 100.

44. "Proceedings Had at the Appeal Hearing in Reference to the Appeal of Doctor H. Chandler Davis to the Senate Sub-Committee on Intellectual Freedom and Intellectual Integrity Held at Hutchins Hall . . . ," 3, found in Niehuss Papers, Box 21, MHC.

45. Nickerson went to Canada, taking a job at the University of Manitoba.

46. Davis, too, got to Canada eventually: the University of Toronto. He first served a prison term for contempt of Congress.

47. It is instructive that back in 1948 the integrity test helped determine the fate of philosopher Irving Copilowish in a case that appears to have been kept out of the press (neither the *Ann Arbor News* nor the *Michigan Daily* refers to Copilowish during the relevant period, September 18 through 24, 1948). I learned of it quite by accident, while scanning the minutes of the LS&A Executive Committee for 1948–1949. The story of this remarkable case—so far as I have been able to piece it together—proceeds as follows. When Copilowish joined the Department of Philosophy in the fall of 1948, he warranted that he had never advocated the violent overthrow of the government, but, in fact, he had once been involved in a Trotskyist group then construed to be subversive. A day or two after having deceived an administrative officer of the university about this matter, he confessed that he had lied and gave his colleagues in Philosophy an extensive account of his political past. Since the final approval of Copilowish's appointment as assistant professor was still to make its routine way through the regents, LS&A dean Kenniston wanted to be prepared to defend Copilowish. Philosophy chairman William Frankena was flown in from Harvard, where he was on sabbatical, to convene an extraordinary meeting of his department, the results of which were conveyed in a letter written to Kenniston that same afternoon. "We confidently believe," Frankena reported on behalf of his department, "that Copilowish has genuinely and entirely renounced his questionable connections, opinions, and activities, and has no intention of returning to them." We detect "nothing subversive or radical in his thinking," Frankena continued, and we find in him no "Marxist or other [b]ias." (See William Frankena to Hayward Kenniston, September 22, 1948, Dean's Files, Department of Philosophy, College of LS&A, Box 81, MHC; See also Box 65 of the same collection, Minutes of the

Executive Committee in 1948–1949, 7 and 8.) The Executive Committee of LS&A was delighted, and Kenniston immediately informed Provost James P. Adams that Copilowish was not "today a supporter of subversive and revolutionary ideas." (Hayward Kenniston to James P. Adams, September 23, 1948, Dean's Files, Department of Philosophy, College of LS&A, Box 81, MHC.) Copilowish was kept on. Kenniston was apparently the crucial force in saving him. (See Frankena's undated letter to Kenniston expressing his department's gratitude, ibid. I have also been helped by the recollections of these events shared with me by Frankena himself; interview, July 14, 1988.) Kenniston told Frankena, according to the latter's recollections, that Kenniston had carried his own letter of resignation when he went to see Adams, but was not obliged to present it because Adams accepted the college's position on the matter. Copilowish, after changing his last name to Copi, wrote an exceedingly successful textbook in logic: Irving M. Copi, *Introduction to Logic* (New York, 1953). This book is now in its seventh edition. Copi left Michigan in 1969 to accept a position at the University of Hawaii. The Copilowish/Copi case is worth this summary here because it falls instructively at the opposite extreme from that of Chandler Davis: Copilowish apparently told his colleagues all, threw himself on their mercy, uncompromisingly renounced political radicalism, and was willing to have it said of him that his "ideas," not simply his political conduct, were devoid of Marxism. The issue of Copilowish's candor was apparently reviewed again when he was granted tenure; a substantial folder dating from that era is closed until Copi's death, "Papers 1950–51, Copilowish (Copi), Irving," Provost, Box 13, MHC.

48. Some evidence of this was found in the spring of 1955, when sixty-one Michigan social scientists were interviewed by a survey research team from Columbia University interested in the impact on faculties of the widespread pressure for ideological conformity. The individual questionnaires seem to have been lost (Schrecker, *No Ivory Tower*, 416), but "patterns of caution" in scholarship, teaching, and lunchroom conversation are a major theme in the published results of the survey, which also included hundreds of social scientists from many other American colleges and universities. See Paul Lazarsfeld and Wagner Thielens, Jr., *The Academic Mind: Social Scientists in a Time of Crisis* (Glencoe, Ill., 1958), esp. 192–236. The Columbia investigators interviewed more faculty from Michigan than from any other single institution; see 434. The failure of Lazarsfeld and Thielens to disaggregate their data by specific institution is an early example of sociologists' tendency, mentioned above in n. 14, to treat the elite professoriat as a single entity.

49. Klein was approved by a departmental vote of 16 to 2. The Executive Committee of LS&A and its then dean, Charles Odegaard, also backed Klein. Odegaard was careful to cover the integrity ground when recommending Klein's appointment, and to contrast Klein favorably in this respect to the three who had refused to answer the questions of the HUAC subcommittee (see Charles H. Odegaard to Marvin L. Niehuss, March 31, 1955, in "Lawrence Klein," Niehuss Papers, Box 5, MHC. Most of the documents relevant to the Klein case are in this file, and in one with the same label in Box 4 of the Niehuss Papers).

50. There is a helpful account of this episode in Marjorie Brazer, "The Economics Department of the University of Michigan: A Centennial Retrospective,"

[1980], 131–140, Department of Economics, Box 5, MHC. The same collection contains typescripts of interviews Brazer conducted in 1979 with the principals of the case, including Klein, Ackley, Paton, Haber, and Katona. Of special significance is Brazer's interview with Ackley, October 29, 1979. I have also profited from Ackley's recent comments about the case; interview, May 16, 1988.

51. William Paton to Marvin L. Niehuss ["Dear Dix"], August 2, 1955, in "Lawrence Klein" folder, Niehuss Papers, Box 5, MHC. Paton sent copies of this letter to five regents and advised his old friend Niehuss of this fact. The regents were obviously moved by Paton's letter. Niehuss's response three days later reminded Paton of Klein's exceptional credentials and of the care with which the department and the college had prepared the argument, but continued cautiously that "in view of all the circumstances" Niehuss was unwilling "at this time" to recommend Klein for tenure. (See Niehuss to Paton, August 5, 1955, ibid.) Although Niehuss eventually supported efforts to appoint Klein to a full professorship without tenure in the hopes of retaining him until regental opposition moderated and tenure could be awarded, Klein, then on leave at Oxford, wrote that he found this compromise gesture to Paton morally repugnant. (See Klein to Niehuss, December 9, 1955, and Klein to Gardner Ackley, same date, both ibid.) Klein accepted a position at the University of Pennsylvania. He paid a return visit to Ann Arbor in 1977, to receive an honorary degree from a university then eager to express its regrets.

52. Robert K. Merton, *Social Theory and Social Structure* (Glencoe, Ill., 1949; 2d, expanded ed. 1957); Ernest Nagel, *The Structure of Science* (New York, 1961); David Truman, *The Governmental Process* (New York, 1951); C. Wright Mills, *The Sociological Imagination* (New York, 1959). The Michigan contribution most comparable to the books by Merton and Truman is Philip Converse, "The Nature of Belief Systems in Mass Publics," in *Ideology and Discontent*, ed. David Apter (New York, 1964), 206–261. The Michigan work most comparable to Nagel's is Abraham Kaplan, *The Conduct of Inquiry: Methodology for Behavioral Science* (San Francisco, 1964). As its subtitle implies, Kaplan's work was designed more explicitly for social scientists than was Nagel's more comprehensive treatise in philosophy of science. "The work is not a formal exercise in the philosophy of science," Kaplan's readers were assured in an introduction by Leonard Broom, "but rather a critical and constructive assessment of the developing standards and strategies of contemporary social inquiry" (xvii). Although this disclaimer suggests a book less sophisticated philosophically than Kaplan's work actually is, the disclaimer is consistent with the distinction I want to make between Kaplan's more "practical" approach and Nagel's greater concern with the classical issues of epistemology and logic. The two books were cited with almost equal frequency by social scientists between 1966 and 1985; see *Social Science Citation Index*, cumulative vols., 1966–1970, 1971–1975, 1976–1980, and 1981–1985. Yet Kaplan's role in the culture of Michigan is not remotely as great as Nagel's at Columbia. Nagel was a Columbia man from 1931, when he began to teach philosophy there, until his death in 1985; Kaplan was at Michigan from 1963 to 1973.

53. Compare my observation about Michigan's presidents, n. 19, above. Although two volumes of methodological essays published in the early 1950s out of Columbia's Bureau of Social Research and Michigan's ISR have much in com-

mon—as noted by Converse, *Survey Research*, 385–386—the Michigan book was a narrower, more practical collection eschewing the "philosophy of social science" which made up seventy pages of the Columbia equivalent. See Paul F. Lazarsfeld and Morris Rosenberg, eds., *The Language of Social Research: A Reader in the Methodology of Social Research* (Glencoe, Ill., 1955), and Leon Festinger and Daniel Katz, eds., *Research Methods in the Behavioral Sciences* (New York, 1953). Lazarsfeld had to face Mills in the elevator, but Converse finds (534) no evidence that ISR social scientists made any effort to respond to criticisms of their brand of social science, including that of Loren Baritz, whose *The Servants of Power: A History of the Uses of Social Science in American Industry* (Middletown, Conn., 1960), she notes, makes frequent reference to ISR authors. But Baritz, interestingly, also cites the early (pre-Michigan) work of Theodore Newcomb as having been written from a refreshingly prolabor standpoint, and some of the work of Daniel Katz as a rare example of self-awareness on the part of social scientists of the function in social conflict of certain styles of "objectivity"; see Baritz, *Servants*, 136–137, 203–204, and 258.

54. For convenient lists of Columbia humanities and social science faculty through the mid-1950s, see R. Gordon Hoxie et al., *A History of the Faculty of Political Science, Columbia University* (New York, 1955), 310–316, and John Herman Randall, Jr., et al., *A History of the Faculty of Philosophy, Columbia University* (New York, 1957), 289–296.

55. I employ the male gender here because the Columbia scholars I list were indeed exclusively male.

56. It is striking, too, how many prominent Columbia scholars addressed McCarthyism in their professional work. The Lazarsfeld and Thielens study mentioned above (*The Academic Mind*) is such an example; so, too is Richard Hofstadter and Walter Metzger, *Academic Freedom in the United States* (New York, 1955), and Daniel Bell, ed., *The New American Right* (New York, 1955). If there was a comparable outpouring of critically engaged social scientific and humanistic scholarship at Michigan, it has eluded me. Kenneth Boulding's occasional efforts along these lines were not so widely noted. Columbia's record in dealing with suspected subversives, incidentally, is very different from Michigan's; see Schrecker, *No Ivory Tower*, 255–256, who notes that President Grayson Kirk knew very well that committees of his faculty would resist inquiry into the "outside activities" of radical colleagues, so was less inclined to convene such inquiries.

57. Such speculation can begin, for example, with the fact that New York institutions are home to most of the sixty-odd academics mentioned in a recent overview of the political discourse of intellectuals between American entry into World War II and about 1960: Richard Pells, *The Liberal Mind in a Conservative Age: American Intellectuals in the 1940s and 1950s* (New York, 1985). Those not affiliated with Columbia, NYU, or one of the CUNY campuses are almost exclusively from other urban campuses, especially Harvard and Chicago. Pells's book is largely a retelling of stories familiar to readers of *Commentary* and *New Republic*, and it would not do to accept uncritically Pells's notion of just what should count as the history of "American intellectuals" during the era. A weakness of the book is, indeed, its obliviousness to mainstream professional scholarship. Yet for my purposes, the book's scope is very much to the point: Pells confronts us with

the most successful of the most journalistic endeavors of American academics during twenty years of the epoch I am addressing. That he finds no occasion even to mention *anyone* from Michigan helps us to determine just where Michigan faculty have and have not made an impact. Efforts to measure the standing of individuals outside their disciplines are even more impressionistic than the rankings of graduate programs. One scholar has tried to apply the techniques of survey research to the task; he produced a list of the "top seventy" American intellectuals as of 1970: Charles Kadushin, *The American Intellectual Elite* (New York, 1974). Kadushin's list is heavily weighted toward nonacademics (e.g., Susan Sontag, Norman Mailer) but includes many academics. For whatever the survey is worth, no Michigan scholar made the top seventy. Even within the "top twenty," Columbia placed three (Bell, Hofstadter, and Trilling). See Kadushin, 30–31.

58. Bates, a native of Grand Rapids, was an entomologist in his technical work. He published a number of popular works that went through several editions during his tenure at Michigan (1952–1971); the best-known were *The Forest and the Sea* (New York, 1960) and *Man and Nature* (Englewood Cliffs, N.J., 1961).

59. Marjorie C. Brazer, "Department of Economics," *Encyclopedic Survey*, 6:144–148.

60. Kenneth Boulding, *The Meaning of the Twentieth Century* (New York, 1967). Boulding cast his claim in the form of a version of modernization theory.

61. Angus Campbell, Philip Converse, Donald Stokes, and Warren Miller, *The American Voter* (New York, 1960). The characterization quoted is that by Robert Booth Fowler, *Believing Skeptics: American Political Intellectuals, 1945–1964* (Westport, Conn., 1978), 187.

62. See, e.g., the discussion by Seidelman and Harpham, *Disenchanted Realists*, 151–169, esp. 152–153.

63. Rensis Likert, *New Patterns of Management* (New York, 1961); George Katona, *The Powerful Consumer: Psychological Studies of the American Economy* (New York, 1960).

64. For Katona's explicit reference to "middle-level theories," see his methodological appendix, *Consumer*, 263. When the distinction between middle-range and grand, or systematic, theory is now applied to the most influential social scientific works produced in the 1950s and early 1960s, Michigan's middle-range orientation is clear. Consider, for example, the rather different character of the Michigan and Harvard contributions listed among the one hundred works most frequently cited by social scientists between 1969 and 1977. Two of the three Michigan items on this list are middle-range classics, *The American Voter* and Likert's *New Patterns of Management*. The third, Daniel Katz and Robert L. Kahn's *The Social Psychology of Organizations*, much influenced by the systems theories of Parsons and von Bertalanffy, is perhaps a borderline case. It may be worth noting that Leon Festinger had left Michigan for Minnesota several years before he published *A Theory of Cognitive Dissonance* (Stanford, Calif., 1957), by far the most frequently cited work of social psychology in the Garfield study. Several Harvard entries on this list, however, are quintessentially grand theory: Talcott Parsons, *The Social System*; B. F. Skinner, *Science and Human Behavior*; and John Rawls, *A Theory of Justice*. Harvard's entries also include John Kenneth Galbraith's *The New*

Industrial State, which might be classified as middle-range theory but is broad enough to push the category to its limit. See Eugene Garfield, "The One Hundred Books Most Cited by Social Scientists, 1969–1977," in Garfield, *Essays of an Information Scientist*, 9 vols. (Philadelphia, 1963–1987), 3:621–632, reprinted from *Current Comments*, September 11, 1978. All of these Harvard books of grand theory are by single authors; yet two of the three Michigan works have multiple authors. Grand theory is almost always done by single minds—the collaborations of Marx and Engels are salient exceptions—while a major setting for team research in the social sciences has been the project of developing middle-range theories on a quantitative base, a project for which Michigan's ISR-dominated social science establishment has proven to be ideally suited.

65. Abraham Kaplan did write in a more popular vein shortly before his departure from Michigan in the early 1970s, e.g., *In Pursuit of Wisdom: The Scope of Philosophy* (Beverly Hills, Calif., 1977), but the work through which Michigan philosophers were then making their mark is better represented by Frankena's *Ethics* (Engelwood Cliffs, N.J., 1963), a work distinguished, incidentally, by its accessibility as well as by its analytic rigor.

66. O. M. Pearl, "Department of Classical Studies," *Encyclopedic Survey*, 6:136–139. Michigan's classicists have established a distinguished record in epigraphy, numismatics, law, and especially papyrology but with few significant exceptions have not been as engaged by the more interpretive literary and philosophical dimensions of classical scholarship. The Wesleyan classicist Brown published *Life against Death: The Psychoanalytical Meaning of History* in 1959.

67. See the complete list of publications of the law faculty through 1959 in Brown, *Legal Education*, 804–919.

68. The history of the Department of English written for the *Encyclopedic Survey* by Richard W. Bailey focuses on the department's teaching record; the dictionary is the one scholarly project Bailey mentions (6:148–152, esp. 152).

69. I refer to 1959 through 1971, during which time the Department of History, by far the leading Michigan producer of Guggenheim fellows, won ten. During the entire half-century between 1938 and 1988, the Department of English won only nineteen Guggenheim Fellowships, while Michigan's historians won twenty-nine, all since 1957. When the rate of Guggenheim production is considered in relation to departmental size, only Michigan's philosophers—ten Guggenheims during the relevant fifty years—compare to Michigan's historians in this distinction. These figures have been compiled from the annual *Reports of the President and the Treasurer* of the John Simon Guggenheim Foundation. During the past quarter-century Michigan has been the fifteenth-ranking institutional producer of Guggenheim fellows; the leaders are Berkeley, Harvard, Columbia, Yale, Stanford, and UCLA.

70. Warren was a devout but idiosyncratic Anglican, who crossed himself when passing portraits of Charles I. In understanding Warren's role at Michigan I have been helped by the recollections of Warner Rice (interview, May 6, 1988) and Otto Graf (interview, June 23, 1988).

71. See Gerald Graff, *Professing Literature* (Chicago, 1987); Walter Sutton, *Modern American Criticism* (Englewood Cliffs, N.J., 1963); René Wellek, *American Criticism, 1900–1950*, vol. 6 of *A History of Modern Criticism* (New Haven, Conn.,

1986). Grant Webster, *The Republic of Letters* (Baltimore, Md., 1979), points out that among "critics," Warren was something of a "scholar," if not an antiquarian. See esp. 163.

72. Of the nearly one thousand names mentioned in a study of the first ten years (1963–1973) of the *New York Review*, I recognize only one that has ever been affiliated with the University of Michigan: Harold Cruse, professor of history and Afro-American studies; see Philip Nobile, *Intellectual Skywriting: Literary Politics and The New York Review of Books* (New York, 1974). The index of Nobile's book, while not a comprehensive list of contributors, is a helpful indicator of just who was and was not part of the milieu of this periodical during the 1960s and early 1970s.

73. Lewis Coser, *Refugee Scholars in America* (New Haven, Conn., 1985).

74. The chief institutional beneficiaries of the migration in the humanities and social sciences appear to have been Chicago, Columbia, and Harvard. The pattern is much the same in the natural sciences and mathematics, although in those fields Berkeley and NYU also hired many émigrés. See Jarrell C. Jackman and Carla M. Bordman, eds., *The Muses Flee Hitler: Cultural Transfer and Adaptation, 1930–1945* (Washington, D.C., 1983); Bernard Bailyn and Donald Fleming, eds., *The Intellectual Migration, 1930–1960* (Cambridge, Mass., 1969); Laura Fermi, *Illustrious Immigrants: The Intellectual Migration from Europe, 1930–1941*, 2d ed. (Chicago, 1971); and Robin Rider, "Alarm and Opportunity: Emigration of Mathematicians and Physicists to Britain and the United States 1933–1945," *Historical Studies in the Physical Sciences* 15 (1984): 107–176.

75. See the list of faculty through 1959 in Brown, *Legal Education*, 470. S. Chesterfield Oppenheim, who joined the law faculty in 1952, was a convert to Christianity. In 1955 Eric Stein, a Jewish émigré from Czechoslovakia, was appointed.

76. Although there were a number of Jews in the Department of Economics by 1955, William Haber believed that Paton's opposition to Lawrence Klein derived in part from Paton's antipathy toward Jews. See Haber, in transcript of Marjorie Brazer interviews of May 1979, Department of Economics, Box 5, MHC. See also, in the same location, the 1979 recollections of Gardner Ackley, who said that Paton opposed Klein for two reasons, "his former communism" and "pure anti-Semitism." Ackley "never spoke to Bill Paton again" after Paton "came over to explain to me" that the initiative to hire Klein "was all a plot" to "solidify Jewish control of the department."

77. Carrter, *Assessment.*

78. These quotations are the characterizations of Terman offered by Stuart W. Leslie, "Playing the Education Game to Win: The Military and Interdisciplinary Research at Stanford," *Historical Studies in the Physical Sciences* 18 (1987): 55–88, esp. 57–58.

79. These presuppositions inform Kerr's *University* and a host of contemporary works, including one of the most thoughtful treatises on science policy ever written: Don K. Price, *The Scientific Estate* (New York, 1965).

80. Michigan's Department of Political Science, for example, ranked fourth in quality but first in number of publications; History was fifth in quality but second in productivity; Anthropology second in quality, first in quantity; Economics fifteenth in quality, eighth in quantity. The pattern did not extend to

the natural sciences, incidentally, where Michigan's programs were generally ranked lower in all categories but had relatively higher ratings for intellectual quality than for number of publications. The study did not provide quantitative indicators for the humanistic disciplines. See *An Assessment of Research-Doctorate Programs in the United States*, printout by Daniel J. Fox, Statistical Research Laboratory, University of Michigan, April 26, 1983. I have been informed by Philip Converse, one of this study's designers, that the study included some twenty pages of caveats and qualifications concerning the interpretation of these data; these caveats and qualifications were not attached to the printouts distributed by Daniel Fox. Close attention to these methodological refinements may well invalidate my interpretation of the study's significance. In any event, in the gross results, only one of Michigan's six leading social science departments, Psychology, ranked lower in quantity of publications than it did in overall faculty quality. It was only fourth in the nation in quantity, but second in quality. Sociology ranked third in both categories. In the ten natural science programs addressed in this study, five Michigan programs did better in quality than in quantity; three the reverse, and two were tied. The figures, by program: Chemistry, twentieth in quantity and thirty-first in quality; Geoscience, fifth and twenty-fourth; Mathematics, eleventh and eleventh; Physics, twenty-fourth and twenty-third; Statistics, twentieth and twentieth; Biochemistry, thirtieth and nineteenth; Botany, seventeenth and eighth; Molecular and Cellular Biology, seventh and twenty-eighth; Microbiology, twenty-eighth and seventeenth; Physiology, thirteenth and seventh.

81. Between 1954—the year that the Center for Advanced Study in the Behavioral Sciences was founded—and 1987, Michigan produced seventy fellows, making it the fifth-ranking producer of CASBS fellows (after Berkeley, Stanford, Harvard, and Chicago). Statistics from CASBS carry an interesting hint about patterns of mobility: of the seventy-seven scholars who were at Michigan when appointed to CASBS prior to 1988, at least twenty-seven later left Michigan for other institutions, mostly in California and the Boston-Washington corridor, while of the forty-six CASBS fellows at Michigan in 1988, only seven had been recruited from outside, and of these only one was a social scientist (as opposed to a medical professional) recruited from a major university in California or the eastern corridor (that one recruitment took place in 1987, from Stanford).

82. Michigan membership in the National Academy of Sciences has never been large. Still, its four members in 1938 represented a larger segment of the total academy membership than its eight members in 1963 and its thirteen members (plus one emeritus member) in 1988. The difference between 1963 and 1988 represents a considerable decline in regard to the natural sciences: in 1963, all eight of Michigan's academicians were natural scientists, but in 1988, by which time the academy itself had become larger and all of Michigan's salient peer institutions had sharply increased their numbers, only seven of Michigan's thirteen active members were natural scientists. The other six were social scientists. The academy did not admit social scientists until the early 1970s. In 1988, Michigan was not close to being among the top fifteen universities in academy membership, even when social scientists are counted. The following are the fifteen highest-ranking research universities (excluding Rockefeller, which is not

the same kind of institution): Harvard (including medical school), 111; Stanford (including medical school), 85; Berkeley, 83; MIT, 80; Caltech, 52; Yale, 50; Chicago, 45; UC San Diego, 44; Princeton, 37; Wisconsin, 36; Cornell, 35; UCLA, 28; Columbia, 26; and Illinois, 24. These figures are based on the affiliations given for academy members on the membership list distributed by the academy. Although I have not tried systematically to sort out the social scientists among the members from all of these other universities, it is obvious that for none of the fifteen institutions listed above do social scientists account for more than a small fraction of the figure given. Michigan is exceptional among major research universities in having so many social scientists in the academy, and in having so few natural scientists.

CHAPTER EIGHT

Science as a Weapon in *Kulturkämpfe* in the United States during and after World War II

The "conflict between science and religion" is a set phrase that historians of the United States associate the most directly with the second half of the nineteenth century, and for good reasons. It was in the wake of the Darwinian revolution in natural history that American Protestants displayed their most acute anxiety about the relation of scientific innovation to inherited Christian doctrine. This anxiety, which was often expressed through the argument that the very idea of a "conflict" between science and religion was based on a misunderstanding of the issues, had long since diminished by the middle decades of the twentieth century. But in the milder culture wars of the era of World War II and immediately following, one can hear several echoes of these earlier spiritual disputes. At the center of these American Kulturkämpfe was a program for secular culture organized around what its adherents represented as the core values of science. This program drew upon a number of elements of earlier, Enlightenment-inspired projects, especially those developed in Victorian Britain by John Stuart Mill and his contemporaries and in early-twentieth-century America by John Dewey and his. Dewey himself survived long enough to participate in some of the quarrels of the midcentury decades.

This secular, "scientific" program and the several rivals against which it was directed during the 1940s and 1950s form the central subject of this essay, which builds upon several of the other studies reprinted here, especially "The Defense of Democracy and Robert K. Merton's Formulation of the Scientific Ethos." I take up some of the changes in the discussion of science that resulted from the essential triumph, within academic circles by the early 1960s, of the science-appreciating, cosmopolitan intellectuals. In closing, I suggest that the faults now routinely found in the work of Merton, Dewey, and their fellows diminish somewhat in significance if one invokes a long-term historial perspective. In this perspective, the blind spots we now identify in the work of many midcentury advocates of a more enlightened America reflect generational differences within what I, at least, am willing to acknowledge as the continuum of Enlightenment purpose stretching back to the seventeenth century. I hope such acknowledgments can make us both more generous toward the midcentury intellectuals and more

*humble about the critical achievements of which our own generation has become
so proud.*

*This essay was prepared as a lecture presented to the History of Science Society
at its annual meeting of 1994. It was published in the society's official journal,
Isis 86 (September 1995).*

ON THE DAY of Pentecost, the Medes and the Galileans and the Meso-
potamians found themselves, along with people from every nation,
speaking to one another with cloven tongues of fire, each hearing the
other as though alterity spoke in one's own language. This is one of the
most moving of the myths we inherit from antiquity, one that depicts
human beings in the process of recognizing a common destiny and addressing that destiny across the lines that divide cultures. This mythic
narrative can be read as a prophecy directed at our own era of multiculturalism, when we defer so quickly to the claims of particular cultures,
and when we suspect universalist projects of harboring imperial and
hierarchical structures. But the distinctive cultures of the world do not
lose their identity in this ancient story of *e pluribus unum*; at Pentecost,
the dispersed children of the earth retain their tribal integrity while
being able to understand each other through a distinctive linguistic
bridge. The topic of this jubilant discourse, as described in the second
chapter of the Acts of the Apostles, was the Christian gospel.[1] Yet the
vision of discursive solidarity, of the epistemic unity of all humankind,
has persisted in secular genres, especially science.

It is said that science, whether a Western innovation transmitted elsewhere or a collection of indigenously developed strategies for coping
with the world, engages, as no other human invention ever has, realities
that impinge potentially on every member of the species. Public knowledge, witnessed by diverse souls in an ever-expanding community of perception and intersubjective reason, shall enable the tribes to see beyond
their own idols to a common fate. Although a range of intellectual movements have claimed the name of science, prominent among these movements are universalist and cosmopolitan protests against the authority of
blood and history. These protests have been developed by liberal and
radical parties in the cultural wars of many times and places. Here, I am
going to talk about one of these settings for universalist, cosmopolitan
constructions of the cultural meaning of science, the United States in
the era of World War II and following. This is a vast topic, and my treatment of it here will be necessarily sketchy.

The central term in this episode is the adjective *scientific*, as used to
modify nouns such as *approach, spirit, method, ethic, ethos, values,* and *culture.* Now, this usage is sometimes taken as an empirical claim about the
process of producing knowledge. In this view, "the scientific spirit" or

"the scientific method" denotes a reality visible in the laboratory and in the field, subject to elaboration in terms that may be complex or simple, depending on the sophistication of the speaker and the needs of the audience. An example of this kind of discourse well known to historians of science is the discussion surrounding Robert K. Merton's formulation of "the scientific ethos." The extent to which Merton's famous norms—universalism, disinterestedness, communism, and skepticism—play a role in what scientists do was a matter of some contention not so many years ago, when Merton's critics insisted that these norms were rather beside the point and some of his followers continued to hold that the old norms still did have some utility as analytic tools for understanding how science works.

Another way of reading the adjective *scientific*, when connected to this class of nouns, is to take it less seriously as an empirical claim and to treat it instead as a bit of evidence about the character of general programs for culture. In this view the significance of Merton's norms is found not in their degree of utility as a description of the practice of producing natural or social knowledge, but in the witness they bear to the moral aspirations of the speaker. When the ideal of being somehow "more scientific" is upheld as appropriate for voters in a democratic polity, for believers in a religious fellowship, for practitioners of the arts, for actors in a set of economic relationships, and for others far removed from laboratories, it follows that this language teaches us less about how science works than about the cultural conflicts in society at large. This point can apply to many of the programmatic writings of Karl Pearson, Charles Sanders Peirce, John Stuart Mill, and many public moralists in the Enlightenment and in the Baconian movement. According to many of these intellectuals, science was valuable in part because it was an agent of cosmopolitan liberation in a particular society.

The specific case at hand is a "scientifically" oriented cultural program designed by a host of intellectuals of Merton's generation for the society of the United States, and to some extent for all societies in a modernizing world expected by many proponents of this program to follow the lead of the United States. I want to sketch this program in very broad terms, to indicate some of the concerns that drove it, and to review several major texts in the articulation and defense of this program by American intellectuals in the 1940s, 1950s, and 1960s. I want then to address briefly the period from the 1960s to the 1990s and, finally, to suggest that the increasingly aggressive role of Christianity as a rival program within the United States today should remind us of some long-term continuities in the *Kulturkämpfe* of the North Atlantic West.

Although I promise to move rapidly beyond Merton, I will stay with him just a moment longer because he is so common a referent, and because his role in what he himself, in 1942, called the "revolutionary conflict of cultures" is now widely recognized. Merton was one of many American and British intellectuals to enlist science as an ideological adhesive in the Allied cause against the Axis powers. Merton gave distinctive shape to a then-widespread assertion that science and democracy were expressions of each other and that both were threatened by Nazism. Among the other writings in the same genre so popular with the coming of World War II, one very similar to Merton's was by Mark A. May, the director of Yale's Institute of Human Relations, who was at the time a more prominent social scientist than Merton. May also had his list of elements in the "morality of science," which he, more explicitly than Merton, advocated as the basis for a culture that should sweep the United States and the world, so that ordinary citizens would live by the code of the scientist: the code of honest, free inquiry, the code of critical, interactive, evidence-based, universalistic, antiauthoritarian, and hence "scientific" conduct. Let all of humankind imitate the fellowship of science, May suggested.[2]

We learn something of the character of the struggles in which this variety of scientific idealism was then being mobilized if we look closely at the two venues in which Merton and May presented their papers. Merton's legendary essay of 1942 was published in the *Journal of Political and Legal Sociology*, edited by an émigré from Hitler's Europe, Georges Gurvitch, and was obviously directed against fascism. May's paper was contributed the next year to a Conference on the Scientific Spirit and Democratic Faith held in New York City and directed not so much at fascists as at Catholics. To be sure, Hitler and Mussolini constituted the larger frame of reference, but this conference, organized by Jerome Nathanson of the Society for Ethical Culture, with the support of Horace Kallen and other well-known defenders of ethnic and religious "tolerance," was designed to counteract specifically Christian formulations of American democracy.[3]

A number of American Catholic intellectuals, inspired in part by the example of the émigré theologian Jacques Maritain, had begun to talk about the need for "values" in a secular society, about the allegedly indispensable role played by religion in the creation of values, and about the crucial contribution to democracy made by the Christian religion, in particular. These Catholic intellectuals often identified the influence of science as a source of the nation's apparently deficient value system. This ideological line was not limited to birthright Catholics; the University of Chicago philosopher Mortimer Adler declared in 1940 that Nazism was not nearly so great a threat to democracy as was John Dewey.[4]

Adler's remark was not an isolated incident. We need to remember several other features of the setting in which Merton, May, and some of their liberal contemporaries spoke up for what they represented as the values of science. Even after Mussolini's invasion of Ethiopia in 1935 and Franco's revolt against the Spanish republic in 1936, Catholic periodicals and substantial sections of the Catholic hierarchy in the United States were openly sympathetic to the fascist cause in Italy and Spain. Moreover, it was a Catholic judge in New York in 1940 who, responding to a civil suit by an individual citizen, voided Bertrand Russell's faculty appointment at the City College of New York on the grounds that Russell was an atheist and a sexual libertine and thus not fit to instruct callow youth, at least not on a salary furnished by the taxpayers of New York City.[5] This dismissal of one of the world's most eminent philosophers and a militant freethinker, chosen by CCNY to succeed the retired Morris Raphael Cohen, is not much remembered today, but it was a cause célèbre in the culture wars of the early 1940s.

While some Catholics did hold "progressive" views, and while some were themselves the victims of Protestant prejudice, the Protestant, Jewish, and agnostic intellectuals who rallied to the banner of science and democracy had strong reasons for believing that Roman Catholic priests and their fellow-traveling intellectuals were a genuine and formidable enemy in a struggle over the future of American culture. An example of the conflict generated within learned societies took place within the American Historical Assocation in 1944. The Catholic historian Carleton J. H. Hayes, who blamed the decline of traditional religion for many of the world's ills and who was friendly to Franco's regime, was almost denied the presidency of the association when nearly a third of the voting members opposed him in what was to have been an uncontested election.[6]

We need to remind ourselves that in those years the notion of a "Christian" culture still carried vivid connotations of anti-Semitic barriers to the employment of Jews in higher education, especially in the humanities and social sciences. Not a single Jew held a tenured appointment in any department within Yale College until 1946. In Columbia's English department, the appointment of Lionel Trilling as assistant professor in 1939 was a breakthrough so striking that its story is still told by aging English professors around the country, in tones that Civil War buffs reserve for describing the battle of Gettysburg. T. S. Eliot was still holding forth on the virtues of a "Christian society" in the late 1930s and early 1940s, and many of the liberal intellectuals who rallied to the banner of scientific culture remembered well his notorious lecture at the University of Virginia, given only a few years before, when one of the century's greatest poets and critics declared, even after Hitler's purge of the German universities, that "any large number of free-thinking Jews" was "undesirable."[7]

Merton and May thus wrote in the context not only of the military struggle between the Allies and the Axis; they wrote also in the context of a *Kulturkampf* going on within the United States. One force in this struggle was a secular, increasingly Jewish, decidedly left-of-center intelligentsia based largely but not exclusively in the disciplinary communities of philosophy and the social sciences. In about 1945 the most engaged of these people included, in addition to Merton and May and Kallen, the philosophers Sidney Hook, Ernest Nagel, Adrienne Koch, Herbert Schneider, Max Otto, and John Herman Randall, Jr., as well as the social scientists Robert M. McIver, Melville Herskovitz, Robert Lynd, and Margaret Mead. The presiding spirit was the aging John Dewey himself, still contributing occasional articles and addresses to the cause.

These men and women saw themselves not simply as supporters of democracy's fight for survival against the international fascist menace, but as the guarantors of a particular vision of democracy: one authentically Jeffersonian, but being subverted by the perpetuation of old-fashioned religious and ethnic prejudices and being inhibited by a psychologically immature and socially provincial predilection for absolutes that portended an authoritarian political culture for the United States. They were cosmopolitan intellectuals fighting against a variety of unfortunate provincialisms that some conservative intellectuals had the outrageous audacity to support. Moreover, most of these secular-liberal, largely social scientific intellectuals saw themselves—in the wake of the Moscow Trials, the Nazi-Soviet Pact, and Stalin's support for Lysenko's destruction of Soviet genetics—as opponents of a generalized "totalitarianism" present in Communism as well as in fascism. What was most suspect about the ostensibly secular Communist movement, indeed, was its "religious" character, which brought it neatly into place alongside the Catholic Church and the old hegemonic Protestantism as rivals to the values of these cosmopolitan intellectuals. "I used to sneer when I read that Communism was a substitute religion, but I don't anymore," the young Richard Hofstadter wrote to his friend Harvey Swados in 1939, when Hofstadter himself was pulling away from the Communist movement. "I hate . . . the simpering dogmatic religious-minded Janizaries that make up the CP," he exclaimed, then went on to declare his belief in "a certain set of values—freedom of individual intellectual inquiry, scientific attitude of mind, respect for facts, a certain cultural latitude. . . ."[8]

Science offered itself to Hofstadter and to many of his secular contemporaries as a magnificent ideological resource. Or, to put the point more sharply, these men and women selected from the available inventory those images of science most useful to them, those serving to connect the adjective *scientific* with public rather than private knowledge, with open rather than closed discourses, with universal rather than local standards of warrant, with democratic rather than aristocratic models of authority.

Bland as most of their formulations might seem from afar, to these intellectuals it mattered enormously to be "objective," to look upon factual realities "without prejudice," to "actually test with experience" one's opinions, and to report "honestly" the results of one's inquiries. These men and women saw a world filled with "prejudice" and with efforts to "impose certain opinions by force." Against these evils one must affirm "free inquiry" and "open-mindedness" in order that our society might be organized realistically on the basis of the conditions life actually presents. If this was what scientists did, then the idea of imitating scientists, of following a "scientific approach," was a capital idea. Margaret Mead said so in *And Keep Your Powder Dry*, her 1942 morale-boosting book that focused on critical thinking and tolerance and democratic virtues and reached its homiletic climax with an incandescent call to the public to have "faith in the power of science."[9]

This faith was resoundingly affirmed at war's end in Harvard University's famous "red book," *General Education in a Free Society*, the committee report that defined the terms of theoretical discussion of American higher education from 1945 through the 1960s, exactly the quarter-century of American academia's most phenomenal growth. This document repeatedly invoked the ideal of Christian education, and for good reason. Even in the 1930s this old ideal had been perpetuated on a nonsectarian basis at public as well as private institutions. To this anachronistic Christian ethos the Harvard authors contrasted their own educational ideal: the creating and maintaining of a democratic community of free but mutually obligated individuals. The report explicitly identified "science" as the foundation of "the spiritual values" of a democratic humanism and declared that American democracy needed citizens with "the habit of forming objective, disinterested judgments based upon exact evidence." Our society needs both tradition and innovation, they said, and it needs both tolerance and conviction. How to balance the two? The answer was clear: "the scientific attitude," as set forth in the writings of William James and John Dewey.[10]

Alongside this widely circulated manifesto for secular education in the scientific spirit, there soon appeared *On Understanding Science*, which Harvard president James B. Conant presented in the form of lectures in 1946 and published the following year. This book is known to historians of science primarily as a record of Conant's initiation of history of science instruction at Harvard, on the "case method."[11] But the historical significance of *On Understanding Science* is much broader. Conant's text was first presented as the Terry Lectures at Yale, endowed for the purpose of nurturing "the Christian spirit" in the light of knowledge.

Conant, his generation's most influential figure in the transition to a more secular higher educational system in the United States, began on his very first page with the concept of secular culture, and he was determined to make his contemporaries understand that the sober and deliberate spirit of science was just what a modern, diverse, technologically advanced society needed if it were to perpetuate the finest values that had once been carried forward by Christianity. Why do "so many feel lost in the modern world?" Conant asked. The prescribed answer, given throughout the 1930s by countless college presidents—and given obligingly even today by political evangelists ranging from Bill Clinton to Dan Quayle—is that folks have not kept the faith of the fathers, that the values associated with religion are what we need more of. But this was not Conant's answer. Conant said that the people who feel lost have "failed to assimilate science" into their culture.[12]

But nothing in Conant's *On Understanding Science* is more fascinating, historically, than a peculiar turn in the argument at a vital point. Even while advocating a more scientific culture, Conant scorned the putting of the scientist "on a pedestal." We should save our pedestals for those who can think and judge like scientists without the constant scrutiny of "peers," without the support of a "self-propagating social phenomenon" that makes impartiality for working scientists an unheroic "routine." Conant did not use the words *profession, community,* or *surveillance* to talk about the social interaction of scientists, but he was clearly going down exactly this path, which we might call the path of Thomas Kuhn. Conant was obviously divided between his proto-Kuhnian insights into the socially disciplining power of technical communities and the individualism he simultaneously associated with democracy. So Conant had it both ways; he entered his caveats, explaining that scientists had the great advantage of daily support for their practice of the scientific spirit, and then he praised as the true heroes of civilization those individuals who could do it on their own.

Who were they? Who were these ideal citizens, the people who could apply intersubjective reason within their own subjectivity? Conant invoked the names of Petrarch and Machiavelli, and Rabelais and Montaigne—freethinking critics of religious orthodoxy—along with the various "honest explorers and hardheaded statesmen and military commanders" who without the benefit of institutional reinforcement "courageously" came to "conclusions based on reason."[13] It is, then, in the service of providing our society with more such people—nonscientists guided by evidence that would be recognized by a larger community of witnesses—that we study cases of scientific experiment. The point is not to imitate the social life of scientists as that life actually is, but *to behave scientifically in social environments very different from the one in which science actually proceeds.*

Conant's thinking in 1946 prefigured the sharp distinction finally made popular in the early 1960s between the tightly organized scientific community and the rest of society. But between World War II and the 1960s, the general program for a culture of open-minded, reasoned deliberation free from prejudice and authority went forward in the name of science with very little attention to the distinctive social arrangements of scientific work. Indeed, William H. Whyte's instant classic of 1956, *The Organization Man*, remained loyal to the old, individualist sense of the scientific spirit; Whyte had none of Conant's insight into the positive value of the socially disciplining features of scientific organization. If Kuhn and his contemporaries just a few years later were to make scientists into "organization men," the journalistic book by a professional business writer that gave us this buzzword still tended the flame of heroic individualist science and lamented science's bureaucratization by industrial laboratories.[14]

Examples of the cultural program I am tracing are easy to find in the academic writing of the 1950s, a decade in which the secular, left-of-center, increasingly Jewish intelligentsia was coming to occupy more and more space in the universities being expanded under the economic aegis of the "GI Bill" and under the ideological leadership of Conant. In this period it was, of course, the Soviet Union rather than Nazi Germany that provided the global context for American *Kulturkämpfe*. Writings by many natural scientists, including the physicists I. I. Rabi and J. Robert Oppenheimer, contributed to the cause.[15] I will concentrate on two texts from the 1950s that illustrate the great range of disciplines and discursive contexts in which agents of this cultural program can be found.

The first is the émigré philosopher Hans Reichenbach's *The Rise of Scientific Philosophy*, a 1951 book designed as a popular exposition of the outlook commonly known as "logical positivism," although Reichenbach himself did not like that term. Another thing Reichenbach disliked was the mushy moralism he attributed to most traditional philosophy, through which philosophers pretended to tell people what was right and good. In keeping with the austere self-image of the analytical philosophers of his milieu, Reichenbach proclaimed the inability of scientists or scientifically oriented philosophers to vindicate moral ends. Moral ends were, of course, matters of volition, and the varieties of emotivist ethical theory took pride in their ability to distinguish Is from Ought. These familiar features of the logical positivist agenda might lead one to expect Reichenbach's book to be an attack on the very idea of a scientific culture. One might expect from Reichenbach a dissent from the cultural program I have been tracing; one might expect an effort to distinguish sharply between the "facts" of science and the "values" of culture. Quite the contrary.

Once the preference for democracy over other forms of governance was accepted—and that evaluation Reichenbach did place beyond the scope of scientific reason—virtually every other issue of social concern within a democracy was cognitive, not strictly emotive, was a matter for resolution by rational assessment of cause-and-effect relationships in the real world. Should, for example, private property be abolished? This was a matter for the infant science of sociology to decide on an empirical basis. It sounded like a moral issue, Reichenbach explained, but actually it was a scientific one. Reichenbach confidently listed, as examples of aspects of life that can be organized on a scientific basis, "education, health, sex life, the civil law, the criminal code, and the punishment of criminals." Individual wills may differ on such matters, but these wills are to be "harmonized" through group interactions that are guided by "cognitive relations," facts about the relationship of means to ends. Reichenbach made a great production of renouncing the application of science to moral issues, but the renunciation was a hollow one in the context of the discourse of American intellectuals to which this book was contributed: as an artifact in that discourse, *The Rise of Scientific Philosophy* announced that virtually every issue his readers cared about was potentially an empirical one, not a moral one, and that the scientific spirit was all the more appropriate as a foundation for culture. On the very last page of the book, Reichenbach conventionally invoked the scientist as an exemplar.[16]

The critical thinking exemplified by the scientist was felt to be much in need as a countervailing force against the outlook and style of Senator Joseph McCarthy, whose activities helped to stimulate my second example from the 1950s, the 1955 book *The Development of Academic Freedom in the United States*, by the historians Richard Hofstadter and Walter Metzger. At the ideological core of this book is something the authors explicitly called "the morality of science." It is to the scientific enterprise, more than any other historical influence, Hofstadter and Metzger declared, that we owe the values of "tolerance and honesty, publicity and testifiability," and "universalism" and "disinterestedness." Hofstadter and Metzger outlined American and European academic history since the seventeenth century, showing these values alternately gaining ground or being subverted by religious and political authority. This deeply engaged product of the intelligentsia's fight against McCarthyism not only presented the morality of science as the theoretical foundation of academic freedom for all disciplines, including the humanities, but left no doubt that the morality of science was the foundation for an entire way of life.

In its opposition to prejudice, in its defense of freedom of conscience and open discussion, the morality of science has become "an ethic of human relationships and an ideal of personal fulfillment."[17]

From Hofstadter and Metzger, one would never get the impression that "humanistic" and "scientific" culture were in serious conflict with one another or were widely perceived to be. The traditional rivalry between these modes, exemplified by the disputes between Matthew Arnold and Thomas Henry Huxley in Victorian Britain, was soft-pedaled during the postwar expansion of higher education but was suddenly called into the open in 1959 by the British scientist and novelist C. P. Snow. *The Two Cultures* created a prodigious dispute among American as well as British intellectuals, but for reasons that are not always recognized. Snow did not simply blast humanists for their ignorance of the second law of thermodynamics, nor did he criticize humanists simply *as* humanists. He attacked a highly particular literary culture, the literary culture of modernism associated with Yeats and Lawrence and Dostoevsky and their professorial advocates. The faults he found with this culture, moreover, were less cognitive than moral. Snow accused the literati of perpetuating and celebrating a mythology of blood and history that had politically reactionary consequences. The modernists were basically crypto-fascists, Snow implied, while the scientific professions carried "in their bones" a humane and democratic orientation toward the future. Scientists, declared Snow, "are freer than most people from racial prejudice; their own culture in its human relations is a democratic one. In their own internal climate, the breeze of the equality of man hits you in the face . . . that is why scientists would do us good all over Asia and Africa." Scientists are the vehicles for the open-minded, liberal-democratic, egalitarian values the whole world needs.[18]

Humanists on both sides of the Atlantic generally reacted with outrage. Snow's ideas were in harmony with the particular cultural program I have been tracing, but he did not direct this program against the usual targets of the American intellectuals of his generation: McCarthyites, conservative boards of trustees, a legacy of anti-Semitic quotas, Catholic versions of democracy, Nazis, Communist totalitarians, and, above all, the old Protestant cultural hegemony. Rather, Snow directed this program against the English department. No wonder it created such a stir.

Now, the literary professoriat had been rather quiet about the moral mystique of science during the postwar era, being glad for the expanded political and professional space this mystique had helped them to achieve. They did their work on Kafka and Conrad and Joyce and Yeats without worrying too much about any possible political coordinates. Indeed, in 1946 this literary critical establishment had largely defended the Library of Congress's award of the Bollingen Prize to the bona fide fascist and anti-Semite Ezra Pound, even when the philosopher William Barrett and some social scientific intellectuals had protested. Poetry was not about politics, the English departments explained, it was about art.

After Snow's intervention, what had been only an implicit conflict between two postbiblical, cosmopolitan, secular programs for culture housed demographically within the same part-WASP, part-Jewish intelligentsia was more open. One of these programs was built around science, of course, but the other was built around the creative genius of the individual, alienated artist. This second program, which often went by the name of modernism, was more frankly elitist than the program for scientific culture, and it was often merely ambivalent rather than hostile toward the claims of blood and history opposed by the celebrants of science.[19]

Not until about the time that Snow wrote *The Two Cultures* did Lionel Trilling and a few other leaders of modernist literary culture in the United States openly begin to question the "sympathy for the abyss" and the "hostility to society" that Trilling acknowledged to be disquieting features of the modernist program.[20] Trilling and his contemporaries had been carrying out their project in a relatively cloistered setting, while their social scientific and philosophical colleagues beat the drums for a culture organized in the scientific spirit. Snow had hit a nerve, and he did so just when some literary critics were brooding among themselves over their own misgivings about canonical modernism. But most of these literary men and women exploded against Snow; for whatever might be the moral deficiencies of Lawrence and Yeats, the English professors were not going to grant the standing to make such judgments to so poor a novelist as C. P. Snow.

Some of this literary cohort withdrew, one might say, and regrouped, and came out some years later under the cover of Michel Foucault and postmodernism to attack science as itself crypto-fascist and to claim for literature the badge of democracy and equality and human decency. But that is an episode of some years later, and its character owes something to the perceived triumph, in the meantime, of the cultural program of the cosmopolitan intellectuals, at least in some sectors of American life.

By the middle of the 1960s the notion of a "closed society" was most often used to refer to the white racist South, as in James Silver's popular book *Mississippi: The Closed Society*. By then the Ivy League universities were anything but closed, in the sense that they had been when Merton and May and Kallen invoked openness as an ideal two decades before. The ethnodemographic transformation of elite academia proceeded apace with higher education's postwar growth, with the result that while Jews constituted only 3 percent of the population of the nation they accounted for 17 percent of the faculties of the elite universities by the end of the 1960s; in some disciplines, such as sociology, economics, and law, the percentage was much higher.[21] This ethnodemographic transformation was not brought about in response to any belief that the disciplines needed "a Jewish perspective"; rather, these faculty appointments were understood to have been made on the basis of prevailing professional standards, which were understood, in turn, to be universalistic.

The massive entry of Jewish intellectuals into the academy from the late 1940s through the 1960s was a crucial victory for the cosmopolitans. The attendant de-Christianization of American public culture was sometimes openly proclaimed—by Leslie Fiedler, for example, who in 1967 celebrated what he called "the great take-over by Jewish-American writers" of the task of speaking for all Americans. In the meantime, the relationship of Catholic commitment to American intellectual and political life had been transformed by the replacement of Spanish and Italian fascism with the "Godless" Communist menace of the Cold War, by the political success of President John Kennedy, by the liberalization of Vatican II, and by the influence of John Courtney Murray.[22] The tension between the secular intelligentsia and Catholicism was dramatically diminished; Catholics were no longer assumed to be enemies of liberal intellectuals.

The sense of triumph in the 1960s to which I refer had two specific manifestations that I want to dwell upon for a moment. One was a social scientific triumphalism marked by the buzzwords *modernization theory* and *the end of ideology*. The second is what I hope it is not a conceit to call the "science studies renaissance," the emergence of a body of scholarly writing about the scientific enterprise itself that took almost for granted the political security of the enterprise of science.

In the social scientific triumphalism flagged by *modernization theory* and *the end of ideology* we see American social scientists delighted with the progress made by Americans in absorbing or at least appreciating "the scientific attitude." We also see these intellectuals offering science to the rest of the world in much the same perspective from which their loquacious ally Snow was calling for the spread of the scientific spirit to Africa and Asia. *The Dynamics of Modernization*, by the Princeton historian Cyril Black, identified "the scientific attitude" as the most important single motor of the entire modernization process from early modern Europe to the present. Industry, technology, and democracy followed eventually in the wake of this distinctive mentality.[23]

The modernizing process was generally understood to entail the making of the entire world over according to the model of what the United States had become by the early and mid-1960s. What was that? The "end of ideology" debates raged over this question. Although one theme in these debates was the insistence of some critics that the United States still had a lot of problems to solve and that old-fashioned interest group politics was bound to be involved in dealing with these problems, what defined the terms of the debates was instead the idea that most traditional political practices and ideologies had been rendered obsolete by the growth of knowledge and by a new political culture responsive to knowledge. Daniel Bell's name is commonly associated with "the end of ideology," but a rendition more pure and less ambivalent than Bell's was provided in 1966 by the Yale political scientist Robert E. Lane. In "The Decline of Politics and Ideology in a Knowledgeable Society," Lane actually cited Auguste Comte's notion of the gradual transition from religion to metaphysics to science and analyzed his own contemporary society in terms of the triumph of the scientific attitude not only within the educated elite, but within a substantial segment of the population at large, even in Congress. Lane acknowledged that belief in God was still found among some "businessmen, bankers, and lawyers," but by and large these and other professionals were moving beyond all that. Lane's newly emerged "knowledgeable society" was one in which democracy had moved to a new stage, guided not so much by the give and take of various conflicting interests and ideologies as by scientific knowledge, especially as produced by social scientists, and by a widespread willingness simply to apply the available information to whatever problem came up. Lane rejoiced in signs that lobbyists, whom an unsophisticated observer might think were still operating in the domain of old-fashioned politics, were now making more and more of their arguments to legislators on the basis of "information."[24]

Now, during the years 1962–1965, the heart of the period in which both modernization theory and the end of ideology were prominent preoccupations of American social scientific intellectuals, there appeared in print a number of books and articles about science that served to make the study of the scientific enterprise a more substantial scholarly endeavor than it had been. These works addressed science's cultural role in terms considerably less defensive or evangelical than had been the case in most of the writings I have cited. I have in mind especially Derek Price's *Little Science, Big Science*, Fritz Machlup's *The Production and Distribution of Knowledge in the United States*, Warren Hagestrom's *Scientific Community*, Don K. Price's *The Scientific Estate*, Thomas S. Kuhn's *The Structure of Scientific Revolutions*, Karl Hill's edited volume *The Management of Scientists*, and Joseph Agassi's "Toward a New Historiography of Science."[25] I do not want to imply that these works prove a genuine end of ideology, nor to suggest that they lacked any function in the cultural struggles of their own time. But I hope it is fair to observe that these works are less directly engaged in a struggle to establish and defend a scientific public culture in the United States than were the bulk of the writings I have mentioned.

Price, Price, Kuhn, et alia published their most enduring works just at a moment when academic intellectuals of a scientific orientation were being widely recognized as the basic arbiters of culture and the most vital policy resource for the nation. Walter Lippmann, still one of the country's most trusted weather vanes for the direction of the winds of doctrine, declared in the *New Republic* that communities of inquiry housed in universities were the chief basis for the society's future. Clark Kerr brought out *The Uses of the University*, one of the most complacent treatises on the social standing of secular-liberal academic intellectuals ever published in the United States.[26]

Complacent may be too loaded a word for the scholarly works that made the "science studies renaissance" of the early 1960s, but in clarifying the relation of this academic boom to the story I am telling about *Kulturkämpfe* I want to remind us of the character of four individual voices that were part of the animated conversation about science going on in the 1960s. One is the policy analyst and longtime government official Don K. Price; and a second is Kuhn. The third is a figure who did most of his work in the era of World War II but suddenly became part of the action in the early 1960s, the British philosopher Karl Popper.[27] The fourth is Merton, by then recognized as one of the most creative social scientists of the age.

Don K. Price's unabashedly establishmentarian case for the "scientific establishment" was the culmination of twenty years of concern with the autonomy of professional researchers in a society with democratic aspirations. Price showed relatively little interest in the broader issues in national culture that engaged Conant, Reichenbach, and Hofstadter and Metzger, but he remained engaged on behalf of what had, by the 1960s, come to be routinely called "the scientific community." The crucial strategy in Price's political defense of science was to classify science outside the exercise of power. Price's ideal types of power and truth, lodged at opposite ends of a single spectrum, resonated comfortably with Lane's contrast between "pure politics" and "pure knowledge."[28] Although Price wrote in classically liberal-pluralist fashion about a system that was working reasonably well, he at least understood that the welfare of the scientific enterprise was always at risk, depending on the character of the larger polity of the society in which science is practiced.

It is exactly this understanding to which Kuhn was so persistently unresponsive. Kuhn focused on the political dynamics within scientific communities and thus succeeded in "politicizing" all thought.[29] Kuhn himself seems not to have expected this reading of his work, and he soon proved ambivalent toward it. One can easily see a continuity between

Kuhn's notion of how scientific communities work and his mentor Conant's ideas as expressed in *On Understanding Science*, but Kuhn, unlike Conant, did not address the general public or offer prescriptions for the culture of that public. Kuhn's description of scientists following dogmas uncritically and behaving more in a totalitarian than in a democratic manner suggests that he was not terribly worried that a nondemocratic image for science might weaken the position of science, or of democracy, within American society.

But Popper was still terribly worried about the standing of both science and democracy, and, unlike the more narrowly focused Kuhn, Popper was a cultural warrior in the grand manner, still fighting the battles of the Enlightenment and of the 1930s and 1940s against totalitarianism and religious obscurantism. Popper's annoyed reaction to Kuhn derived in part, I suspect, from his political engagements, from his authentically world-historical vision, and from his sense that reason is still a cultural force ranged against a series of historic enemies that the apparently naive Kuhn did not recognize.[30] Popper spoke for a generation that saw the world almost lost to a regime that distinguished Aryan physics from Jewish physics, and almost saved by a regime that distinguished proletarian science from bourgeois science. If it is not too far-fetched, one can imagine the worldly-wise Popper playing Cardinal Bellarmine to Kuhn's Galileo, conscious of how complex and fragile is a whole system of thought and practice built up through years of struggle, and trying to explain it to a youngish fellow who just wants to speak the "truth," oblivious to what in today's idiom would be called "the social responsibility of intellectuals."

While the agonistic voices of Popper and some of his followers fulminated against Kuhn for not affirming the critical aspects of the scientific process, the irenic voice of Merton, stronger than ever as a result of the triumph of his general theoretical contributions to sociology, spoke compellingly to the opportunity to develop sociology of science as an organized discipline. Merton's work from the 1930s and 1940s, gradually detached from its original *Kulturkämpfe* contexts, was reprinted yet again and elaborated on in new studies by Merton and younger sociologists inspired by his work. The point of this new work of the Mertonian sociologists was, of course, to advance the scholarly study of science, not explicitly to advance a program for culture. When I contrast Merton's role in the 1960s to his role in the late 1930s and early 1940s I do not mean to say it is one or the other, *Kulturkampf* or discipline building, but only that the balance between these two missions is very different in the two periods.[31]

Of these four voices, only Kuhn's survived to be a major referent point in what came to be called "postmodern" discussions of science. Kuhn was, of course, the youngest of the four, and the least restrained by awareness of the social and political settings in which scientific communities operate and of the role that general ideas about science play in the cultural politics of a modern society. Although Kuhn's work was quickly absorbed into academic science studies in a Mertonian mode, and soon helped to inspire several schools of thought that embedded knowledge more deeply in social interests than the Mertonians did, I invoke postmodernism to remind us of the familiar story of Kuhn's appropriation and use by intellectuals of the 1970s and 1980s who depicted science as an authoritarian, "totalizing" project that impedes rather than promotes truly democratic and egalitarian values. Under the influence of Foucault, in particular, there spread in the C. P. Snow–burned literary circles, especially, the notion of "power/knowledge"—a far cry from Lane and Price—and the additional sense that knowledge was, in Foucault's memorable phrase, "not made for understanding; knowledge is made for cutting."[32]

The representation of science in postmodernist discourse is so close to us today that I need do no more in this lecture than allude to it. Yet there is one element in the contemporary scene to which I want to call attention in closing. This is the recent, increasingly assertive claim of conservative Christians that Kuhn and Foucault and their followers have disproven the objectivity of science and thus have rendered an orthodox version of the biblical episteme cognitively legitimate once again. This turn in the *Kulturkämpfe* of our own time is surely an arresting development in a society in which almost half of the population—so the polls say—are creationists.[33]

I do not want to imply that the mid-1990s present the same challenges presented by the mid-1940s, nor to assert that the unamended ideas of Merton and Mead, of Conant and Hofstadter, could serve us well today. Indeed, few indulgences are more satisfying for historians of science now than to point out how our own work, and the work of our colleagues in philosophy and sociology, has shown the pathetic inadequacy of the ideas about democracy and science and gender that prevailed forty or fifty years ago.

But it is all too easy for us to patronize that generation of American cosmopolitan intellectuals and to forget the specific concerns that animated their activities as public moralists. I believe that the proponents of a scientific culture for the United States in the 1940s, 1950s, and 1960s were more admirable ideologically than were most of the people they struggled against. I have employed a partly ironic voice to describe their strivings, but in the end I do not want to deny an element of intellectual and political kinship with some of them. Science alone is not a sufficient foundation for culture, but were it within my power to design a multiculturalist pentecost,[34] a jubilee morning when the curse of Babel shall be revoked and the dispersed children of Adam and Eve return to Eden to testify with cloven tongues of fire, the language in which they would testify would be the language of Newton and Locke, the language of intersubjective reason, the language of science.

NOTES

1. Acts 2:1–21.

2. Robert K. Merton, "A Note on Science and Democracy," *Journal of Legal and Political Sociology* 1 (1942): 115–126, on 116; and Mark A. May, "The Moral Code of Scientists," in *The Scientific Spirit and Democratic Faith*, ed. Eduard C. Lindeman (New York, 1944), 40, 43–44, 46. For a fuller account of the immediate political context of Merton's development of the notion of the "scientific ethos" in the late 1930s and early 1940s, and for an overview of the tradition of ideological writing about science upon which he drew, see David A. Hollinger, "The Defense of Democracy and Robert K. Merton's Formulation of the Scientific Ethos," *Knowledge and Society* 4 (1983): 1–15, reprinted as chapter 5 of the present volume.

3. This group sponsored a second conference a year later, even more pointed than the first in its suspicion of Christian designs on American culture. The proceedings of this conference reveal much about the "culture wars" of that period and prefigure some of those being fought in our own time; see Jerome Nathanson, ed., *The Authoritarian Attempt to Capture Education* (New York, 1945). Among the contributors were many prominent intellectuals of the era, including the psychologist F. H. Allport, the geneticist A. J. Carlson, the journalists Bruce Bliven and Gerald Wendt, and the philosophers E. A. Burtt, Arthur E. Murphey, Sidney Hook, and Charles W. Morris. The volume opened with an essay by the nation's leading secularist, John Dewey, then eighty-six.

4. Mortimer Adler, "God and the Professors," in *Science, Philosophy, and Religion*, ed. Louis Finkelstein (New York, 1941), 120–149.

5. Awareness of the importance of this event has been helpfully reawakened by George Marsden, who alludes to it in *The Soul of the American University: From Protestant Establishment to Established Nonbelief* (New York, 1994), 383. Examples of Catholic voices addressing the issue of fascism can be found in John P. Diggins, *Mussolini and Fascism: The View from America* (Princeton, N.J., 1972), 182–197, 299–301, 329–333, 390–394.

6. This incident is discussed in Peter Novick, *That Noble Dream: The "Objectivity Question" and the American Historical Profession* (Cambridge and New York, 1988), 321–322. Novick observes that the movement to stop Hayes's election included Richard Hofstadter, Kenneth Stampp, Richard Current, Dwight Dumond, Frank Freidel, and Fred Shannon. See also Novick's account of Hayes's expressed political and religious views (243–244).

7. T. S. Eliot, *After Strange Gods: A Primer of Modern Heresy* (London, 1934), 20. See Dan A. Oren, *Joining the Club: A History of Jews and Yale* (New Haven, Conn., 1985), 261, 326. Prior to 1946 Jews did hold tenured appointments in several of

Yale's professional schools, but not in Yale College, the undergraduate liberal arts college at the heart of the university. The first Jew to hold the rank of professor in Yale College was the philosopher Paul Weiss.

8. Richard Hofstadter to Harvey Swados, September 30, 1939, October 10, 1939, quoted in Susan Stout Baker, *Radical Beginnings: Richard Hofstadter and the 1930s* (Westport, Conn., 1985), 150–151.

9. Margaret Mead, *And Keep Your Powder Dry: An Anthropologist Looks at America* (New York, 1942), 262.

10. Paul S. Buck et al., *General Education in a Free Society* (Cambridge, Mass., 1945), esp. 39, 43, 47, 50. Marsden offers a helpful account of the "red book" in *Soul of the American University*, 388–390, but he fails to convey the sense of liberation that secularism brought to many educators of the period.

11. Indeed, Conant's use of Boyle's pump in his teaching program provides the very first footnote in a classic of today's historiography: Steven Shapin and Simon Schaffer, *Leviathan and the Air-Pump: Hobbes, Boyle, and the Experimental Life* (Princeton, N.J., 1985), 4.

12. James B. Conant, *On Understanding Science: An Historical Approach* (New Haven, Conn., 1947), unpaginated epigraph and 1–3.

13. Ibid., 7, 9, 10–11.

14. Whyte's disgust at the "bureaucratization of science" is a sign of how deep his resistance is to the Conant-Kuhn trajectory. See William H. Whyte, *The Organization Man* (New York, 1956), 225–238.

15. Rabi's essays from this era were collected in I. I. Rabi, *Science: The Center of Culture* (New York, 1970), and many of Oppenheimer's in J. Robert Oppenheimer, *The Open Mind* (New York, 1955). See also the posthumous collection: Oppenheimer, *Atom and Void: Essays on Science and Community* (Princeton, N.J., 1989).

16. Hans Reichenbach, *The Rise of Scientific Philosophy* (Berkeley, Calif., 1951), 295, 297–298, 326.

17. Richard Hofstadter and Walter P. Metzger, *The Development of Academic Freedom in the United States* (New York, 1955), 365–366.

18. C. P. Snow, *The Two Cultures: And a Second Look* (Cambridge, 1963), 48, 87–93. This edition included Snow's 1963 elaboration of arguments made in his original lecture of 1959. Snow's attack on modernist literary culture is more pronounced in the 1963 segment than in the 1959 text.

19. This is not the place even to outline this alternative cultural program. I have addressed it in David A. Hollinger, *In the American Province: Studies in the History and Historiography of Ideas* (Bloomington, Ind., 1985), 74–91, 203–206; and Hollinger, "The Knower and the Artificer," in *Modernist Impulses in the Human Sciences, 1870–1930*, ed. Dorothy Ross (Baltimore, Md., 1994), 26–53, 311–317.

20. Lionel Trilling, "On the Teaching of Modern Literature," in *Beyond Culture: Essays on Literature and Learning* (New York, 1965), 3–30. This essay first appeared in 1961 in *Partisan Review*.

21. James W. Silver, *Mississippi: The Closed Society* (New York, 1964). For statistics on Jewish representation in the universities see Stephen Steinberg, *The Academic Melting-Pot: Catholics and Jews in American Higher Education* (New York, 1974), 103.

22. Leslie Fiedler, "Master of Dreams: The Jew in a Gentile World," *Partisan Review* 34 (1967): 339–356, esp. 347. The role played by John Courtney Murray, *We Hold These Truths: Catholic Reflections on the American Proposition* (New York, 1960), in the greater integration of Catholics into American intellectual life remains largely unappreciated today outside the circle of Catholic intellectuals. The career of Murray, a Jesuit priest, is helpfully addressed in Patrick Allitt, "The Significance of John Courtney Murray," in *Catholic Polity and American Politics*, ed. Mary Segers (New Haven, Conn., 1990), 53–67.

23. C. E. Black, *The Dynamics of Modernization: A Study in Comparative History* (New York, 1966), esp. 70.

24. Robert E. Lane, "The Decline of Politics and Ideology in a Knowledgeable Society," *American Sociological Review* 31 (1966): 649–662.

25. Derek Price, *Little Science, Big Science* (New York, 1963); Fritz Machlup, *The Production and Distribution of Knowledge in the United States* (Princeton, N.J., 1962); Warren Hagestrom, *Scientific Community* (New York, 1965); Don K. Price, *The Scientific Estate* (Cambridge, Mass., 1964); Thomas S. Kuhn, *The Structure of Scientific Revolutions* (Chicago, 1962); Karl Hill, ed., *The Management of Scientists* (Boston, 1974); and Joseph Agassi, "Toward a New Historiography of Science," Beiheft 2 of *History and Theory*. I have addressed elsewhere this remarkable outpouring in relation to debates over science's claims to political autonomy; see David A. Hollinger, "Free Enterprise and Free Inquiry: The Emergence of Laissez-Faire Communitarianism in the Ideology of Science in the United States," *New Literary History* 21 (1990): 897–919, reprinted as chapter 6 of the present volume.

26. Walter Lippmann, "The University," *New Republic*, May 28, 1966, 17–20; and Clark Kerr, *The Uses of the University* (Cambridge, Mass., 1964).

27. Only in 1959 was Popper's mid-1930s treatise on philosophy of science brought out in English as *The Logic of Scientific Discovery* (London, 1959).

28. Price, *Scientific Estate*.

29. One of the first scholars to develop this understanding of Kuhn's implications was the historian J.G.A. Pocock: "Languages and Their Implications," in *Politics, Language, and Time: Essays on Political Thought and History* (New York, 1971), esp. 13–17.

30. See, e.g., Karl Popper, "Normal Science and Its Dangers," in *Criticism and the Growth of Knowledge*, ed. Imre Lakatos and Alan Musgrave (Cambridge, 1970), 51–58.

31. The role played by Merton's work in the various decades is addressed in Hollinger, "Defense of Democracy."

32. Michel Foucault, *Language, Counter-Memory, Practice: Selected Essays and Interviews*, ed. Donald F. Bouchard, trans. Bouchard and Sherry Simon (Ithaca, N.Y., 1977), 154.

33. See, e.g., George Marsden, "The Ambiguities of Academic Freedom," *Church History* 62 (1993): 221–236; and Ronald L. Numbers, *The Creationists* (New York, 1992), ix (polls regarding creationism).

34. I want to acknowledge that this formulation is inspired, in part, by Herman Melville, *Redburn* (1849; reprint, Harmondsworth, Middlesex, 1976), 240.

Index

About the Author

DAVID A. HOLLINGER is Professor of History at the University of California, Berkeley. His previous books are *Postethnic America: Beyond Multiculturalism, In the American Province: Studies in the History and Historiography of Ideas,* and *Morris R. Cohen and the Scientific Ideal.*